See No Evil

See No Evil

A Guide to Protecting Our Children from Media Violence

Madeline Levine, Ph.D.

Jossey-Bass Publishers • San Francisco

Jossey-Bass books and products are available through most bookstores. To contact Jossey-Bass directly, call (888) 378-2537, fax to (800) 605-2665, or visit our website at www.josseybass.com.

Substantial discounts on bulk quantities of Jossey-Bass books are available to corporations, professional associations, and other organizations. For details and discount information, contact the special sales department at Jossey-Bass.

For sales outside the United States, please contact your local Simon & Schuster International Office.

 Manufactured in the United States of America on Lyons Falls Turin Book. This paper is acid-free and 100 percent totally chlorine-free.

Library of Congress Cataloging-in-Publication Data

Levine, Madeline.
    [Viewing violence]
    See no evil : a guide to protecting our children from media
violence / Madeline Levine.
        p.   cm.
    Originally published: Viewing violence. New York : Doubleday.
1996.
    Includes bibliographical references and index.
    ISBN 0-7879-4347-9 (pbk.)
    1. Mass media and children.   2. Mass media and teenagers.
3. Violence in mass media.   I. Title.
HQ784.M3L48   1998
302.23'083—dc21
                                                                98-15191

PB Printing   10 9 8 7 6 5 4 3 2 1

Contents

Acknowledgments

Looking back over the past five years, I am astounded by the kindness and generosity of the many people who took an interest in this project.

Although we agreed, disagreed, and occasionally locked horns, I am very grateful to Dick Wolf, Charles Rosin, and Greg Weisman for helping me understand the complex and often conflicting demands placed on those who create some of our best and most popular television programs.

The staffs of former Senator Paul Simon and Representative Edward Markey were tireless in tracking down obscure government documents and keeping me current on legislation that changed with mind-numbing speed.

My greatest debt is owed to those researchers whose work on media violence and children has illuminated this important and troubling aspect of our culture. For the many hours it took to make sure that I understood their research thoroughly, I would like to thank Leonard Eron, L. Rowell Huesmann, Leonard Berkowitz, Jerome Singer, Joanne Cantor, Albert Bandura, Edward Donnerstein, Ronald Drabman, Aimee Dorr, Sarah Stein, and Don Roberts. Special thanks to Calvin Settlage, whose early comments on values were particularly important to me.

Two people deserve special mention for their interest in this book and their largesse of time and spirit. George Gerbner, who has spent a lifetime clarifying the ways in which media affect us and our children, was exceedingly generous with his time and knowledge. Most important, however, during the arduous task of writing this book, was his contagious conviction that people can have a significant effect on righting wrongs. I am profoundly grateful to him. To Richard Heffner, whom I cannot place in any category because his intelligence and breadth of knowledge are so great that he defies categorization, my deepest thanks. Our many discussions made me think and then rethink my assumptions about rights and responsibilities.

To Eric Simonoff, my agent and sometimes therapist, friend, baby-sitter, and sounding board—thank you for the vote of confidence long before I deserved it. There is no greater gift than to take seriously someone's need to be heard. To Eadie Klemm, his assistant, thanks for always knowing when all I really needed was a sympathetic ear.

To Alan Rinzler, who had unswerving faith in this project, thank you for never giving up. Thank you, Cathy Mallon, who did an outstanding job copyediting. To my publisher, Jossey-Bass, who picked up the ball and made sure this book would remain in print, thank you for your vote of confidence and for the integrity to promote an issue of pressing public concern regardless of its "marketability."

To my dear friend Dee-Dee Epp, thanks for your love and for keeping me connected to the outside world. Thank you, Margarita Sanchez—you loved and cared for my children so thoroughly that I had the peace of mind to devote myself to this project. And to my Uncle Obbie in Florida, who would regularly call at two in the morning just to make sure I knew "what that jerk said about television"—thanks for the late-night humor and for watching out for me.

Thanks to Nancy Boyden who helped with mountains of photocopying and difficult librarians. And a very special thank you to researcher Karen Capadona, who took every one of my phone calls starting with "You'll never be able to find this out" and somehow managed to find it all out anyway.

To my mother, Edith Levine, for her unflagging support and belief in me. Thank you for listening to hours of frustrated, euphoric, jagged phone calls. To my husband, Lee, who barely let a day go by without taping some clipping or commentary to our bathroom mirror. Thank you for your love and support and for allowing me the space to complete a project that took me away from the family more than any of us liked.

And most especially to my three sons Loren, Michael, and Jeremy. Thanks for enduring late carpool pickups, missed basketball and soccer games, and endless nights of frozen pizza and takeout food. I have learned more from you three than from all the psychology courses I ever took. Thanks for letting me use all those embarrassing anecdotes about you. You won't get teased for long; kids' memories are short. You three guys are the greatest blessings I will ever know.

Kentfield, California
July 1998

Madeline Levine

This book is lovingly dedicated to my father, Louis Levine, who taught me to follow both the rules and my heart.

See No Evil

Introduction

Two days shy of his twelfth birthday, my oldest son asked me if he could see the movie *The Silence of the Lambs*. Having recently seen it, I said no without hesitation. Cannibalism, murder, and mutilation seemed to be the stuff of nightmares, and I saw no reason to expose him to such ferocious brutality. Our ensuing discussion was predictable. I said that *The Silence of the Lambs* (or *The Terminator*, or *Die Hard*, or *Nightmare on Elm Street*) was not appropriate for his age. He said, "It's just a movie, Mom. It can't hurt my development." Being the son of a clinical psychologist, he has learned, in self-defense, to speak his mother's language.

I was struck by his insistence that he was the only one of all his friends who had not seen the movie. As a psychotherapist and the mother of three boys, I am not easily fooled into believing the anthem of adolescence, "I'm the only one." He assured me that he was telling the truth, and I was certain that he was exaggerating.

"Go ahead and call," he suggested. So I did, believing that other parents would share my point of view. After all, we live in a middle-class, well-educated community with parents who are genuinely and regularly involved in their children's activities. I was certain that other parents would agree that a movie like *The Silence of the Lambs* was an experience to shield children from.

One by one I called his friends' mothers, all women I had known for years and who were, without exception, good moms. Yes, their sons had seen the movie, some with parental permission, some without. Some of the parents and all of the kids felt "it was just entertainment." A few of the more outspoken boys even questioned why I found it difficult to "distinguish reality from fantasy." Although all of the kids felt that the movie was "very scary," none said that they had any nightmares related to it.

So here I was, a forty-five-year-old Ph.D., mother of three, significantly disturbed and shocked by a movie that eleven- and twelve-year-olds had taken in stride. My training and experience as a psychologist told me that these children should have been traumatized by the psychotic, graphic sadism of Dr. Hannibal Lecter.

Developmentally, young adolescents are concerned with issues of physical growth, awakening sexuality, the replacement of parental values with peer values, and an emerging sense of identity. At its best, *The Silence of the Lambs* simply does not deal with the emotional issues relevant to young adolescents. At its worst, it presents a sadistic, perverted central character in an intriguing and even playful way. In addition, I would expect this movie to raise anxiety about sexuality and physical vulnerability. Yet these children were remarkably unmoved. Why weren't they upset by this movie? Why weren't they horrified?

Almost every week, I am approached by a concerned parent who asks me, "How much TV is safe for my child? When does it become harmful?" I am frequently asked my opinion about the suitability of one movie or another. Parents appear to be simultaneously concerned with and indifferent to the amount of media violence seen by their children. On the one hand, we read articles, attend lectures, and consult with experts on how media violence affects our children; on the other hand, these same children are exposed to levels of media violence inconsistent with everything that is known about healthy child development.

I have written this book both as a psychologist and as a mother. A great deal is known about the harmful effects of media violence on children, but much of the research is technical and inaccessible to the average parent. Without this information, parents are likely to continue to underestimate the harmful effects of media violence.

As a psychologist, I hope to sharpen parents' awareness of the unique ways in which children at different stages of development experience the media. I will present what social scientists have long known about media violence: that it encourages aggression, desensitization, and pessimism in our children. But since all passion inevitably flows from personal commitment, I have written this book because I do not want my three sons growing up in a society that routinely glorifies violence and denies social responsibility.

This book is divided into three parts. The first part looks at the role of the media, and particularly media violence, in the lives of our children. Both television programs and movies are used to provide examples. Although the majority of research has been conducted on television, it seems likely that many of the findings are equally applicable to movies, which feature far more brutal and graphic depictions of violence than broadcast television. The first part traces the development of television in this country and examines more than forty years of research on the subject of media violence and children. I try to untangle the thicket of research, focusing on those findings that parents will find most significant and useful in understanding how their children are affected by media violence.

The second part of the book examines how children at specific stages of development think, act, and feel. Parents will be helped to see the world through the eyes of their children. The effects of the media will be considered in detail for children at different ages. Examples and suggestions will help parents decide which films and programs are appropriate and which are inappropriate. Although I have tried to keep my television and film examples reasonably contemporary, sometimes an older, better known movie or show is cited because of its familiarity to the public.

At the end of each chapter in Part Two is a checklist to help parents focus on the major issues affecting children at each stage of development. These checklists are included for easy reference, particularly when parents are on the fence about the appropriateness of a movie or television show for their child. Two or three no's suggest finding something else to watch. The checklists are divided into sections on attachment, aggression, cognitive development, and moral development so that parents can pay particular attention to those categories that may be troubling for their child. For example, if you are concerned about your child's being too aggressive, even a single no in the aggression category should alert you that this particular movie or television program is a poor choice for your child.

A Television Hall of Fame (and a Hall of Shame for preschoolers) following these checklists is offered as a jumping-off point for ideas about programs and movies that I consider either outstanding or particularly terrible. There is no Hall of Shame for kids past preschool because by middle childhood most of what kids watch is not children's television programming. So whereas *NYPD Blue* is inappropriate for an eight-year-old, the show is outstanding for an adult audience. Feel free to add your own picks and pans. Don't discount movies that are unfamiliar; there are many gems that deserve to be seen.

Some shows and movies have almost universal appeal and may be found in more than one age category. Don't be surprised if the movies contain some violence or deal with disturbing material. As this book should make clear, the point of parental supervision is not to shield children from all the disquieting aspects of life but rather to allow children to be exposed to difficult things in ways that enhance their ability to deal effectively with life's problems. A number of the movies, particularly in the older age groups, are R-rated. Some deal with upsetting or controversial content, so you might want to check them out yourself first.

For the most part, however, I tried to recommend interesting, thoughtful, and optimistic movies. At times, a good laugh is recommendation enough. There are a number of books on the market that give a brief synopsis of thousands of movies. Roger Ebert's *Video Companion* is particularly thoughtful and well written.

Finally, the third part of the book focuses on how parents, as well as government, schools, and the media, can best approach the problems created by a system at odds with itself. Is it possible both to "serve the public interest, convenience, and necessity" and to "recognize the special needs of children" while still turning a profit?[1] How can we, in our varying capacities as parents, educators, politicians, entertainers, and most important of all, citizens preserve a healthy cultural environment for our children? A list of resources at the end of the book provides parents with phone numbers and addresses of the major networks and government agencies involved with media regulation. This directory also helps parents and other concerned citizens locate organizations active in the area of media reform and media literacy.

PART ONE

Warning:

Viewing Violence Is Dangerous to Your Child's Health

1

What We Know

The debate is over.

Violence on television and in the movies is damaging to children. Forty years of research concludes that repeated exposure to high levels of media violence teaches some children and adolescents to settle interpersonal differences with violence, while teaching many more to be indifferent to this solution. Under the media's tutelage, children at younger and younger ages are using violence as a first, not a last, resort to conflict. Parents, eager to protect their children from the damaging influences of media, find that they are unable to find useful, accessible information about what is harmful.

Locked away in professional journals are thousands of articles documenting the negative effects of the media, and particularly media violence, on our nation's youth. Children who are heavy viewers of television are more aggressive, more pessimistic, less imaginative, less empathic, and less capable students than children who watch less. With an increasing sense of urgency, parents are realizing that the real story about media violence and its effects on children has been withheld.

Speaking before the U.S. Senate Committee on Governmental Affairs, Leonard Eron, one of the country's foremost experts on media and children, said:

There can no longer be any doubt that heavy exposure to tele-vised violence is one of the causes of aggressive behavior, crime and violence in society. The evidence comes from both the laboratory and real-life studies. Television violence affects youngsters of all ages, of both genders, at all socioeconomic levels and all levels of intelligence. The effect is not limited to children who are already disposed to being aggressive and is not restricted to this country.[1]

Every major group concerned with children has studied and issued position papers on the effects of media violence on children. The Surgeon General's Scientific Advisory Committee on Televi-sion and Social Behavior, the National Institute of Mental Health, The U.S. Attorney General's Task Force on Family Violence, the American Psychological Association, the American Academy of Pediatrics, and the National Parent-Teachers Association have all called for curbing of television and movie violence. Their findings represent the inescapable conclusions of decades of social science research. Doctors, therapists, teachers, and youth workers all find themselves struggling to help youngsters who, influenced by re-peated images of quick, celebratory, and gratuitous violence, find it increasingly difficult to negotiate the inevitable frustrations of daily life.

The United States has become the most violent nation in the industrialized world. Homicide is the leading cause of death for large segments of our country's youth, and we have more young men in prison than any other country in the world. The roots of violence in our society are complex. We are well informed about the contributions of poverty, child abuse, alcoholism, and drug abuse, but we must also consider the role played by the images that our children see on the television screen during their average three and a half hours of daily viewing.

A major gap exists between research findings and what the public knows about the harmful effects of media violence on chil-dren. This is not surprising. Public education often lags behind research, especially when economic stakes are high. For example, until recently, tobacco executives were still insisting that "the scientific proof isn't in yet to link smoking and cancer."[2] The entertainment industry stands to lose a great deal of money if violence, a particularly cheap and reliable form of entertainment, becomes less popular.

Ordinarily, when science discovers a matter of pressing public concern, it relies on the cooperation of the media to ensure that this information reaches a wide audience. Much of the success of the antismoking campaign was due to the media's active efforts at educating the public. Similarly, the media have played a significant role in educating Americans about the advantages of wearing seat belts, the need for child car seats, and the inadvisability of drinking and driving. As a result we have seen a significant reduction in children and teenagers dying in motor vehicle accidents. Yet violence among youngsters and teenagers has skyrocketed. Researchers speak with one voice in telling us that this is partly due to the incessant glamorization of violence in the media. However, the entertainment industry's self-protective stance has resulted in these findings' being ignored, denied, attacked, or misrepresented.

In May 1995 presidential hopeful Bob Dole delivered a blistering attack on the entertainment industry. "A line has been crossed—not just of taste but of human dignity and decency." He called for an end to the "mainstreaming of deviancy." Dole struck a chord of national discontent even though he freely admitted that he had not personally seen much of what he attacked and seemed to ignore the paradox of calling for an end to violent images while simultaneously supporting a repeal of the ban on assault weapons. Headlines across the country announced "Dole Scolds Entertainment Industry."

In typical punch-and-parry fashion, the entertainment industry responded within hours. "Hollywood Scoffs at Dole's Rebuke of Show Business"[3] proclaimed feature articles the next day. Using characteristic hyperbole, director Oliver Stone called Senator Dole "a modern-day McCarthy."[4] But of the dozens of articles crossing my desk in this frenzy of accusations and counteraccusations, not one dealt with substantive issues. The entertainment industry can ill afford to scoff at the legitimate concerns of parents who feel that their children are awash in images of violence and cruelty. Nor can concerned citizens simply rebuke the entertainment industry without being knowledgeable about the problems. *Informed* dialogue precedes change. The importance of the effects of media violence on child development is far too great to be abandoned to the arena of parental grumbling and political opportunity.

It seems that we are regularly presented with articles connecting horrible crimes with exposure to the media.

- Serial killer Nathaniel White described how he killed his first female victim while imitating a scene from the movie *Robocop 2*. "I seen him cut somebody's throat then take the knife and slit down the chest to the stomach and leave the body in a certain position. With the first person I killed I did exactly what I saw in the movie."[5]

- Two young adolescents murdered a disabled man in California by kicking, stabbing, beating, and finally choking him to death. When asked by the police why they poured salt in the dying man's wounds, one of the boys responded, "Oh I don't know. I just seen it on TV."[6]

- Nine-year-old Olivia Niemi was sexually assaulted with a discarded beer bottle on a deserted beach in San Francisco. The four girls who took part in the attack said they were imitating a scene from *Born Innocent*, an NBC television movie they watched three days before committing the crime.[7] The movie, which takes place in a girls' reform school, shows a new inmate cornered by four girls and graphically raped with the handle of a plumber's helper.

It is time to move past the debate of whether or not the entertainment industry is responsible for these crimes. The question is not whether the media are the cause of crimes like these (they aren't) but whether the media are an important ingredient in the multiple causation of crime (they are). Violence is frequently the end point of many different personal, social, and environmental factors. Television has become a powerful environmental source of behaviors, attitudes, and values. In many homes it threatens the traditional triumvirate of socialization—family, school, and church. *Excessive and gratuitous media violence is an easily reversible contributor to crime.* Quite simply, we need to tell our children stories that contribute to their healthy development and encourage positive behaviors rather than allowing the media to encourage negative ones.

By the time they graduate from high school, children will have spent 50 percent more time in front of a television set than in front of a teacher. The average American household has television turned on more than seven hours a day, and the average American child watches three to four hours a day.[8] The vast majority of this time is spent watching programs not targeted to a children's audience—game shows, soap operas, and MTV. Television makes no distinctions among viewers. If you are four years old and able to turn on the television, then you are privy to the same information as a fourteen-year-old or a forty-year-old. Television is promiscuous. It shows itself to anyone who wants to take a look. Neil Postman, author of many outstanding books on the effects of technology on children, has wisely observed:

> Indeed, it is a common enough observation, particularly favored by television executives when under attack, that whatever else may be said about television's impact on the young, today's children are better informed than any previous groups of youngsters. The metaphor usually employed is that television is a window to the world. This observation is entirely correct, but why it should be taken as a sign of progress is a mystery. . . . It means that in having access to the previously hidden fruit of adult information, they are expelled from the garden of childhood.[9]

Television has eradicated many of the traditional barriers that protected children from the harsh facts of adult life. No wonder youngsters who are heavy viewers of television are more pessimistic than light viewers. They have been exposed to a world of violence, sex, commercialism, and betrayal far beyond their emotional capacities. Hours spent watching the O. J. Simpson trial make the world of adults look grim indeed.

George Gerbner, dean emeritus of the Annenberg School of Communication, believes that television "tells most of the stories to most of the people, most of the time."[10] Television "cultivates" the viewer's perceptions of society, encouraging the belief that the real world is more or less like the fictionalized world of television. Television has become the melting pot of the twentieth century. It provides us with a shared set of beliefs and assumptions about how the world works. Television is such a fundamental part of life that one in four Americans say that they wouldn't surrender their sets for a million dollars.[11]

Network executives are quick to exploit our sense that television is a kind of cultural glue binding us together as a nation. In a *TV Guide* interview, Judy Price, vice president for children's programming at CBS said, "A kid can't be the only one on the playground not to watch *Power Rangers*."[12] This statement highlights one of the prime objectives of media promotion. In addition to making things familiar and desirable, the media must create an appearance of social necessity. "A kid can't be the only one on the playground not to watch *Power Rangers*" implies that the child who is prevented from partaking in this quintessential American experience will be denied full participation in the social life of his or her peer group. While shared media experiences are certainly part of group conversation at playgrounds, workplaces, and homes around the country, parents should not be made to feel guilty when they act to protect their children from excessively violent programming.

These manipulations by people in the entertainment industry are revealing as well as distressing. Media executives loudly demand that parents take more responsibility for their children's viewing.

"When are you going to stop blaming the media and start looking at the home environment and the fact that parents are supposed to monitor what their children are watching?" admonishes a well-known Hollywood producer.[13] However, parents and politicians who lobbied for the V-chip (which would allow parents to screen out violent programming) were told by industry leaders who opposed the V-chip that violence must be evaluated on a case-by-case basis. When the V-chip became inevitable, the industry then fought long and hard against providing an appropriate rating system for parents. It is no accident that parents feel so helpless about controlling access to media they disapprove of. While giving lip service to the need for adult supervision, television executives aggressively act to circumvent parental authority.

Television itself should not be demonized. It can serve as an effective instrument for human development and enrichment. Wonderful programs, including many on the Public Broadcasting Service (PBS), have proved that television can teach children new skills, enlarge their worldview, and promote prosocial attitudes and behaviors. But commercial television has a different agenda than personal and cultural development. Commercial television's agenda is to round up the largest and most affluent audience it can and deliver that audience to an advertiser.

Advertisers like programs with good track records and proven formulas for gaining an audience. That is why so much of what television offers appears repetitive and formulaic. We may have access to hundreds of stations, but in fact the kinds of stories we see are surprisingly limited. As a result television cultivates a common perspective. All too frequently that perspective includes a reliance on violence as a habitual, acceptable, and even admirable way of resolving conflict. This trivializes the enormous human toll that violence always exacts.

The media, as major disseminators of attitudes, assumptions, and values, can ill afford to ignore their responsibilities while asserting their rights. While the National Rifle Association insists that "guns don't kill people; people kill people," the fact is they do it with guns. Similarly, television doesn't kill people, but it encourages antisocial behavior by providing the ideas, the social sanctions, and often even the instructions. Those who profit from the enormous opportunities for financial gain and status that the entertainment industry provides must act as citizens as well as businesspeople. And it is the responsibility of all citizens, not just parents, to provide children with a culturally healthy environment.

The effects of the media are not trivial. For example, it is well known that suicide rates increase after the suicide of a celebrity *if* there is extensive media coverage. The highly publicized suicide of Kurt Cobain, lead singer for the rock group Nirvana, resulted in many copycat suicides, mostly of male adolescents. "When Kurt Cobain died, I died with him" was the note left by an eighteen-year-old who, along with two other friends, executed a suicide pact following Cobain's death.[14] This is not to suggest that the news should not have been reported. But science has provided us with enough research to be able to predict that the kind of sensational and repeated coverage that Cobain's suicide received was bound to result in an increase in adolescent suicides. Parents need to be aware that sensational coverage of crime and suicide by young celebrities can be emotionally devastating for vulnerable teens. Parental awareness, supervision, and discussion are critical variables in heading off additional tragedies.

Although examples of copycat crimes are particularly distressing, they underscore the power of a medium that reaches into virtually every household in the United States. Setting social norms can never be considered a trivial task. If you are elderly, it is not trivial that the media insist on reducing you to a dotty simpleton. If you are an African American, it is not trivial that the media vacillate between worshiping you as a sports hero, laughing at you as a buffoon, or reviling you as a thug. If you are a woman, it is not trivial that every female newscaster must be ten or twenty years younger than her male counterpart. If you are a parent who tries to convey the values of hard work and good education to your children, it is not trivial that Beavis and Butt-Head have become the supermodels of teenage sloth and indifference.

Images have consequences, often distressing and even tragic ones. My eleven-year-old son and I turned on the news one evening to hear a quick disclaimer about "disturbing images" followed by scenes of dead and critically injured children. In a neighboring community, a van had slammed into a school playground, killing one child and critically injuring several others. In the two seconds it took for me to reach over and change channels, those blood-soaked images were burned into our minds. My son had great difficulty sleeping and experienced many nightmares that night. Were those scenes necessary? As news, did that footage teach us anything we need to know about the world or how to conduct our lives? I don't believe it did. No context was provided for the incident. There was no investigation of why our society tolerates drivers who operate unsafe vehicles or have multiple driving offenses. Rather I believe the television station was following the time-honored bromide "If it bleeds, it leads."

Like so much of what passes for "news," this was simply visual exploitation without any attempt to inform the public about significant underlying social problems. Media executives who invoke First Amendment rights to justify such irresponsible programming are cowards. Grant Tinker, before becoming president of NBC, called poor television programming "a national crime" and suggested that network executives who did not live up to their responsibilities be jailed.[15]

The basis of all societies is a reasonably shared set of values. We may define ourselves individually as Democrats or Republicans, liberals or conservatives, antigovernment or progovernment. However, most Americans would agree that there is a basic set of values that define our society. These include loyalty, responsibility, family, integrity, and courage. Respect for individual rights, accompanied by a tolerance for diversity, has characterized the United States (at least in theory) since its founding.

The word *rights* came up repeatedly in my discussions with various media executives: individual rights, creative rights, and most predictably, First Amendment rights. I am not a political scientist, and this incessant referral to First Amendment rights as a way of deflecting criticism sent me scurrying to my son's high school social studies text to refamiliarize myself with the Constitution and the Bill of Rights. I had almost forgotten that there is a Preamble to the Constitution that puts forth the overarching principles of our democracy. In the Preamble there is no mention of rights. Rather, the tone and language recognize that the United States was founded on the notion of communal responsibility rather than on individual rights. The Preamble talks of "*common* defense" and "*general* welfare."

The Bill of Rights, the first ten amendments to the Constitution, is familiar to the public. Whether it's the gun lobby invoking a self-serving version of the Second Amendment or First Amendment absolutists like director Oliver Stone, who echoes the sentiments of many in the entertainment industry when he equates criticism with censorship, the United States has turned its attention from responsibilities to rights. Rights are not entitlements; they are immunities. None of us, whether we are parents, politicians, media executives, or members of special-interest groups, can afford to forget that along with the extraordinary range of rights that we enjoy in this country comes an equally extraordinary range of responsibilities.

When executives in the entertainment industry insist that profits come before responsibility, they do not live up to their commitment to serve the public. When we as parents allow our children to sit and watch hours of thoughtless violence, we do not live up to our commitment to protect and nurture our children. Our children are being hurt. They are hurt when they are the victims or perpetrators of mindless violence illustrated and glorified by the media. They are hurt when they see the world as a corrupt and frightening place in which only consumer goods bring satisfaction and peace of mind. They are hurt when they have become so dependent on rapid-fire, prefabricated visual effects that they can no longer conjure up their own images or dream their own dreams. It is time to stop hurting our most vulnerable population. It is time to start protecting our children.

MASS MEDIA MYTHS

True or false?

- Media violence is just entertainment. It has no real effect on the way people think or behave.
- Americans are particularly enchanted with violence and so the entertainment industry is only giving us what we want.
- Watching violence is cathartic. It actually makes people less aggressive by allowing them to "blow off some steam."
- Parents have a pretty good understanding of what their children are watching and how it is affecting them.
- The airwaves in the United States are owned by the large networks.
- Cartoons are not really frightening to children and do not influence their behavior.
- Children with high IQs are less affected by media violence than children with lower IQs.
- Over the past two decades, the entertainment industry has responded to the demands of parents, educators, and politicians and has significantly reduced the amount of violence shown on television.

ALL OF THESE STATEMENTS ARE FALSE!

2

Television in the USA

Television was introduced to the American public by the Radio Corporation of America at the New York World's Fair in 1939. Not incidentally, the first image to be publicly broadcast on a television screen was the dollar sign.[1] At that time television was viewed largely as an object of curiosity, although the well-known journalist and children's author E. B. White wrote with uncanny clairvoyance, "I believe television is going to be the test of the modern world, and in this new opportunity to see beyond the range of our vision, we shall discover either a new and unbearable disturbance of the general peace or a saving radiance in the sky. We shall stand or fall by television—of that I am quite sure."[2]

Not even E. B. White's prescience could have prepared him for the kinds of experiences that television would soon be bringing into virtually every American household. We would see some of our most beloved political leaders—John F. Kennedy, Robert Kennedy, and Martin Luther King Jr.—murdered before our collective eyes. We would watch televised courtroom trials during which serial killers Jeffrey Dahmer and Ted Bundy described crimes of unspeakable inhumanity. We would see seven popular astronauts reduced to a plume of smoke in the *Challenger* disaster. Ninety-five million people would sit in rapt absorption as O. J. Simpson, a sports superstar, fled down a Los Angeles freeway allegedly to avoid arrest for the double murder of his ex-wife, Nicole Brown Simpson, and her friend Ron Goldman.

We have been delighted by, indifferent to, or offended by characters like Archie Bunker, Murphy Brown, and Roseanne. Television and the movies have become such a common reference point that Vice President Dan Quayle made Murphy Brown's pregnancy a political issue in his 1992 bid for reelection. President Bush appropriated a line from Clint Eastwood's *Dirty Harry* movie and invited the Iraqis to "make my day" during the Persian Gulf War. Following the release of Spike Lee's popular film *Do the Right Thing*, members of Congress saw fit to use that phrase sixty-seven times in a four-month period.[3] Presidential hopeful Bill Clinton appeared on MTV to bring his agenda to the program's fifteen million potential voters.[4]

Almost every child in this country knows Big Bird, Bert and Ernie, and the Cookie Monster. Barney, a purple dinosaur created by a mother in Texas unhappy with the programming available to her young son, has proved wildly successful. Seventeen kindergartners sang his "I Love You, You Love Me" anthem as they cringed in terror in a disabled elevator during the New York World Trade Center bombing. For nearly thirty years Mister Rogers has played friend, educator, and psychotherapist to children, reassuring them that "you're special" and "I like you just the way you are." Karate has become the social interaction of choice as youngsters pay homage to the Teenage Mutant Ninja Turtles and Power Rangers in playgrounds around the country.

Americans, regardless of race, religion, gender, age, or socioeconomic group, have been bound together by the shared cultural experience of television. We have watched with attention, interest, and sometimes disbelief as television has poured the world into our living rooms and bedrooms. Television, which was in only 9 percent of American households in 1950, is now in 98 percent of them.[5] Most homes have two or more televisions as well as cable and a VCR, all of which allow access to an ever-expanding range of media offerings. Children are watching, on average, close to twenty-eight hours of television every week.

George Gerbner has observed, "The longer we live with television, the more invisible it becomes."[6] Television and the media in general have so successfully saturated our culture that we barely recognize their influence. Major U.S. corporations spend over $45 billion a year on advertising designed to cultivate desire and change our behavior.[7] Our attitudes and actions are shaped in ways that are subtle, persuasive, and often outside our consciousness. Many people in this country cannot remember a time before television.

Though Americans have embraced television, the concerns about its role and influence are long-standing. In 1961 the recently appointed chairman of the Federal Communications Commission, Newton Minow, delivered his famous "vast wasteland" speech. In his inaugural address to the National Association of Broadcasters, he said:

> When television is good, nothing—not the theater, not the magazines or newspapers—nothing is better. But when television is bad, nothing is worse. I invite you to sit down in front of your television set when your station goes on the air and stay there without a book, magazine, newspaper, profit-and-loss sheet, or rating book to distract you—and keep your eyes glued to that set until the station signs off. I can assure you that you will observe a vast wasteland. You will see a procession of game shows, violence, audience participation shows, formula comedies about unbelievable families, blood and thunder, mayhem, violence, sadism, murder, western bad men, western good men, private eyes, gangsters, more violence, and cartoons. And, endlessly, commercials—many screaming, cajoling, and offending.[8]

Thirty years later, on the anniversary of this speech, Minow observed, "In 1961 I worried that my children would not benefit

much from television, but in 1991, I worry that my grandch
will actually be harmed by it."[9]

Minow's worries are shared by all those interested in the effects
of media on child development. Historically, there has always been
concern about the ways in which children can be manipulated by
"outside ideas." In Plato's *Republic*, Socrates asks, "Then, shall we
simply allow our children to listen to any stories that anyone happens to make up, and so receive into their minds ideas often the
very opposite of those we shall think they ought to have when they
grow up?"[10] All forms of media have been the subject of widespread
concern at one time or another. Radio, silent movies, and comic
books have all had their share of critics. Mass media bring into the
home ideas and sensibilities that are beyond the control of, and
often in conflict with, parental values.

As American society changes, fragments, and, too frequently,
explodes, concern about the effects of media on children has accelerated. We now live in a country where ten-year-olds murder
babies and fourteen-year-olds march into schools fully armed and
mow down classmates. In 1971 there were about 550 studies on
children and television. In 1990, this number soared to almost
3,000.

Parents today feel less able to control their children. Isolated
from extended family and often economically stressed, American
parents spend less time with their children than parents in any
other nation in the world.[11] Many would argue that television has
replaced all other institutions as the single most powerful transmitter of cultural values.

Both common sense and my experience as a psychologist tell
me that parents are still the most active agents in a child's socialization. However, there is no question that television teaches children many things about our culture. Television reflects, creates, and
perpetuates our social order. It teaches who's in charge and who sub-
mits. It illustrates who gets away with things and who is likely to be
punished. Television takes us behind the scenes of our society. Here,
men dominate the airways, women are a subservient minority, real

minorities barely exist, and when they do it is usually only in stereo-typed fashion. Television communicates the hierarchy of power re-lations in our society. Too frequently it teaches boys how to be perpetrators and girls how to be victims.

Research on the effects of media has focused on several areas, effects on children being the most prominent. Is violence on tele-vision harmful to children? In what ways? Who is most likely to be harmed?

Unusual circumstances have allowed social scientists to look at what happens to communities when television is introduced. In 1973 Tannis McBeth Williams and colleagues were presented with the opportunity to study an ordinary Canadian town about to receive television for the first time.[12] The town, which the re-searchers named Notel, was not an unusual or particularly isolated town, but because of its location in a deep valley it had been unable to receive television signals. The researchers had a year in which to accumulate data on many variables, including children's level of aggression before television transmitters were installed. For comparison, data were also collected on two nearby towns, one called Unitel, with limited television service, and one called Multitel, with ordinary television service. The results of the study were unequivocal. Two years after the introduction of television, children in Notel displayed a significantly increased level of ag-gression. This increase took place regardless of gender or initial level of aggression. The study also showed that the introduction of television decreased children's reading scores, creativity, and involvement in community activities. Sex-role stereotyping increased as well.

Although this study took place in Canada, the bulk of research on the effects of media violence has been conducted in the United States. When researchers have studied media effects in other coun-tries, results have been generally comparable. Unfortunately, but perhaps not surprisingly, despite a large body of scientific knowl-edge, the media have been superficial in coverage of this issue. We are often led to believe that this is an area of debate in the academic community. Minimal differences in research findings are sometimes used as proof that conclusions are unwarranted. But almost without exception, research has consistently shown the damaging effects of television's showcasing of excessive and gratuitous violence.

The truth is that violence is not generic and neither are children. Different kinds of children at different ages are affected by violence in different ways. The reasons for the social problems of this country are long-standing and complex. Many other factors besides media violence—lack of job opportunities, availability of guns, drugs, and poverty—must be considered when making a thoughtful assessment of this country's high murder rate and high rate of incarceration. It is foolish to suggest that television, or any single factor, is responsible for these problems. But television's contribution is real and needs to be understood. The next chapter looks at some of the major studies that have been conducted on the effects of media violence on children. Research has identified and focused on three major areas of concern:

1. Does media violence encourage children to act more aggressively?
2. Does media violence cultivate attitudes that are excessively distorted, fearful, and pessimistic?
3. Does media violence desensitize children to violence?

The research answers each of these questions with a disturbing yes. A familiarity with these studies and their implications provides the backbone for later chapters designed to help parents make informed decisions about their children's viewing.

3

Research and Theory

Despite its title, this chapter is quite practical. It takes a quick look at some of the major research that has been conducted on media violence and children. Its purpose is to familiarize parents with the fact that a large and respected body of research supports what most parents know intuitively: that watching people behave violently does not promote healthy child development. The facts in this chapter should encourage parents to give greater consideration to their gut feeling that regular viewing of violent media is bad for their children.

DOES MEDIA VIOLENCE ENCOURAGE CHILDREN TO ACT MORE AGGRESSIVELY?

Children are great imitators. Even in the earliest months of life, infants can mimic the facial expressions of their caretakers. Children learn how to eat, dress, use the toilet, and begin to interact with others because people around them, particularly their parents and other caretakers, as well as peers and siblings, are constantly providing examples of how to do things. Children are not particularly selective in what they imitate; countless parents have been reminded to pay attention to their language when their three-year-old utters "damn it" in frustration. Sometimes it seems as if nothing escapes the attention of the young child. Although imitation is not the only way that children learn, it is the earliest and sets the stage for future learning.

Given that children are relentless in their imitation of people around them, it is logical that they would also imitate people they see on television and in the movies. From Davy Crockett coonskin caps to Teenage Mutant Ninja Turtle bandannas, costumes based on television characters have always been extremely popular. This type of imitation of screen characters is not limited to young children. A generation of adolescents rolled up their T-shirt sleeves and cultivated the sneer and swagger of James Dean and Marlon Brando. Many of today's teenagers seem to have shopped at a single store, so alike are they in their choice of flannel shirts and baseball caps, a style of dress begun and perfected by the grunge bands of MTV. Throughout the life cycle, we imitate others in order to learn new things and to reinforce our identity with a particular group.

Stories of children imitating characters from the media with tragic results are reported with some regularity.

- A five-year-old boy set his home on fire, killing his two-year-old sister, following a *Beavis and Butt-Head* episode. The boy's mother described him as addicted to Beavis and Butt-Head—two moronic preadolescent MTV cartoon characters who enjoy setting fires and other antisocial acts.[1]
- An adolescent boy was killed by a car and several of his friends seriously injured while imitating a scene from the movie *The Program*. The scene shows young men attempting to prove their courage by lying down between car lanes on a busy road.[2]
- A thirteen-year-old boy and his friend acted out the Russian roulette scene from the movie *The Deer Hunter*. The young boy died instantly after shooting himself in the head.[3]

These stories are tragic, but thankfully they are also rare. Clearly most children do not simply imitate what they see on the screen.

Instead, out of the multitude of behaviors, images, attitudes, and values that children are exposed to, they choose only certain ones to make their own. When frustrated, one child cries in a corner while another kicks and punches and yet a third seems to take the frustration in stride. Though imitation may be the earliest form of learning, children do not become carbon copies of the people around them. As for the effects of media violence on children, if imitation were the only or even the primary form of learning, we could predict tomorrow's headlines from today's *TV Guide*. We cannot, of course, and that is because what children learn from the media is usually far more complex than simple imitation.

Some of the earliest research on the effects of media violence on children was conducted by Albert Bandura at Stanford University in the 1960s. For more than three decades, Bandura has looked at the ways in which children construct their selves out of the range of possibilities available to them. His early work focused on the circumstances under which children became more aggressive by observing aggression. His Bobo doll studies are considered classic experiments in psychology and have done much to illuminate the ways in which children are likely to learn from media violence.

Bandura's Bobo doll is a large inflatable clown that is weighted to pop back up when hit. In a typical experiment, Bandura divided nursery school children into three groups: one control group and two experimental groups. All children were initially put into a room filled with attractive toys. The control group was then excluded.

One experimental group watched a filmed sequence on a simulated television set.

The film began with a scene in which [an adult male] model walked up to an adult-size plastic Bobo doll and ordered him to clear the way. After glaring for a moment at the noncompliant antagonist, the model exhibited four novel aggressive responses each accompanied by a distinctive verbalization. First, the model laid the Bobo doll on its side, sat on it, and punched it in the nose while remarking, "Pow, right in the nose, boom, boom." The model then raised the doll and pummeled it on the head with a mallet. Each response was accompanied by the verbalization "Sockeroo . . . stay down." Following the mallet aggression, the model kicked the doll about the room, and these responses were interspersed with the comment "Fly away." Finally, the model threw rubber balls at the Bobo doll, each strike punctuated with "Bang." This sequence of physically and verbally aggressive behavior was repeated twice.[4]

The children in the other experimental group saw the same sequence performed live by an adult male. After this, all three groups of children were brought into a room containing many toys, among them balls, a pegboard, mallet, guns, and dolls. Children who were in the control group displayed few or none of the aggressive behaviors. However, children who had viewed the attacks on the Bobo doll, either on television or live, displayed a considerable number of aggressive behaviors similar to those they had observed.

What was perhaps most interesting about Bandura's findings were the novel ways children found to express their aggression. One little girl took a doll and twirled it around by one leg, slamming it into the Bobo doll. Another young boy grabbed a pistol and began shooting the Bobo doll. Not only did the children imitate adult displays of aggression, but they also added their own particular spin. This is why we say that children frequently "model" their behavior rather than simply imitate what they see.

There were a number of criticisms of Bandura's research. Detractors said that of course children learn behavior from adults, but that doesn't mean that they would copy television, particularly cartoon violence. Others said that a child acting aggressively toward a toy doesn't mean that the child would be aggressive toward a person. Further research laid these objections to rest. Children who were aggressive with the Bobo doll were also more aggressive toward peers. Other studies found that children could learn aggressive behavior from a cartoon figure just as readily as from a live adult.[5]

The fact that a child does not act aggressively after observing violence does not mean that the child has not learned about aggression. Performing and learning are not necessarily the same. Of the children who observed the adult acting aggressively toward the Bobo doll, most became more aggressive and some did not, but they all *learned* about behaving aggressively. Many of us have had the experience of reacting angrily in some trivial situation, such as being cut off on the freeway and responding with obscenities and an itchy middle finger. A few minutes later we may wonder, "Where did that come from?" It comes from the large repertoire of aggressive responses that we have learned and stored but generally have enough control to bypass. Because a child does not go out and shoot someone after watching *Demolition Man* does not mean that the child has not learned that shooting might be a plausible solution to frustration and anger. Actual aggressive behavior may appear only in situations where controls have been reduced or self-esteem is seriously threatened.

To look for a direct relationship between violent programming and children's behavior is simplistic and not particularly useful. As children grow past the preschool years, their aggressive behavior becomes less imitative and more reflective of their developing interpersonal style. Although a three-year-old may imitate a Teenage Mutant Ninja Turtle kick more or less exactly, the older child, with a larger repertoire of behaviors, just seems to get more physically aggressive. Watch a theater full of young adolescents after a showing of *Lethal Weapon*. They leave the theater pushing and shoving and generally more physically active than if they had seen a comedy. Though they are not exhibiting a new behavior, it has become easier to express an old aggressive behavior such as pushing or shoving. Provocation or frustration increases the likelihood that learned aggression will find expression. Several cities have experienced melees and even homicides following the showing of particularly provocative movies. The ordinary jostle that one might experience leaving a crowded theater becomes a trigger for barely contained rage.

Although true imitation of a fictional crime is rare, it does happen. In 1987 a disturbed young man named Michael Ryan committed Britain's worst mass murder. Dressed in full Rambo gear, he slaughtered sixteen people, including his mother, before turning his gun on himself. The most appalling example of movie imitation is that twenty-six people have shot themselves through the head playing out the Russian roulette scene from the 1978 Vietnam war epic *The Deer Hunter*.[6] More recently, fourteen-year-old Michael Carneal walked fully armed into his school in West Paducah, Kentucky, and shot down a group of teenagers as they began a prayer circle. Three of the girls died, and five more students were seriously injured. Carneal admitted to police that the scene of carnage he left behind was something he had seen in the movie *The Basketball Diaries*.

To ask the right questions, we need to switch the focus from "Do television and movies teach children to be more aggressive?" (they do) and instead ask "How effectively is aggression taught?" Under what circumstances are children most likely to express the violent solutions they have learned? An extensive body of research suggests that several important variables determine how effective a media message will be in teaching aggression to children:

- Do children identify with the character?
- Is the violence reinforced? Does crime pay?
- Is the violence seen as real or make-believe?

Parents must have some understanding of each of these factors because they all play an important part in answering our basic concern, "Is this likely to teach my child to behave aggressively in response to conflict and frustration?"

Do Children Identify with the Character?

Common sense tells us that we are more likely to imitate people who are attractive, respected, and powerful. Jacqueline Kennedy's pillbox hats and simple suits were as popular among aspiring young women in the 1960s as Eddie Vedder's flannel shirts and ripped shorts are among adolescent suburbanites in the 1990s. Within their respective groups, these two stylish individuals—contemporary, talented, and powerful—were seen as models worthy of imitation. Imitating people who are prestigious and powerful allows us the illusion of borrowing some of their authority and privilege.

Research studies have shown that the more we identify and empathize with a character, the more likely we are to imitate that character.[7] For this reason many psychologists are particularly concerned about "good guy violence." Contrary to popular opinion, the good guys do almost as much killing as the bad guys. Of course, these murders are presented as necessary and justified. As a result the audience is likely to retain sympathy for the police officer whose partner was murdered, or husband whose wife has been raped, or parent whose child has been abducted. It is not uncommon in a movie theater to hear applause and shouts of approval when the bad guy is finally blown to pieces by the heroic avenger.

Clint Eastwood, Charles Bronson, Sylvester Stallone, and Arnold Schwarzenegger have all been wildly successful in their roles as vigilante heroes. The police and judicial system are dismissed as trivial and incompetent. At the end of *Dirty Harry*, we see Clint Eastwood toss his badge into the water, a dramatic gesture suggesting that the institutions designed to serve justice in this country are disposable. Many of our most popular movies carry messages suggesting that violence, not due process, is the manly and appropriate solution to crime. Equally distressing is the blurring of boundaries between good and evil.

We see the awful consequences of this point of view in our newspapers daily. Young men are murdered for "dissing," or being disrespectful to, another young man. Children are killed for their jackets or their sneakers. These are the tragic end points of a culture that glorifies violence, neglects the complexities of social problems, and elevates men who are vengeful and ruthless to icon status. If we truly want less aggressive and more compassionate children, we will have to come up with different role models for our children to admire and emulate.

There are bright spots to be considered. Knowing that children are most likely to model their behavior after characters they like and identify with helps us choose programs that feature healthy role models. Just as children become aggressive following exposure to antisocial programming, they can also become more cooperative after exposure to prosocial programming.

Sesame Street, the most watched children's television program of all time, has been the subject of intense scrutiny. Volumes of research have been written on the academic and social effects of the program. Because it is multicultural and avoids gender stereotypes, children find many characters to identify with. Not surprisingly, children who are regular viewers show enhanced social skills and attitudes. Minority children show increased cultural pride, confidence, and interpersonal cooperation.[8] Caucasian children show more positive attitudes toward children of other races.[9] Positive effects of *Sesame Street*, in terms of acquiring academic as well as social skills, are stronger if the child watches with a parent.[10] This point will be stressed repeatedly throughout this book. *Parental involvement greatly enhances the prosocial effects and reduces the antisocial effects of media on children.*

Is the Violence Reinforced? Does Crime Pay?

Young children see things in black and white. They reach moral conclusions by observing which behaviors get punished and which don't. Numerous studies have shown that children are most likely to imitate violence that has been rewarded. In one variation of Bandura's Bobo doll studies, one group of children watched an adult beat up the Bobo doll and then be rewarded with stickers and juice. The adult was told that he was a "strong champion." Another group of children saw the adult punished by being spanked with a rolled-up magazine and told, "If I catch you doing that again, you big bully, I'll give you a hard spanking. You quit acting that way." Both groups of children were then left in a room with many toys, including the Bobo doll, and were told to play while the experimenter left for a few minutes. Needless to say, children who had seen the adult being rewarded for his aggressive behavior were far more likely to act aggressively than children who had seen the adult being punished.[11]

It is comforting to know that research confirms what most parents know intuitively. Few of us would consider resolving our conflicts at home by smacking or shooting each other. We are constantly trying to shape our children's behavior by rewarding their cooperative efforts and punishing their aggressive and inappropriate behavior. The media's sanctioning of violence as a respectable solution can be either exaggerated or extremely subtle. This book is filled with examples of the kind of in-your-face, out-of-control violence found in movies such as *Die Hard* and *Con Air*. However, in the popular movie *Kindergarten Cop*, a kinder, gentler Arnold Schwarzenegger assaults a child molester. He is then called into the principal's office, expecting to be chewed out for fighting in front of the children he teaches. Instead, after a dramatic pause, the principal asks, "How did it feel to punch out that son-of-a-bitch?" Schwarzenegger is congratulated for his aggression. The applauding audience, along with the principal, considers Schwarzenegger's aggression appropriate, even heroic.

Of course, taken as a single example, this seems trivial. Where's my sense of humor? It was a funny scene. But this book is about the *cumulative effects* of media violence. It is about the fact that we hardly even notice anymore that conflict is routinely solved by aggression. In real life, aggressive solutions are rarely rewarded or seen as funny. The truth is that aggressive children and adolescents tend to be ostracized, not lionized, by their peer groups.

Like violence that is rewarded, violence that seems justified is far more likely to be imitated than violence that seems unjustified. Psychologist Leonard Berkowitz and his colleagues at the University of Wisconsin have carefully researched the topic of justified aggression. In a typical study, Berkowitz had male subjects angered by being insulted. The subjects were then divided into two groups. One group saw a violent movie in which a bad guy was beaten up.

The other group saw the same violent movie, but this time a good guy was beaten up. After the movie, the subjects were allowed to punish the student who had insulted them earlier. Those who had seen the bad guy beaten up were much harsher in their punishment than those who had seen the good guy beaten up. Berkowitz interprets these differences by saying that the movie violence against the bad guy was seen as morally justified, whereas the violence against the good guy was morally unacceptable. The subjects in the experiment tended to see their own behavior in the same light. Justified aggression on the screen made these young men feel that their own aggression was similarly justified.[12]

Ethical considerations prohibit studies in which people are actually allowed to injure others. However, some particularly creative studies have strongly suggested that people who feel they are justified in acting aggressively would do so if given a chance in the real world. Stanley Milgram, at Yale University, conducted a well-known series of experiments on obedience to authority. He studied the willingness of people to administer electric shocks to another person. The person being shocked was actually a partner of the experimenter and the shocks were not real, although the subjects did not know this. Instead they were instructed to continue "shocking" the person despite screams and pleas for mercy. When subjects hesitated to proceed, the experimenter emphasized the necessity of conducting the experiment. More than 63 percent of the subjects completed the experiment, despite the fact that it appeared they were torturing another human being. Later questioning revealed that those administering the shocks felt they were justified because they were "following instructions."[13]

The world has repeatedly experienced devastation by people who felt that their brutality was justified because they were "just following orders." Media for children should emphasize responsibility for individual action rather than encourage blind obedience to authority. *Teenage Mutant Ninja Turtles*, for example, is structured so that the Turtles take much of their instruction from the old rat

Splinter. Although Splinter is portrayed as a wise character, his orders are arbitrary and often condone violence. Most important, the Turtles never question his orders or think about the implications of behaving aggressively. As parents we spend years encouraging children to take responsibility for their own actions ("If everyone jumped off the bridge, would you?"). Programs for children should encourage reflection and consideration of consequences.

One of the most significant and frightening findings in the research on justified violence concerns attitudes toward rape and the abuse of women in general. Edward Donnerstein, a leading researcher in the field of aggression and pornography, has repeatedly demonstrated that when subjects are given information that endorses aggression and then are shown violent pornography, their own aggression toward women increases.[14] Exposure to films that are both violent and pornographic and in which the sexual aggression is seen as either justified or not harmful ("she liked it," "she was just asking for it") encourages attitudes of callousness toward women.

Many media portrayals of sexual abuse suggest that women like to be treated roughly by men. Pornography invariably portrays women as lusting after a sexual encounter regardless of their initial protests. However, this portrayal of women is hardly limited to pornography. Mainstream movies, such as The Getaway, portray women as readily debasing themselves in order to experience the kind of sexual excitement that only some psychopathic killer can provide. Looking for Mr. Goodbar, Fatal Attraction, and 9½ Weeks, all show women humiliated and even murdered as a result of their sexual "addictions."

Almost all of the peripheral women in MTV videos are portrayed as either sexual accessories or nymphomaniacs. Even teachers and rocket scientists are ready to rip their clothes off at the merest invitation of some irresistible aging male rocker. Research tells us that media promoting the ideas that women enjoy sexual aggression and that men are justified in their use of force against them contribute to attitudes that are tolerant of rape and other forms of sexual abuse.

Is the Violence Seen as Real or Make-Believe?

Violence that is realistic is more likely to have an effect on people than violence that is unrealistic. Realistic violence is seen as "telling it like it is"—a truer reflection of the world than violence that is obviously fictionalized. For older adolescents and young adults, television's realism is the most important consideration in the relationship between viewing violence and behaving aggressively.[15] Many cities experienced a rash of violence after the showing of particularly realistic movies such as *Colors* and *Menace II Society*. Though the body count may be higher in movies like *Mortal Kombat* or *Robocop*, these movies are overblown and unrealistic, making real violence less likely.

Seymour Feshbach, professor of psychology at the University of California, Los Angeles, looked at the role that realism plays in cultivating aggression in children. In one experiment children were shown a movie of a riot. Half the children were told that they were watching a fictitious Hollywood movie. The other half were told that they were watching news footage of an actual riot. After viewing the film, the children were given the opportunity to push a peer. Feshbach found that the children who believed they were witnessing real violence were more aggressive than those who thought they were watching fiction.[16]

Children at different ages consider very different things to be real. This point will be fully developed later in the book, but it is important to note that Big Bird is real for the three-year-old, the Incredible Hulk is real for the five-year-old, and Roseanne is real for the seven-year-old. It is not until a child is almost nine years old that "real" means about the same thing that it does for adolescents and adults. For younger children, "real" tends to be anything that could possibly happen. For adolescents and adults, "real" is something that is probable, not just possible. From this difference in the concept of what is real, it is easy to see how much more vulnerable young children are to being frightened by the media. It is possible for a big, bad wolf to come knocking at the door, and the young child is accordingly afraid that this could "really" happen. The older child knows that this is most unlikely and doesn't waste a lot of time worrying about such a doubtful possibility.

Research studies show that parents consistently underrate how frightened their children are by things that parents don't consider "real."[17] Joanne Cantor and Sandra Reilly, at the University of Wisconsin, found that parents' estimates of their children's exposure to scary media were far lower than the children's reports.[18] This probably represents a lack of awareness on the part of parents about what their children are watching as well as a lack of understanding about how easily and frequently children are frightened by what they see. Although much of what the media present is clearly unreal to adults, it is perceived as real by children, particularly younger children. Many parents took very young children to see *Jurassic Park*, assuming that their children would understand that dinosaurs posed no threat. Although this was a perfectly entertaining and even thought-provoking movie for older children, it was a nightmare for the many young children who were carried out of the theater screaming. Not all dinosaurs are created equal, and *Jurassic Park* is a far cry from *Barney & Friends*.

Children understand at a very early age that cartoons are different from other media offerings, that they are less real. After about age three, children use animation as a cue that what they are watching is not to be taken as seriously as other forms of media. According to some researchers, television violence should have the least effect when children watch cartoons in which aggression is punished, negative consequences are shown, and the perpetrator is a totally bad person. But before we plunk our children down for hours of Saturday morning cartoons, it is important to remember that even though young children may understand that cartoons are not real, repeated exposure to cartoon violence still increases aggression.[19] Perhaps it's better for a youngster to watch *Biker Mice from Mars* than *NYPD Blue*, but this is not the only choice a parent has to make. If we take the time to review the media's offerings carefully, we can find wholesome, thoughtful, and appealing programming for our children.

DOES MEDIA VIOLENCE CULTIVATE DISTORTED, FEARFUL, AND PESSIMISTIC ATTITUDES?

According to FBI figures, less than 1 percent of Americans are victims of violent crime in a given year.[20] Why do most Americans believe that crime rates are going up when actually they have been stable over the past two decades and have recently begun to decline? Why do so many of us greatly overestimate the likelihood of being a victim of violence?

George Gerbner has studied this question for more than thirty years. His research suggests that because television reaches so many people and delivers such a consistently violent message, it creates a worldview that is accepted by most people, even though it is false. Gerbner and his colleagues have found that heavy viewers of television differ systematically from light viewers on many issues, assumptions, and beliefs.[21] Heavy viewers are more likely to overestimate their chances of involvement in a violent crime, to believe that their neighborhoods are unsafe, and to assume that crime rates are rising. Heavy viewers of television see the real world through a lens that focuses disproportionately on violence and victimization. Historically, prime time television offers us, on average, five acts of violence per hour, and cartoons typically subject children to twenty-three acts of violence per hour.[22] Over half of all major characters on television are involved in some kind of violence every week. On Saturday morning children's shows alone, more than 90 percent of the programs and more than 80 percent of the characters are involved in violence.[23] No wonder people who watch a lot of television have exaggerated perceptions about the amount of violence taking place in the real world.

Gerbner defines heavy viewers of television as people who watch more than three hours a day and light viewers as people who watch less than two hours a day. This puts most Americans into the heavy viewing category. Even when controlling for a large range of factors such as age, gender, socioeconomic status, and race, Gerbner found that "violence-laden television tends to make an independent contribution to the feeling of living in a mean and gloomy world." Gerbner labels this the "mean world syndrome."[24]

This is not to suggest that danger does not exist in our world. As earlier figures made clear, Americans have good reason to be concerned about violence. Although the overall crime rate may be relatively stable, crime has become more random, and certain age groups, young men in particular, are at greater risk of victimization than ever before. Whatever real dangers do exist, however, heavy viewing of television intensifies the fears and insecurities of both adults and children. This leads to behaviors such as purchasing weapons "for protection" that are likely to cause additional violence. It is well known that homes in which there are guns are far more likely to be involved in violence than homes without guns.

A large-scale epidemiological study looked at the risk associated with keeping firearms at home. After studying well over a million people over a five-year period, the researchers concluded that "home can be a dangerous place." For every fatality resulting from the use of a gun for self-protection they found forty-three suicides, criminal homicides, or accidental gunshot deaths.[25] People buy guns to safeguard themselves and their families only to find that they are far more likely to be the victims of their weapons than protected by them.

Regardless of any particular television program or movie, mass media collectively draws us into a symbolic world with a particular set of values. Although this book will discuss many particular movies and television programs, it is important to keep in mind that *it is the aggregate of television and other media that is at issue, not any individual piece of programming.*

Certainly *Power Rangers* is a poor viewing choice for preschoolers and *Nightmare on Elm Street* an even poorer choice for adolescents. This book provides information to help parents with the decisions they face every day when their children ask, "Can I watch this?" But I hope it also illuminates the idea that the mass media, *on the whole*, present us and our children with a consistently inaccurate, pessimistic, and violent view of the world. It is foolish to argue that such a worldview—presented hour after hour, day after day, year after year—does not affect our children. We are all affected by what we see, and children are particularly influenced by the media because they have fewer alternative sources of information. Although occasional exposure to screen violence is not likely to be damaging to the vast majority of American children, a steady diet of it promises to contribute to an increasingly violent, impulsive, and desensitized society.

DOES MEDIA VIOLENCE DESENSITIZE CHILDREN TO VIOLENCE?

Perhaps the greatest concern that parents have about media violence is that their children seem increasingly desensitized to violence. Given the large amounts of violence witnessed under the guise of entertainment, it seems reasonable to ask whether children's feelings as well as their behaviors are affected by the thousands of acts of violence they have seen. Parents, educators, and therapists are appalled that so many children seem to take even the most horrifyingly graphic depictions of violence in stride. As we have seen earlier in this chapter, there is no question that media violence encourages real-life violence among some children. The question of desensitization to violence is equally compelling and more complex, and it probably affects larger numbers of children.

A mother consulted me after taking her two sons, ages eleven and thirteen, to see the popular action movie *Demolition Man*. She accompanied her sons because she wanted to see "what all the fuss is about." In a particularly gruesome scene, Simon Phoenix, played by Wesley Snipes, holds up a bloody eye that he has just gouged out of another man's head. The mother reflexively let out a scream and covered her eyes with her hands. Both sons turned to her in disgust and embarrassment and told her, "Be quiet! It's just a movie." Neither son seemed the least bit upset by what he had just seen. The mother wanted to know whether this was a "normal" reaction or whether her sons had become desensitized to media violence. She worried that their lack of concern about violence on the screen would translate into a general lack of concern about people and a reluctance to be helpful to others.

This mother, along with the many stricken parents who find that their children seem strangely unaffected by even the most sickeningly graphic scenes, has good reason to be concerned. Two decades of research on the question of whether media violence can desensitize people have consistently shown that repeated exposure to violence blunts emotional reactions and makes people less likely to intervene or seek help for victims.

University researchers find that their experiments dealing with aggression are being delayed because their student assistants are unable to identify aggressive acts. Graduate students hired to help code aggression on television do not always record pushing, shoving, hitting, and in some instances using a gun as acts of aggression. Research assistants need to be educated that physical assault of one person by another is by definition an act of aggression. Depictions of violence in the media have become so routine that normal people no longer recognize it.

What exactly is desensitization? It is a type of learning that makes us increasingly less likely to react to something. When we are first exposed to a new situation, whether to a violent movie, an upsetting argument, or an attractive member of the opposite sex, our bodies respond automatically. Scientists who study arousal and its opposite, desensitization, use physiological measures, such as heart rate, and psychological measures, such as attitude checklists, to determine level of arousal.

The relationship between desensitization and learning is easy to see. If we are sitting at home working on a project and it begins to rain heavily, it may startle us at first, but we quickly become accustomed to the sound and are able to go on with our work. If the rain continued to demand our attention, raised our heart rate, and made us anxious, we would accomplish very little. By itself, desensitization is neither good nor bad but simply a type of learning.

Very young children are aroused by aggressive scenes on television. Research studies have shown that preschoolers show higher levels of emotion when watching aggressive television programs as compared to more neutral programs.[26] Much like the preadolescent who finds himself hacking and choking after his first cigarette drag, young children are initially distressed by threatening and violent images. This arousal diminishes with repeated exposure as the child becomes desensitized to the violence.

Numerous studies have shown that the more people watch media violence, the less sensitive they become to it.[27] This explains why children seem increasingly capable of tolerating more and more explicit scenes of violence in the media. Over and over, in gruelingly graphic movies such as *Natural Born Killers*, *Seven*, or *Interview with the Vampire*, it is inevitably adults who walk out in distress or disgust. The large numbers of teenagers in the audience stay put. This is partly because one of the rites of passage of adolescence is to remain unfazed by horror movies. However, it also reflects a lessening of the impact of violence on those who have been exposed to a steady diet of visual abuse from the time they could talk. The more we watch violence, and the less distressed we are by it, the more we risk becoming tolerant of real-life violence.

Are Desensitized Children More Likely to Behave Violently?

The phenomenon of desensitization has been studied for many years. Public outrage over several well-publicized events in the 1960s and 1970s accelerated scientific study in this area. In 1964 Kitty Genovese was raped and murdered outside her New York apartment building. Although more than forty people were aware of her distress, no one came to her aid. The My Lai trials in 1971 revealed that during the Vietnam War, American soldiers witnessed and participated in the killing of unarmed civilians and children with a shocking level of unconcern. Researchers became increasingly interested in the question of whether people who have been exposed to a great deal of prior violence, either directly or vicariously through the media, might eventually exhibit a kind of psychological and physiological tuning out of the normal emotional responses to violent events.

In an early study of desensitization, a team of researchers exposed their subjects to films of a tribal ritual involving painful and bloody genital mutilation.[28] Though initially very distressed, the subjects became less emotionally responsive with repeated viewing of the film. Repeatedly exposing a person to a frightening stimulus in order to lessen anxiety is called systematic desensitization, and it is frequently used to treat individuals with phobias. It is a process all parents are familiar with as they try to coax a frightened child into approaching a feared situation or object. Many a mother, with a fearful child attached to her leg, has slowly approached a neighborhood dog while reassuring her child, "You don't have to touch the doggy, just watch Mommy touch her. See, that wasn't so bad." Over time, the parent's patience and reassurance, as well as the child's repeated exposure to the animal, help the child to be less fearful. Desensitization then can help children engage in activities that were previously anxiety-provoking.

Unlike the beneficial effects of desensitization described, desensitization to violence works against healthy development. One particular study can serve as a model for the many done on this subject.[29] This study was designed to determine whether children who watched a lot of television were less likely to be aroused by violence than children who watched little television. Researchers divided the children into two groups: heavy viewers and light viewers. The children watched several neutral films and a brutal boxing scene from the Kirk Douglas movie *Champion*. The choice of a boxing scene is important because scenes of violence alternated with nonviolent scenes as each round came to an end and the boxers returned to their corners.

Heavy and light viewers showed no differences in arousal to the neutral films. However, when both groups were exposed to the filmed violence, the low-viewing group became more emotionally aroused than the high-viewing group. Interestingly, even during the nonviolent segments of the boxing movie, children who watched little television tended to be somewhat more aroused than the frequent viewers. It seems that it was harder for them to recover from having witnessed violence. The scientific literature as well as common sense tells us that it's easier to participate in an activity that doesn't make us anxious than in one that does.[30] It may be exactly this decreased anxiety about aggression that encourages aggressive behavior after watching violent media. Kids who no longer feel anxious about violence are more likely to participate in it.

Does Desensitization Diminish the Capacity to Show Care and Concern for Others?

Studies by psychologists Ronald Drabman and Margaret Thomas show that children who have been exposed to more violent programming are less likely to help younger children who are in trouble.[31] In a study with third- and fourth-graders, children were randomly divided into two groups; one group watched a violent television program and the other did not. The children were then led to believe that they were responsible for monitoring the behavior of a group of younger children whom they could observe on a videotape monitor. The children on the videotape played quietly at first and then became progressively more angry and destructive with each other. Whereas 58 percent of the children who had not seen a violent program sought adult help before the angry children began physically fighting with each other, only 17 percent of the children who had seen a violent film sought adult help before actual physical fighting broke out. The researchers concluded that children who are exposed to media violence may be more likely to consider fighting a normal way to resolve conflict or may be more desensitized to and less aroused by violence.

Arousal is highly correlated with swift intervention in an emergency situation.[32] An experiment that examined how bystanders respond to emergencies found that an increased heart rate and the speed of intervention in a staged emergency situation were substantially correlated. More aroused people came to the aid of others in trouble more quickly than those who were less aroused. As we have seen, repeated viewing of media violence lowers arousal level.[33]

In a world in which genocide still comes to us on our nightly news, where random violence has become the most common form of murder in this country, and where handguns are the leading cause of death of large segments of our population, desensitization is perhaps the greatest threat of all. We are losing our awareness of what it means to be human as we become less responsive to human suffering. Although we may never engage in violent acts or endorse violence ourselves, we may not dislike it nearly as much as we should.

SUMMARIZED RESEARCH FINDINGS

True or false?

- Media violence encourages children to act more aggressively.
- Media violence encourages attitudes that are distorted, fearful, and pessimistic.
- Media violence desensitizes children to real-life violence.
- Desensitized children are more likely to be aggressive than children who are not desensitized.
- Desensitization interferes with a child's capacity for empathy.

ALL OF THESE STATEMENTS ARE TRUE!

PART TWO

Through the Eyes of a Child

___

How Children "See" the Media

4

The Cartoon Dilemma

Ages Three, Four, and Five

It's quite a stretch for an adult to see the world through the eyes of the preschool child. Young children are not little adults. They do not think like adults, act like adults, or experience things as adults do. Preschool children inhabit a world that is magical, unique, and quite distinct from that of grown-ups, teenagers, and even older children. For example:

- A four-year-old will be heartbroken to discover that the tooth fairy has forgotten to leave a gift under her pillow.
- Allow a three-year-old to play with a red car. While the child watches, place the car behind a green filter that makes the car appear to be black. Ask the child what color the car "really" is, and he will say black.
- Show a four-year-old two identical tall glasses of water. As the child watches, pour the water from one tall glass into a wide, short glass. The child will believe that the tall glass contains more water than the wide, short glass.

These few examples illustrate that a child's thinking differs qualitatively, not just quantitatively, from that of adults. Young children do not simply have less experience than adults. The nature of their thinking and the very ways in which they experience the world are entirely different.

GENERAL DEVELOPMENT

To make good choices about what preschoolers should watch, we need to appreciate the nature of the young child's world. Children's beliefs that the tooth fairy is real, that a car can magically change its color, and that volume depends on the shape of the container are not occasional aberrations in ordinary thinking. They accurately describe the world of the preschool child, where magic is real and the laws of science as we know them don't exist.

"Why is the sky blue?" "Why do cherries have pits?" "Where does God live?" "Who is older—Grandma Edith or Abraham Lincoln?" The questions of the young child are endless and often unanswerable. Infants and toddlers come to know the world exclusively through their senses; preschoolers seek explanations.

When explanations aren't apparent, preschoolers will gladly make them up to suit the situation and satisfy themselves. Many children this age believe that little people live inside the television set. This belief actually shows great cognitive advancement over the toddler's thinking. The preschooler is searching for an explanation instead of simply taking things at face value. Although there are no little people inside the television, the preschooler is aware that some force is active in making things appear on the screen. Things don't just happen; there are reasons.

Children at this age are into everything. They are budding scientists who seem to be driven to touch and take apart anything they can get their hands on. Before you can turn around, the roll of film has been pulled out of the camera and is laying exposed on the bed. While you answer the doorbell, the television's remote control is being quietly disassembled. Mothers are often exhausted in their attempts to keep the house in order. Children at the beginning of this stage frequently appear insatiable in their quest for knowledge.

The question children ask most often at this stage of development is an incessant "Why?" Parents can be driven to distraction.

Although there are certainly individual differences among children, curiosity and playfulness appear to be innate. Children do not need to be taught how to play. Bring young children to a playground or a toy store, and if they feel secure, they will play. No one ever had to teach a child how to use a sandbox. Researchers have shown that humans and other primates appear to have an inborn desire for discovery.[1] Adults must provide children with environments that are safe, stimulating, educational, and fun. Though it can be trying at times to answer all those "Why?" questions, a youngster's enthusiasm should be cultivated. A child's level of curiosity and exploration is an important indicator of overall adjustment. By the end of this stage of development, as young children become increasingly capable of controlling themselves, things begin to quiet down. Hang in there. Try to see the world through the amazed eyes of your young child.

Preschool children are in a period of accelerated development. On many different fronts, we see emerging capacities for self-control and self-management. Although they were babies only a year or two ago, preschoolers can now stand on line, listen to a teacher, and play with other children without getting into pulling and hitting matches over toys. They can hold a candy bar and wait until after dinner to eat it (well, sometimes they can). Though there certainly are moments when it seems that all of their developmental advances have evaporated, preschool children are consistently (if erratically) moving in the direction of greater self-control.

Erik Erikson, one of our foremost developmental psychologists, calls these preschool years the period of "initiative versus guilt."[2] Erikson believes that children from about three to six are expanding their sense of independence by increasingly taking the initiative in learning about the world and about social relations. "Can I help?" and "I want to do it myself" are common requests at this stage. According to Erikson, the child who is encouraged to take on more responsibility and greater challenges is likely to develop a lifelong feeling of enthusiasm and competency. If your child wants to help you clean the car, give him a rag and thank him for his help. In contrast, the child who is challenged or criticized for his attempts to become independent is likely to feel guilty and lose faith in his abilities.

The preschool child's move toward greater independence is supported by a number of newly developing abilities. First, children this age possess impressive physical skills. They can run, jump, climb, and manipulate objects. More and more tasks are now within their reach. They can pull on their pants, button their buttons, put away the silverware, and wash their own hair. They can climb to the top of the slide, balance on the seesaw, and ride tricycles. Watch the delight of a child who has just found out that she no longer needs her mother's push to get her swing going; her own pumping legs can send her soaring.

Along with increasing physical abilities, preschool children enjoy a host of developing cognitive skills that advance their sense of independence. Language is well developed now, so children are able to ask for what they need and put their feelings into words. They are no longer dependent on a sympathetic interpreter to have their needs met. As children become better able to verbalize their wishes, they begin to see that they have the power to influence their environment. To the extent that they are heard and their wishes treated with respect, the world becomes a reasonably benign and responsive place.

This does not mean you should always grant the wishes of your young child. On the contrary, frustration is an inevitable part of the preschooler's life (an inevitable part of all stages of life, actually). Children of this age are up against an endless barrage of no's: "No, you can't have ice cream before dinner," "No, you can't watch *The X-Files* with your older sister." Their natural enthusiasm and curiosity propel them out into the world, while their parents try to keep them safe and healthy.

Around age four, children begin to develop real friendships. Preschoolers have a great deal to learn from other children, including their own siblings. Competence with peers is important not only for the fun it brings but also because the peer group is a major arena for learning the concepts of fairness, reciprocity, and cooperation. In addition, it is a very important setting in which children learn to manage their aggression. An older sibling may ignore a younger one who calls him a "poo-poo head," and Mom may gloss over the accusation that she's "the meanest person in the world." However, preschool children are not apt to find such generosity among their peers. Whether physical or verbal, expressions of aggression are more likely to be met with retaliation or exclusion than with indulgence.

In addition to an increased capacity to control aggression, preschool children are also beginning to behave in a prosocial manner. Just as controlling aggression depends on increasing self-management skills, so does prosocial behavior. "Do you want some of my candy?" means that the child is able to put aside his own desires and respond to someone else's need. The child who is able to ask this question and share his precious resources sees that there can be value in delaying his own gratification. This is the beginning of altruism.

All of these advances in the preschool child (developing and maintaining friendships, becoming more self-reliant, inferring things about the world that are not readily apparent) depend in large measure on the child's emerging self-control. These developing capacities mark a huge leap forward for the young child and pave the way for one of the major challenges of the next stage of development—school.

No preschooler exhibits these characteristics at all times and under all circumstances. Development at this point is highly variable and changeable. One day a young child is able to resolve a fight with a friend, offer his sister half of his cookie, and straighten up his room; the next day he may throw himself in a screaming heap on the floor when his mother suggests that it is bath time. This is normal. Children's controls at this time are fragile and are easily challenged by fatigue, hunger, and frustration. But overall, the child is moving in the direction of increased control.

CARTOONS AND THE PRESCHOOL CHILD

There are many issues related to the preschool child and the media, but one of them invariably invites passionate concern and disagreement—the issue of cartoons. Are cartoons bad for kids? Why do they need to be so violent? Are there any good ones? Can they actually harm development? Are they addicting? Don't kids know that cartoons are make-believe?

Cartoons are the most violent form of entertainment on network television today. Whereas the average prime time television show has approximately five acts of violence per hour, cartoons typically have closer to twenty-five acts of violence per hour.[3] Unfortunately, our society has decided to subject its most vulnerable members to its most intensely antisocial programming.

Preschoolers see cartoons through naïve eyes. The distinction between reality and fantasy is murky to a child this age, the laws of nature are unknown, and the concept of cause-and-effect is weak. In the eyes of a three-year-old, the sun and the moon move because of him. Certainly, then, flattened rabbits can rearrange themselves, and good guys can be immune to the kind of firepower that in real life would wipe out a small village. Young children's thinking is concrete, literal, and incapable of understanding symbols. Their moral code dictates that might makes right.

These basic facts of child development are often misunderstood and unappreciated by the broadcasting industry. Christine Hikawa, ABC's vice president for broadcast standards and practices, has said, "When scholars and behavioral scientists lump *Tom and Jerry* and *Roadrunner* cartoons with movies like *I Spit on Your Grave* as being equally violent and harmful, their credibility goes out the window."[4] Statements like this, which are consistently used to justify the continuance of violent programming, show a refusal to acknowledge the developmental processes of childhood.

A *Roadrunner* cartoon, with its rapid pace, continuous violence, and seductive appeal, has much in common with *I Spit on Your Grave.* Though the movie is clearly more graphic, both provide similar experiences aimed at different age groups. Both are arousing, vacuous, and violent. It is not any single cartoon, any single movie, or any one video game that is of concern. But parents need to realize that their children are being subjected to a barrage of messages, often violent, stereotypical, and always commercial, that are at odds with the moral values that most parents hope to convey to their children.

Most cartoons have little to offer children. Conflicts are typically resolved by inappropriate force. The symbolism and moral endings that are included in many cartoons, probably to make parents feel that their children are learning a "good lesson," are totally lost on young children. For example, on an episode of *Biker Mice from Mars* that featured explosions, fights, and dangerous motorcycle stunts, the program ended with a "safety message" about buckling up. Such a message is retained by an adult only because of its sheer absurdity; it is not likely to be retained by a four-year-old who has barely recovered from the sensory assault of the preceding thirty minutes.

Most important, the majority of today's cartoon characters do not deal with the issues that are of fundamental importance to young children. Sharing, jealousy, control of impulses, sibling rivalry— these are the kinds of topics that are pertinent to young children. And it is in this arena that television can actually be helpful to youngsters. As we will see later, shows like *Mister Rogers' Neighborhood*, *Sesame Street*, and *Barney & Friends* are so beloved by young children because these shows are familiar with and sensitive to the real-life problems of young children.

During the preschool years, children begin developing the capacity to distinguish fantasy from reality. Contrary to popular opinion, this distinction is not reliably in place until a child is eight or nine years old. In a classic experiment on whether preschoolers can tell what is real from what appears to be real—called the appearance-reality distinction—Rheta DeVries tested a group of children aged three to six.[5] She introduced them to a cat named Maynard and then put a dog mask on Maynard. She asked the children questions such as "What kind of animal is it now?" "Does Maynard say bow-wow or meow?" and "Does Maynard like dog food or cat food?" The younger children believed that Maynard was now a dog. Simply putting a dog mask on a cat had altered reality for the three-year-olds. By the age of six, the children knew that Maynard remained a cat and that reality is not so easily altered. Six-year-olds have begun to understand that their eyes can deceive them.

Given the young children's utter lack of sophistication about what constitutes reality, how are they affected by the cartoons they watch? Is it likely that youngsters will identify with and imitate cartoon characters? The answer appears to be a qualified yes. For many young children, cartoon characters can seem real. Children have been known to imitate, sometimes with tragic consequences, the antics of their favorite characters. Teachers have reported an increase in martial arts interest, as preschoolers karate chop their peers on the playground in imitation of *Teenage Mutant Ninja Turtles*. Parents report that their youngsters are particularly combative after watching superhero cartoons like *Power Rangers*.

Heroes (and today's technowonder equivalents, superheroes) serve an important psychological function for young children and have always been part of their socialization. In a world that is large, frightening, and well beyond the rudimentary understanding of the young child, heroes guide and reassure. By identifying with the persistence and superior abilities of the hero, children come to feel that they too may someday be able to conquer the world, "to leap tall buildings in a single bound." Heroes provide clear rules about acceptable and unacceptable behaviors, and internalizing these rules helps the young child's developing conscience.

Children need stories that help them make sense out of the chaotic and conflicting feelings they frequently have. Most particularly, children need help sorting out their feelings of ambivalence. One moment they love their baby sister, and the next moment, as mother coos and caresses the baby, they wish her dead. Contrary to adult wishful thinking, childhood is often not a sunny and serene time. Rather, young children are frequently awash in nameless anxieties and dark, often violent, fantasies. Fairy tales, because they recognize these realities of the young child's inner life, have remained immensely popular for centuries. They speak to the issues that children care about most: sibling rivalry, ambivalence toward their parents, separation anxiety, and self-actualization.

The popularity of fairy tales reminds us that children's stories do not have to be totally sanitized in order to be appropriate for young children. *Grimm's Fairy Tales* can make an adult's hair stand on end. Both Little Red Riding Hood and her grandmother are eaten alive by a wolf before being rescued by a hunter who slits open the wolf's belly. Little Red Riding Hood and the generations of children who have heard her tale learned important lessons: don't stray off the path, don't talk to strangers, and always follow mother's instructions. That the story is told vividly, even gruesomely, does not diminish its socializing function (reading or being read to allows the child to conjure up the exact amount of "scariness" that she can handle). Children are aided by stories that are clear about good and evil and are ultimately optimistic. Fairy tales acknowledge the conflicts of childhood and help children manage their impulses and make good choices. *Faerie Tale Theatre*, hosted by Shelley Duvall, is an excellent series of videotape versions of classic fairy tales. It's a wonderful alternative to the counterfeit heroes of Saturday morning cartoons.

Preschool children are often more frightened by fantasy programs than they are by more realistic programs. Consistency is very important to preschoolers, and they are particularly frightened by things that change unpredictably from the ordinary to the grotesque. For example, children this age are far more frightened by David Banner's transformation in *The Incredible Hulk* than by the more realistically frightening movie, *Jaws*. However, the *Incredible Hulk* cartoon is less upsetting than the *Incredible Hulk* drama. Many youngsters were apprehensive and even tearful when seeing the movie *Teenage Mutant Ninja Turtles*, although in cartoon form these same turtles seem only to provoke mild euphoria and a tendency to practice karate on the nearest available object. Only very young children seem truly frightened by cartoons. But cartoons are effective at boosting a child's level of aggression.

Suggested violence, which depends heavily on symbolic cues such as lighting and music, is often completely overlooked by the young child. Similarly, much of what is talked about on the news is less upsetting to young children than we might expect. Though graphic photographs and news footage are certainly disturbing, the news is primarily spoken, and children are more attentive—and therefore more vulnerable—to what they see than to what they hear. This is not to suggest that young children should watch the evening news or be allowed to watch more realistic adult programs because "they won't get it anyway." I simply want to emphasize that young children are particularly vulnerable to exactly those media offerings that adults are likely to dismiss as fantasy. *Fantasy is the world in which young children live, and it can therefore be quite disturbing to them when violence is portrayed.*

There is, of course, another side to the debate about television programming for young children. Television has tremendous potential to educate, expand, and enrich the lives of young children. Programs such as *Sesame Street, Mister Rogers' Neighborhood,* and *Barney & Friends* and channels such as Nickelodeon and the Public Broadcasting Service (PBS) all offer wonderful opportunities to youngsters. Research studies have shown myriad benefits from these offerings. Regular viewing of *Sesame Street* has been shown to accelerate academic performance. Watching *Mister Rogers' Neighborhood* for as little as a half-hour per day for two weeks has been shown to increase children's imaginativeness and positive feelings and decrease their aggression.[6]

Although there are exceptions, the majority of children's programming, cartoons in particular, misses the boat. Why? We know a great deal about which children are most vulnerable to media violence, what kinds of programs are most damaging to children at different ages, and the potential of television to educate and socialize. Given all this information, why not simply create programs that take into account a child's developmental level, send prosocial messages, and are both entertaining and instructional? It seems just as easy as creating cartoons that are violent, antisocial, and mind-numbing. Besides, it would quiet down all those whining politicians, parents, and social scientists. How puzzling that television executives don't seem to appreciate the opportunity.

HISTORY OF CHILDREN'S PROGRAMMING

To understand this apparent lapse in clear thinking on the part of the networks, we need to understand a bit about the history of children's television programming. In the 1970s, encouraged by activist groups such as Action for Children's Television (ACT), the Federal Communications Commission (FCC) took an active role in protecting the interests of children. It recognized the differing needs of children at various stages of development and pressured the television industry to introduce more educational programming aimed at particular ages, rather than at children in general. It regulated the amount of time networks could spend on commercials and pushed for less violent programming. The FCC clearly recognized that children are a vulnerable and special audience when it issued a policy statement in 1974 declaring that "broadcasters have a special obligation to serve children."

This protective attitude changed rapidly under President Reagan's policies of deregulation in the 1980s. Mark Fowler, newly appointed head of the FCC, reversed earlier policy and declared that "it was time to move away from thinking about broadcasters as trustees. It was time to treat them the way almost everyone else in society does—that is, as businesses."[7] In 1984 the FCC ruled that networks could devote unlimited time to commercials; thus was born what is kindly called the "program-length commercial." Networks—in conjunction with toy manufacturers and other character licensing industries, such as makers of cereals, linens, lunch boxes, and clothing—began creating characters solely for the purpose of mass marketing. The shows *He-Man*, *Strawberry Shortcake*, *Care Bears*, *Transformers*, and their counterpart products all became enormously popular because of the joint efforts of network executives and toy manufacturers.

The magnitude of the business of selling armies of superheroes, fleets of transforming robots, and stables of long-haired ponies to young children is staggering. In 1995, $28 billion of character licensing products were sold worldwide.[8] Overly muscular, power-obsessed superheroes relying on violence, weaponry, and robots became a generically successful formula for boys. Similarly, long-haired, pastel-colored animals representing splintered emotions appealed to girls. Mr. Fowler's vision of television as nothing more than a business, as "another appliance . . . a toaster with pictures,"[9] took root and flourished in the conference rooms of advertising agencies, toy manufacturers, and network executives who contrived to sell the most products to the largest number of children. Needless to say, educational programming plummeted, as did programming aimed at specific age groups. Commercial children's television moved away from the educational, the developmental, and the prosocial and into the realm of big business.

THE CHILDREN'S GHETTO: CARTOONS AND CONSUMERISM

Saturday morning programming is derisively referred to as the "children's ghetto" by the entertainment industry. Nowhere is the statement "TV is good for 'killing time' for those who like their time dead"[10] more applicable than in these few hours of mindless trash, which a majority of American children watch every week.

Cartoon characters almost without exception fall into one of two categories: testosterone-enhanced superheroes or pathetically witless girl-surrogates like ponies or fairies. Settling in to watch my first few hours of Saturday morning cartoons, I expected to be disturbed by the high levels of violence.

What I did not expect was the astounding stupidity and banality of these cartoons. In talking with many parents, I realized that few have spent any significant amount of time watching these shows. Granted, Saturday morning cartoons generally serve the function of parking the kids for a few hours while parents attend to other matters (or catch up on some well-deserved sleep). However, even parents who have made some attempt to preview what their children are watching report that usually they find themselves drifting away from the television within minutes because the programs are so unbearably crude. I suggest that all parents spend a couple of hours watching Saturday morning cartoons with their children to gain a better appreciation of how poorly their children are being served. After all, we wouldn't send our children to a preschool without spending time there, nor would we hire a baby-sitter without an interview. With children in this young age group watching close to twenty hours of television per week (more hours than many children spend in day care or preschool), it is essential that we put some effort into monitoring what our children watch on television.

What parents are most likely to see on any of the superhero programs (*Turbo Rangers*, *New Voltron*, *Beetleborgs Metallix*, *Teenage Mutant Ninja Turtles*, and so on) is that boys are expected to be fixated on ideas of power and that technology is just as likely to run amok as to be of any benefit. Power is something that is constantly under attack, and cartoon life usually consists of power gained, robbed, withdrawn, and threatened. For reasons that are unclear, many of these power negotiations deal with dire nuclear threats and the disposal of nuclear waste. The great promise of technology to aid humankind has been transformed into an equally likely force of evil, as pet rats gain mammoth proportions and unwitting scientists become walking nuclear time bombs.

Violence on these programs is singularly unconvincing. In fact, most of these programs are notable primarily for their lack of conviction. They are poorly conceived, plot is minimal, dialogue is ludicrous, and animation is often amateurish. The exception to this is the brief period during which, accompanied by loud music and much atmospheric disturbance, the main characters transform themselves into superheroes. These scenes generally are the only minute or two of actual visual excitement out of twenty-two minutes of numbing mediocrity. Teamwork is highlighted in boys' programming because it gives toy manufacturers the opportunity to create an ever-expanding array of new characters for purchase.

Previously popular "girl" cartoons such as *Strawberry Shortcake*, *Care Bears*, and *My Little Pony* are on the verge of extinction, although they continue to thrive on video. Although these cartoons are free of the senseless and irrelevant violence of the superhero cartoons, they present a world of superficial, fragmented emotions. Characters, rather than being whole people (or bears or fairies or ponies), possess only a single identifiable trait, such as loving, caring, sharing, or even (heaven forbid!) grumpiness. Cartoons for girls seem to suggest that all young girls are in need of psychotherapy. These heroines are passive, silly, and constricted. Since the point of most cartoon programs is to hawk the wares of the toy manufacturers and other vendors of licensed characters, this fragmentation of emotion in girls' programming serves the same purpose as teamwork in boys' programming. As writer and social critic Tom Engelhardt points out, "No one wants to sell just one action figure."[11] So manufacturers of licensed products produce dozens of characters for each program. *Care Bear* products include Share Bear, Tenderheart Bear, and Cheer Bear, and *X-Men* manufacturers produce an endless stream of action figures with names like Wolverine, Krule, and Tusk.

Almost without exception, cartoons miss the opportunity to present powerful role models who derive their strength from a capacity for empathy and interpersonal skill, as well as a sense of adventure. Real power for both boys and girls comes from believing that one is valued and capable.

There are attempts to produce cartoons that are exciting and that feature healthier role models. Disney's contribution to the field, *Gargoyles*, is a particularly interesting example. At first glance it doesn't appear very different from any other superhero cartoon, except that its animation is so much better. It's the story of a group of gargoyles who once guarded a medieval Scottish fortress and a thousand years later find themselves guarding New York City. They are alive at night but turn to stone during the day. Goliath, the leader of the Gargoyles, has a singularly egalitarian relationship with Elisa Maza, the female police officer who befriends him and the other Gargoyles. My ten-year-old son, who insisted I watch the program, billed it as "a story about outsiders." It does focus on many of the issues most pressing to children: conformity, feeling different, and intolerance.

Gargoyles is too well written to need superfluous moral tags at the end of the program, and this show weaves its messages into the action. But most of all, it respects the intelligence of children and the social problems, both major and minor, that they are likely to confront. In a particularly serious episode titled "Deadly Force," one of the Gargoyles, excited after seeing a gunfight in a movie, accidentally shoots Elisa with her own police revolver. The rest of the episode focuses on the consequences of the characters' carelessness. Elisa nearly dies, her family is grief stricken, and the Gargoyle runs away, unable to stand the guilt he feels. It actually takes Elisa several episodes to recover from her wounds.

Although this program has the look of a superhero show, it deals thoughtfully with problems that are relevant to children. It is probably better saved for older children who can appreciate some of its complexity. Gargoyles has been well received and proves that children's entertainment can be both profitable and responsible.

In the two years between writing my first book, Viewing Violence, and writing this one, there have been some promising changes in children's programming. Because of legislation mandating three hours of educational programming per week, most of the networks have come up with programs that, though marginally educational at best, are at least less destructive than their predecessors. For the time being, acts of violence per show have been reduced. Cartoons like Madeline and 101 Dalmatians have replaced some of the more vulgar superhero cartoons. This issue will be looked at in detail in the final chapter of this book.

Unfortunately, mandating three hours of educational television per week makes little difference, given that preschool children are watching twenty hours and more per week. The majority of children in this country are watching some portion of Saturday morning cartoons. For the most part, these cartoons continue to reflect an adult world that clings to the relics of Stallone and Schwarzenegger as powerful men because of physical prowess, exorbitant displays of firepower, and their propensity to use violence and intimidation as ways to resolve conflict. Similarly, "good" women are all too often portrayed as long-suffering victims.

Children's television programming unfortunately holds a mirror to our culture. If what we see is an emphasis on power for settling conflict and an admission of how deficient we are in experiencing authentic emotions, then perhaps this is because children's television, created by adults, reflects our own compromised view of the world. Until our adult world chooses to acknowledge that both men and women can be powerful in ways that genuinely serve each other and society, we should not be surprised that children's cartoons simply reflect a balder version of this reality.

PSYCHOLOGICAL DEVELOPMENT AND THE MEDIA

Preschool children are connected to their families by a very short tether. They are in a period of accelerated physical, social, and emotional development. Optimal development occurs when the children's caretakers are loving, available, and firm. According to 1994 Department of Labor statistics, over 60 percent of mothers with preschool children are working. This means that the majority of preschoolers are in day care or nursery school for part or most of every workday. While family is unquestionably the most important influence on preschoolers' lives, the outside world has begun to beckon. With their rapidly expanding cognitive and social skills, children at this age crave and benefit from new experiences.

One of the major responsibilities of parenting during this time is to encourage children's independence while protecting them from danger. "Yes, you can walk to the store with your sister, but you have to hold her hand when you cross the street." "You can ride your bike in the park, but not on the street." "I will let you go to some movies, but not *Godzilla*; it's just too scary for little kids." Many times every day, parents make major and minor decisions about what their youngsters can handle and what is beyond their capabilities. Because parents "dose" the world for them, children are able to have experiences that expand their world but don't overwhelm them. As will be repeated many times in this book, children who feel good about their ability to influence and manage the world and who feel secure about parental availability are likely to have high self-esteem and to be free of excessive worry.[12]

Attachment

Rather than exposing children to media fare that is typically violent, commercial, and beyond the cognitive capacity of young children, it is preferable to encourage play. Preschool children love playacting. Mommy, daddy, teacher, doctor, police officer, and firefighter are all roles that children relish. Providing youngsters with some of the props for these roles adds mightily to their enthusiasm. Every parent has seen their children—boys as well as girls—toddling around in Mom's high heels, pocketbook rakishly thrown over the shoulder, and lipstick smeared somewhere in the vicinity of the child's mouth. For most children of this age, Mom is the center of the universe, and they are only too happy to grab some of her power and try it on for themselves. Though their appearance suggests imitation, the dialogue of preschoolers shows that they are engaging in a more complex process. Children at this age have begun to identify with their parents.

Child development experts understand a great deal about the process of identification, which, along with imitation, is characteristic of this stage of development. At earlier stages of development, children only imitate. Research has shown that infants as young as two to three weeks can imitate facial expressions.[13] By fourteen months of age, children can show delayed imitation of television characters.[14] However, imitation is different from identification.

Identification takes place at a later age and demands more of youngsters. To identify, children have to have some ability to understand
the internal world of the person they are identifying with. So in
addition to putting on Dad's tie and carrying his briefcase, preschool
children will act out some of Dad's attitudes. "Young man, I told you
that you would be punished if you threw rocks again. Go to your
room immediately," says the four-year-old to his baby brother, sum-
moning up Dad's authority and attitudes, as well as his physical
movements. The next time that this same four-year-old is tempted
to throw rocks himself, he will summon up this image of his father,
and this will help him control his behavior. This child is identifying with his father, not simply imitating him.

Imitation and identification help children appropriate adult
power. It is clear to the preschool child where the power in the
house resides. Her parents no longer rush to her side at her slightest
protest, and temper tantrums are generally ineffective (at least they
should be) in having needs met. The toddler's insistent "Me do it"
is replaced by the preschooler's recognition that much of what gets
done depends on the willingness of adults to help. At the same
time, it becomes painfully clear to preschoolers that they really are
not able to navigate the world alone. This is a most unsettling piece
of reality. For the last year or two, they have been wild with excitement at the discovery of their own will, their own beginning ability to regulate themselves. They can pour a drink, go to the toilet,
and dress themselves, all unaided. They are absolutely loath to give
up their newly discovered and intoxicating autonomy.

The realization that parents really run the show and call the
shots sets up an interesting dilemma for preschoolers. Either they
can capitulate and become babyish again, allowing their parents to
take over their hard-won advances, or they can identify with the
parents and incorporate parental attributes into their sense of self.
Children invariably choose the latter solution. Instead of relinquishing their tender new self, children enhance this self by taking
on characteristics of their parents and other powerful adults in their
world. Hence the parade of police uniforms, firefighters' gear, and

superhero costumes, as well as the beloved accouterments of parent-hood: shoes, keys, pocketbooks, toolbelts, telephones, and briefcases.

Conflict with parents is lessened once children begin this process of identification. Because four-year-olds have begun to see themselves as being like their parents, they tend to have much less conflict with their parents than the notorious "terrible" two-year-olds. Self-control is supported because children have begun to internalize parental standards and can begin using these standards as guides to behavior.

We even see the beginning of guilt as children find that their actual behavior frequently does not measure up to their newly internalized parental standards. "You go to your room right now. And don't come out until you can listen," admonishes a four-year-old girl speaking to her doll. This young girl is practicing the powerful parental role—the role that decides what is acceptable, what is not, and what the consequences of such behavior are. One day this little girl will send her own little girl to her room with the same admonishment. She has begun practicing for this day years in advance. In the meantime, her admonishments to her doll remind her of her parents' rules and the kinds of behavior they expect.

Parents have a window of opportunity during the preschool years as their children try on and discard one identity after another. In large measure, the child is trying to expand his limited sense of power by being like Mom or Dad or a Teenage Mutant Ninja Turtle. Although children's programming is often dismissed as frivolous, it provides powerful role models—too frequently negative ones—that are incorporated into the child's sense of self. Too often children's programming, cartoons in particular, celebrates the kinds of nonreflective abuses of power that most parents are opposed to.

Unfortunately, in spite of mountains of evidence to the contrary, most parents do not consider television to be very influential in the lives of their young children. Ninety-two percent of parents with young children do not provide any guidance for television viewing on Saturday mornings. When it comes to television viewing, practice does not make perfect. Those children who watch a lot of television without restriction from their parents show poorer comprehension, greater confusion between reality and fantasy, more restlessness and aggression, and less acquisition of general information than children who come from homes where parents set limits on television viewing.

Jerome and Dorothy Singer, directors of the Family Television Research and Consultation Center at Yale University, recommend that preschool children watch no more than *one hour* of television per day, increasing to two hours in elementary school. The Singers were so impressed with the consistency of their findings that they wrote, "Our results regarding viewing amount are so clear that there is virtually no qualification of the recommendation."[15] Preschool children have so much energy, enthusiasm, and curiosity. Introduce them to butterflies, tadpoles, sunsets, and building blocks. Delay introducing them to television for as long as possible.

Aggression

There is a large body of research focusing on the effects of media violence on preschool children. Almost without exception, this research has found that viewing violence makes children more aggressive, more restless, more fearful, less creative, and less sensitive. In addition, the kind of rapid pacing typically used in violent programming can limit a child's capacity for self-restraint and tolerance of the normal delays of life. No study has ever found any benefit to children from watching violence.

Albert Bandura found that children learn to be aggressive by observing and imitating other people who are acting aggressively. If these individuals, or "models" as Bandura calls them, are rewarded for their violent behavior, children are even more likely to imitate them.[16] Kids learn violent behavior directly by observing others in real life and vicariously through the media.

Over the more than thirty years since Bandura's pioneering studies, much research, as well as the observations of almost any parent, supports the idea that children are learning attitudes and

behaviors from the many hours they spend in front of the television. More recent work by Bandura suggests that not only are
children imitating aggressive behavior, but they are becoming more
tolerant of aggression as well. Children learn how to behave from
the people around them. Both science and common sense tell us
that children who spend their time immersed in a fantasy world of
simple violent solutions to complex human problems are being
poorly schooled.

One of the most significant accomplishments of childhood is
the increasing ability to delay frustration. Counting to ten and taking a walk around the block are strategies that adults have learned
to help them control anger and not get caught up in the heat of the
moment. Young children do not have this capacity and frequently
find themselves grabbing another child's toy or striking out when
they are angry. A study by psychologists Friedrich and Stein found
that one of the most significant features of preschool children who
are exposed to aggressive cartoons is a decline in their ability to tolerate delay.[17] Children with a low frustration tolerance are apt to
rely on aggression as a way to solve problems. This is a poor solution
to frustration, and the child who continues this kind of impulsive
behavior is likely to be penalized at home, in school, and by peers.

In one of their most important studies, Jerome and Dorothy
Singer studied aggression in a group of children beginning at age four
and followed these same children through age nine.[18] Some have
argued that television doesn't make children more aggressive; aggressive children just happen to prefer more violent television programming. Studies such as the Singers' control for initial levels of
aggression and see whether this is the factor that is responsible for
aggressive behavior many years later. In fact, the Singers found that
even when they controlled for initial levels of aggression, "later
aggression in these children is strongly predicted by a combination of
heavier viewing of violent TV shows, preschool heavy TV viewing,
and a family that emphasizes physical discipline and the assertion of
power."[19] *Children who are not particularly aggressive to begin with become
more aggressive as a result of their exposure to television violence.*

The Singers' research began with preschool children, an age group that is often dismissed with the mistaken assumption that "they really don't understand what they're watching." Although children in this age group have varying degrees of comprehension, studies such as the ones described here should convince us that they are being heavily influenced by what they watch. Whereas some of the media's effects on preschool children are readily apparent, others may take many years to manifest themselves. We have good reason to be concerned about short-term effects—preschoolers who are heavy viewers have higher levels of aggressiveness, distractibility, and restlessness—and even more compelling reasons to be concerned with the long-term effects. The four-year-old child who is restless and aggressive after a couple of hours of Saturday morning cartoons may turn out to be the adolescent who has trouble paying attention in class, has difficulty getting along with parents and peers, and ultimately engages in antisocial activities.

Both parents and researchers tend to focus on *behavior*, which is, after all, easily identifiable and measurable. The child who attempts to jump over a barricade with his tricycle or who punches a younger sibling in imitation of some action hero demands our attention. Parents who see these kinds of behaviors in their children tend to take some action, at least in part because they fear for their child's safety or the family's harmony. There are, however, other aspects of media influence that are just as significant, although less readily apparent. These have to do with how the media affect the *attitudes* of children. This topic tends to get more attention where older children are concerned. For instance, the media's influence on how adolescents think about the opposite sex is well documented. But children of three, four, and five are also developing opinions, attitudes, and values, and the media play a significant and frequently overlooked role in this area.

There have been a number of experiments that have looked at the ways in which the media can alter the attitudes of young children. Many television programs aimed at young children, superhero cartoons in particular, showcase aggression as a means of gaining both power and rewards. Does exposure to this attitude on television alter the way children feel about aggression? After all, it seems likely that in many households young children are encouraged to "get along" rather than to impose their will on others. Mothers are forever telling their youngsters, "Learn to share," "You have to take turns," "Don't hit, use your words." Most parents are not telling their preschoolers to "nuke 'em" in order to get their way.

In a clever study designed to look at whether or not rewarding aggression would change preschoolers' attitudes toward it, youngsters were shown manipulated film sequences involving two boys named Rocky and Johnny.[20] In one version, Rocky successfully takes Johnny's toys away and is rewarded with stickers and juice. In the other version, Rocky tries to take Johnny's toys, but Johnny successfully defends his toys and beats up Rocky. Sixty percent of the preschoolers who saw Rocky rewarded for his aggression expressed the desire to be like him. However, only 20 percent of preschoolers who saw Rocky punished for his aggression wanted to emulate him. *Aggression was unacceptable to these preschoolers only if the aggression was punished.* Successful rewarded aggression, even though it was unfair, was seen as positive.

Parents have their work cut out for them. Although an occasional cartoon is not likely to do any damage, parents need to be as involved with their preschooler's television choices as they are with every other aspect of their preschooler's life. Helping children understand what is seen on television is critically important in order to maximize comprehension and minimize apprehension.[21] In particular, parents need to actively supplement their child's moral education by commenting on strategies of violence and aggression that are unacceptable. "X-Men may be able to vaporize people, but in our family it works a lot better to talk things out, even if you're very, very angry."

Children's aggression needs to be acknowledged. Their emotional life is frequently in turmoil, and they are often at the mercy of intense feelings they are incapable of understanding. The ways of the world are still far beyond their grasp. Young children rely on their parents' explanations and illustrations of what kinds of behavior are acceptable and valuable. This is how they learn to become functioning, contributing members of society. The kinds of dilemmas that young children face daily—a sibling taking their favorite toy or a friend refusing to share a cookie—are appropriate arenas for exploring ways to resolve conflict. Shows such as *Sesame Street* and *Mister Rogers' Neighborhood* frequently deal with aggression on this level. Media featuring violence that is excessive, gratuitous, and graphic have no place in the lives of young children.

Cognitive Development

A mother and her three-year-old son walk briskly into their local movie theater for an afternoon showing of *Snow White*. They settle into their seats just as the lights go down. The mother can feel her young son's body stiffen in the darkness. A menacing hooded figure with long, blood-red fingernails appears on the screen and cackles at her reflection in the mirror. The little boy closes his eyes in fear, and as the sinister music builds, lets out a terrified scream. The manager hurries over and offers a prompt refund to the embarrassed mother and sobbing child.

That mother is me, and the child is my youngest son. I use this example to show that parents, even child-care professionals, will occasionally make mistakes about what their child can handle despite education, experience, and the best of intentions. Sometimes these mistakes are the fault of the industry, which has irresponsibly advertised a movie or program to appeal to children. For instance, *The Gun in Betty Lou's Handbag*, which was billed as a comedy and seen by many young children, contained violent and frightening scenes inappropriate for young children. But sometimes parents make mistakes too. We want to see a movie that our child has been pestering us to see, so we take her along, figuring that just this once it won't matter. *Batman* was seen by many young children. Its PG-13 rating should have alerted parents that it would not be suitable for preschoolers, many of whom were very frightened by this movie.

Most of the mistakes that we make when we allow children to watch TV or movies that are upsetting to them is the result of our not appreciating the child's way of thinking. Let's take the opening example of *Snow White* and my three-year-old son to gain some understanding of the preschooler's thinking.

Depending on the child's individual temperament, young children have very different ways of approaching new situations. Studies on temperament identify three different groups of children: easy, slow-to-warm-up, and difficult.[22] Basically, slow-to-warm-up children take a bit longer to adapt to new situations. They need a little extra time to feel comfortable in a new environment. My third son, who is rather quiet, would fall somewhere between easy and slow-to-warm-up. He would have benefited from not being rushed into the theater and from having some extra time to think about where he was. More time would also have given me a greater opportunity to explain what would happen. "Lots of people will come into this room. You probably won't know any of them. But they all live around here and are bringing their children to the movies just like I'm bringing you." Many adults have a hard time walking into a room filled with people they don't know. For those youngsters who don't relish novel situations, a theater full of one hundred or so complete strangers is quite a challenge. Most important, my son was simply too young for *Snow White*.

Disney has made many memorable movies that children enjoy, cherish, and watch over and over again. So why did my three-year-old fall apart? The answer lies in the appearance-reality distinction discussed earlier in this chapter. This body of research looks at children at different ages and assesses whether they can distinguish between what is real and what is deceptive in its appearance.

Interestingly, a number of researchers have attempted to teach three-year-olds to make a distinction between what something appears to be and what it actually is. Children in these studies received training on the meaning of *real* versus *apparent*. For instance, the researcher would take a Charlie Brown puppet and then put the puppet inside a ghost costume, saying, "Charlie Brown looks like a ghost to your eyes right now, but it is really and truly Charlie Brown."[23] Children were corrected repeatedly when they insisted that the figure in front of them was a ghost. In spite of extensive explanations and training, and much to the surprise of the investigators, three-year-olds continued to do poorly on these tasks. Though it is not entirely clear why three-year-old children cannot distinguish reality from appearance, the critical point is that they cannot. Therefore no amount of reassurance, such as telling a child that "it's just a movie" and "not real," is likely to convince a three-year-old that what he sees isn't real. My son's terror was justified. For the young preschooler, what you see is what you get.

The three-year-old has a very tenuous hold on reality, one that is subject to enormous distortion and disruption. Three-year-olds are tender beings, and although their verbal skills are exploding, we must remember that their psychological and cognitive abilities are still very limited. By the age of six, children can easily manage simple appearance-reality tasks, but it is not until several years later that children are fluent in their ability to make this distinction. Disney makes some wonderful movies, and parents are often anxious to expose their children to experiences that they found delightful in their own childhood. But three-year-olds need to be protected from even the most outlandishly unrealistic portrayals of "bad people." The wonderful world of Disney can wait until your child is five or six. At that time it can be enjoyed and marveled at because the child has begun to understand that not everything she sees is real.

Another area in which cognitive development is taking place is in the preschooler's play. Play and fantasy provide children with the skills for effectively managing the world as well as diverting themselves from angry feelings. In the miniaturized world of palm-sized cars, small dolls, and building blocks, children gain confidence and familiarity. Youngsters experience a sense of control that builds feelings of competence and self-esteem. Eventually the cars will be life-sized, as will the babies and the building materials. Imaginative play paves the way for children's success at school, among peers, and ultimately in their adult lives. Here they learn about the world, about fairness and justice, about getting along with other children, and about how to take someone else's point of view. In play, children cultivate inner resources of imagination, creativity, and self-reliance. Imaginative play encourages mental reflection, and mental reflection encourages the development of a personality that is empathic and self-aware.

Television, with its repetitive format and solutions, does not encourage spontaneous play. Rather it encourages rote replication of the same banal plots and resolutions. Children are robbed of the opportunity to develop different perspectives and alternate solutions. Toys based on these same formulas further interfere with the child's creative capacity to come up with novel and interesting solutions. Bypassing creative and spontaneous play is of serious consequence for young children. If your child owns every Batman action figure, try skipping the Batman fortress. Instead of buying a prefabricated fortress, cave, or castle, allow your child to construct one out of blocks or boxes. By doing this, your child learns about planning, design, construction, and physics, along with his or her fantasy play. It is a much richer experience.

Some research suggests that imaginative children and adults are less likely to engage in impulsive acts or in acts of gross aggression.[24] In one of the few studies of its kind, Singer and Singer studied a group of children aged three to eight and tried to establish which variables inhibited or encouraged imagination in children. Four factors were found to predict imagination in children:[25]

1. Organized daily routine
2. Less viewing of television in the preschool years
3. Limited recent viewing of realistic action television shows and less general emphasis on television in the home
4. Extent to which the child's mother values imaginativeness

Preschool children are in Piaget's stage of "preoperational" thinking. Their thinking is "black and white" and completely ego-centric. The three-year-old will clap his hands over his eyes and dare you to find him. From his point of view, which is the only point of view at this stage, you can't see him because he can't see you. One of my young patients used to plug her fingers in her ears and in a louder and louder voice would demand to know if I could hear her. Her plugged ears meant my hearing must be impaired as well. Children at this age have little capacity to adopt a point of view other than their own.

Because their thinking is totally egocentric, preschoolers cannot distance themselves from what they watch. In the movie *Labyrinth*, an older sister, frustrated at being asked to baby-sit for the evening, implores goblins to take away her baby brother. They do, and she spends the rest of the movie trying to undo her wish. This movie fascinated many older children who could still remember the strength of their own wishes to get rid of a sibling but were cognitively mature enough to know that wishing doesn't make it so. However, I saw several young children who expressed concern about this movie, fearing that angry wishes they had made toward a younger sibling might come true. For the preschooler, wishing can most certainly make it so.

Programs such as *Mister Rogers' Neighborhood*, which continually emphasize the difference between reality and fantasy ("Let's go to the neighborhood of make-believe"), help children become increasingly capable of making this distinction. Like a good parent, Mr. Rogers mediates the television experience for young children, answering questions when they are likely to arise, engaging the child in a dialogue, and often restructuring new experiences and information into forms that are easily understood by children. He talks slowly, reflects on what is going on, and speaks to his young audience directly. His kindliness is appreciated by children because he never assumes that they know more than they do.

Fred Rogers' slow pace helps children think about what they are learning. In this respect, *Mister Rogers' Neighborhood* is singularly helpful to young children. It is one of the few programs that has ever filled air space with silence. After hearing a moving performance of cellist Yo-Yo Ma, Fred Rogers invites his young viewers to be quiet and in the silence remember the beauty of what they have heard. This is education at its best, encouraging reflection and imagination, the cornerstones of intellectual development. Children do not have to be hit over the head to learn. On the contrary, they learn best when they are given the opportunity to slowly incorporate new material in a setting that respects their limitations and supports their self-esteem.

In addition to being extremely egocentric, preschoolers are also very literal in their thinking. To a preschooler, a rose is a flower, period. It is not a symbol of love; it is not a symbol of beauty; in fact, it is not a symbol of anything. Symbols are far too abstract an idea for children of this age. The preschooler simply does not have the experience or ability to know that sometimes things stand for ideas or concepts. Abstract concepts, such as justice, duty, and fairness, are beyond the mental capacity of the young child. For preschoolers, fairness isn't a concept, it's simply getting what they want.

Another characteristic of preschoolers is their inability to think in reverse. This is important because it means that the young child does not understand that the man led off in handcuffs at the end of the program is the same man who committed murder at the beginning of the program. As every parent knows, consequences for children's misbehavior need to be swift and relevant. "If you throw the candy again, I will take it away from you right now." Punishing a young child even an hour after a disobedient act is typically both ineffective and confusing.

These examples of limitations in the preschool child's thinking should be borne in mind when making decisions about their viewing fare. Standbys such as *Mister Rogers' Neighborhood*, *Barney & Friends*, and *Sesame Street*, as well as some new programs like *Captain Kangaroo* (yes, back again and updated for the 1990s), *Bear in the Big Blue House*, and *Wimzie's House*, are all excellent choices for this age group. Videotapes are often a good alternative to the more commercial television fare. Both PBS and Nickelodeon do a wonderful job of programming for young children. Media offerings for children this age need to be kept simple, direct, and gentle.

Moral Development

The night before I began writing this section, I found my three-year-old playing with a Lego figure and motorcycle I had never seen before.

"Where'd you get this from, Jeremy?" I asked.

"School," he answered warily, anticipating my response.

"Well, if you got it at school, we'll have to bring it back there tomorrow because it doesn't belong to you."

"I got it at school, but now it's mine because I took it" was his succinct response.

And there, of course, was my opening. For the young preschooler, possession is not nine-tenths of the law—it's one hundred percent. Psychologists see this as an expression of the young child's egocentrism. "If I take it, it's mine. If I want it, it's mine."

Fairness at this age is identical with getting one's way. The high point of Sara's fifth birthday party was a colorful piñata her parents had strung up on the patio. Tired of waiting her turn on line, Sara simply muscled up to the front, declaring, "I'm the birthday girl, and it's unfair to make me wait." One of her young friends responded by pushing Sara aside and stepping into her place. "No, I'm the guest. Everyone knows it's unfair to make the guest wait." Soon there was a melee of five-year-old girls, each asserting that she was being treated unfairly. Sara's parents needed to step in, restore order, and clarify that although each girl wished she could be first, this was not the same as being treated unfairly.

It is not that the young child is selfish in any negative way; he is simply incapable of complex moral thinking, just as he is incapable of complex intellectual thinking. Youngsters at this age cannot really concentrate on two pieces of information at the same time. Piaget called this "centration," the child's tendency to pay attention to only one aspect of a situation. As we saw in the beginning of this chapter, young children will believe that a short, wide glass holds less water than a tall, thin one even though they've just seen the water poured from one glass to the other. In this example, the child is only able to attend to the most prominent feature of the situation, the height of the glasses. He is unable to use other relevant information to understand the problem.

Similarly, when faced with a moral dilemma like "You can't take that truck out of the store because we didn't pay for it," the young child can only attend to one aspect of the situation. In this case, the most prominent feature is the child's desire. In the pursuit of having their desires met, children of this age are quite willing to "lie, cheat, and steal." I have put these rather objectionable words in quotation marks to highlight the fact that their meanings are really quite different when we are talking about a child this young.

Children of three, for the most part, don't understand that manipulations such as lying are wrong. From the young child's point of view, they are simply ways of getting the world to conform to their wishes. The three- or four-year-old can quite innocently say, "I should have lied," when confronted for breaking the rules. Lying is normal and common among preschoolers.

As children move away from the issues of autonomy and separation characteristic of the two- and three-year-old, they begin work on the developmental task of accommodation, of fitting in. Four- and five-year-olds are forming friendships, learning the rules of social interaction, and less likely to be engaged in battles with their parents. They are beginning the process of standing in someone else's shoes. As a result, their thinking about moral issues is also beginning to change. Toward the end of this stage of development, most children appreciate the value of getting along and understand that imposing their will on others is often ineffective. In their new-found spirit of cooperation, four- and five-year-olds look around and see that without a doubt, it is adults who hold the power. This leads them to an interesting conclusion: adults are always right. Children at this age often exhibit unquestioning obedience. "My mother says" becomes an incantation, invoking the highest authority known to the young child.

Lest we be lulled into thinking that the recalcitrant child has suddenly come to his senses and acknowledged the wisdom of adult authority, remember that children come to this conclusion only because adults wield more power. Four- and five-year-olds try very hard to obey adults, but it is almost entirely out of fear of punishment rather than respect for the adult's point of view.

Given that a large part of the preschool years are devoted to acknowledging parental power, it seems reasonable to suggest that parents have a particular opportunity at this time to influence their child's moral development. Parents who are involved with their children, who set limits using reason rather than power to establish their authority, and who actively communicate a set of values tend to have children with higher levels of moral development. For instance, parents who watch television with their children can enhance many of the positive effects of viewing and reduce negative effects. Research has shown that watching television with a parent increases the information children learn from educational television and helps children understand more of what they are seeing.[26]

Parents stand between their children and the world. They protect the young from experiences that are potentially disturbing and help children learn to regulate their desires. These twin functions of discipline and protection are called "mediation." Parents mediate when they set up rules about television viewing—how much can be watched, how late the child can stay up, and what content is appropriate and acceptable. Explanation and clarification are ways of protecting children from being overwhelmed by information or images they are psychologically unprepared to handle.

Parents need to be willing to regulate their youngster's television time and movie choices. The American Academy of Pediatrics recommends that children this age spend no more than two hours a day watching television. As this chapter should have made clear, children have very important social skills to develop at this time, and imaginative play is the arena where this is best accomplished.

Too much television time cuts into the opportunity to play and tends to make children less imaginative, more restless, and more passive. Parents should also set up alternate activities for their youngster. This doesn't mean that the parent is forever doing something interesting and creative with their child; few parents have the time or energy for this kind of attention. Besides, as we have seen, one of the major developmental tasks of this stage is to begin forming relationships outside of the family. Peer play as well as solitary play are both of great importance for the preschool child.

Parents need to help increase their child's understanding of the media. They need to explain that television is not real and that many of the solutions proposed by the media, particularly violent solutions, are unacceptable and are unworkable in real life. For example, you can explain that if one of the Power Rangers really did "nuke" his opponent, he would be placing many people in jeopardy and would be severely punished for his criminal activity. Although some of this may not be clear to the three-year-old, five- or six-year-old children are likely to understand what parents mean. The aggregate of these types of parental messages imparts a sense of values to children.

Many studies have shown that television can foster prosocial behavior. This effect is substantially enhanced when parents and schools provide support in the form of discussion and role playing.[27] In one study, children were shown prepared videos of generous behavior and then given an opportunity to be generous to others. The exposure to the filmed example of generosity increased the children's real life generosity.[28] *Barney & Friends* has been shown to improve children's manners, as well as their vocabulary.[29] *Mister Rogers' Neighborhood* has been shown to enhance a wide range of prosocial behaviors, as well as encouraging curiosity, happiness, and playfulness in young children.[30]

Most parents do not need a battery of social scientists to tell them that watching people behave well, whether in real life or in the media, helps children internalize more wholesome role models than watching people behave violently and impulsively. The fact is that television does exert a significant effect on the young child's developing mind and conscience. Parents can exercise economic clout by boycotting the advertisers of offensive programming and pushing for media literacy programs in the schools.

Finally, the implementation of a true children's network, publicly funded, would go a long way toward proving that we value our children and recognize the power of the media in their lives. Such a network could be geared to the development of children at different ages and would be capable of placing responsibility before profit.

PRESCHOOLER VIEWING CHECKLIST

Attachment

Presents the world as a safe place	yes	no
Adults can be counted on to take care of children	yes	no
Emphasizes thoughtful and cooperative behavior	yes	no

Aggression

Angry feelings are acknowledged	yes	no
Aggression is an unacceptable way of handling conflict	yes	no
Thinking and talking are the preferred ways to solve problems	yes	no

Cognitive Development

Material is simple and understandable	yes	no
Encourages curiosity	yes	no

Moral Development

Clear about who are the good guys and who are the bad guys	yes	no
Bad people are brought to justice and punished for their misdeeds	yes	no
Adults portrayed as using moral authority wisely	yes	no

TELEVISION HALL OF FAME

Sesame Street

Barney & Friends

Shining Time Station

Bobby's World

Mister Rogers' Neighborhood

Lambchop's Play-Along

Rugrats

TELEVISION HALL OF SHAME

Power Rangers

Teenage Mutant Ninja Turtles

Beetleborgs Metallix

X-Men

Biker Mice from Mars

Voltron

MOVIES AND VIDEOS TO CHECK OUT

As I suggested earlier, skip most movies for the youngest children.

Dumbo

The Little Mermaid

Shelley Duvall's Faerie Tale
    Theatre

Lady and the Tramp

Pinocchio

Barney & Friends (video
    series)

ADD YOUR OWN FAVORITES

_____

_____

_____

_____

5

Middle Childhood

Ages Six, Seven, and Eight

The middle years of childhood are typically quite wonderful. Intoxicated with their newly developing skills and relative freedom, children of this age are having a love affair with the world. Life for the child of six, seven, or eight is a challenging, exciting adventure. Transformed children who just a year or two ago depended on mother to meet almost all of their needs now exhort and demand, "Mom, let me do it myself!"

GENERAL DEVELOPMENT

Unlike preschoolers, middle-age children do not live solely in the here-and-now, and as a result they are interested in past, present, and future. Their horizons are expanding with dazzling speed, and they are enchanted by their families, their neighborhoods, their schools, other children, other countries, and outer space. The world has become their oyster.

Remarkably, Freud labeled this period of development "latency," believing that children were quietly consolidating their skills before the onslaught of adolescent sexual awakening. Unfortunately, this view of middle childhood as a period of psychological torpor has, until recently, made the social and emotional development of middle childhood one of the least studied topics in child psychology. True, the whirlwind pace of change that characterized infancy and the preschool years has abated. Physical growth has slowed to a few inches a year, and cognitive and social advances are perhaps less dramatic. However, children of six, seven, and eight are in no way languishing. An increased interest in research in this area has begun to show us that these years are rich in cognitive, moral, social, and emotional changes.

The family remains a major institution of socialization, although school and the peer group are becoming increasingly important. The middle-age child has three important tasks to accomplish during this developmental stage: consolidating a sense of self, forming close relationships with peers, and achieving success at school.

Consolidating a Sense of Self

Preschool children are apt to describe themselves as "tall," "skinny," "a fast runner," or any one of a number of physical characteristics that they associate with themselves. Preschoolers think of the self as a concrete entity and so describe it largely in physical and tangible terms.

Middle-age children, on the other hand, are beginning the process of developing a sense of self that is psychological and enduring over time. By the time a child is eight or so, a self-description will certainly include physical characteristics, but it will also include such psychological attributes as "I'm a good person," "I'm smart," or " I like to take care of people." These more complex descriptions mirror the cognitive shift that is taking place at this age: the ability to think logically, as well as the ability to see things from another perspective. As always, cognitive, moral, social, and emotional development are intertwined.

Although this ability to think psychologically represents a huge leap forward in sophistication, it is just the beginning of a process that will become increasingly refined throughout later childhood and adolescence. Far more sophisticated than they were just a year or two before, children of six, seven, or eight still tend to take people pretty much at face value. One mother tells the following story.

My daughter Terri and her best friend Allison are seven. Allison's goldfish died. My daughter asked Allison if she would like another goldfish for her birthday, which was coming up in two weeks. With lip trembling, Allison said, "No." Later that evening, sitting around the dinner table, my husband suggested it would be a good idea for Allison's parents to get her another fish. My daughter disagreed emphatically saying, "Allison said she didn't want another one." My older daughter, Elizabeth, who is twelve, said it was a good idea to get another goldfish because "Allison's sad now, but she'll get over it."

Terri was baffled when several days later she found Allison happily talking to her new goldfish.

At age seven, Terri takes her friend at her word and does not really consider extenuating factors. She does not have enough experience with people to know that what people say is governed by a number of factors, in this case sadness and loss. It will be several years before Terri understands that motives may not be apparent and that what people say cannot always be taken literally.

Middle-age children are increasingly able to think of themselves as possessing permanent psychological characteristics. One of the most important of these characteristics is gender identity, the understanding that one is either male or female. Boys who a few years ago paraded around in their mothers' shoes and pocketbooks wouldn't be caught dead in such get-ups. Girls who used to play doctor with other girls and boys are certain they will get "boy cooties" if they so much as touch a boy. Children this age believe it is wrong to behave in ways associated with the opposite sex. Play tends to be almost exclusively same-sex with very rigid rules about the circumstances under which cross-gender contact is permissible. Only about 6 percent of play during middle childhood crosses gender lines.[1]

Unfortunately, research shows that parents still have very different attitudes and expectations for their sons and daughters. Studies show that girls are given less freedom, are less likely to be encouraged to be independent, and are expected to be more nurturing and less ambitious than boys.[2] As we will see in the section on school achievement, lower expectations for girls have a profound influence on academic accomplishment as well as on self-esteem.

Forming Close Relationships with Peers

Once a child enters school, the number of hours spent with peers increases dramatically. The family, and most particularly the mother, was the dominant influence on the infant and young child, but now school and peers compete with the family for influence on the middle-age child.

The relationship between grown-ups and children is always unequal in terms of power. When all else fails, parents can and frequently do fall back on their ultimate authority: "Because I said so, and I'm the parent." Relationships between children of approximately the same age are less about authority and more about equality; as a result, peer relationships offer children unparalleled opportunities to learn new skills and new rules of social interaction. No longer do children feel coerced into submitting to the will of those older and bigger. They are now able to negotiate to have their needs met with other children who share a similar level of status and power. "I'll play jacks now if you'll skip rope with me later." Learning how to regulate aggression, how to treat people fairly, and how to offer support and loyalty are some of the skills advanced by friendships during middle childhood. Being a good friend is the theme of many television shows aimed at children, and in this particular area, the media have done a good job of supporting healthy attitudes and behaviors.

Beginning friendships, as well as the structure of school, offer children the opportunity to define themselves not only as individuals but also as part of a group. Preschoolers have very little sense of a collective identity and at best may see things as "us versus them." School begins to reinforce a sense of group identity based on shared interests, abilities, and attitudes. Children are divided into reading and math groups based on differing levels of ability and divide themselves into groups based on interests and abilities, such as athletics or popularity.

Children of six, seven, and eight are beginning to have the cognitive as well as the social skills to understand the nature of the group and that the group has norms and rules that are to be followed in order to maintain membership. "No girls allowed" means exactly that, and woe to the young boy who allows a girl into the clubhouse. He is likely to be expelled, at least temporarily, from the fellowship of his young male friends.

School Achievement

From the moment the six-year-old crosses the threshold into the first-grade classroom, life is irreparably changed. The child is now a full-time student. No longer is it enough to play and to keep out of trouble. New rules, new expectations, and new tasks challenge the youngster at every turn. Even the smallest details of life may be proscribed in new and often unfamiliar ways, such as where to sit, when to sit, and even how to sit. For at least the next twelve years, six hours a day, five days a week, most children will be focused on the task of learning both a body of knowledge and the rules of social interaction. Children face a breathtaking task, and how well they succeed has enormous implications for the rest of their lives.

School is a powerful agent of socialization and demands exactly those behaviors that are required of people in the working world. In the classroom, children are expected to be punctual, respectful, and organized. They are also expected to be competitive and to value achievement. They are required to follow rules, to obey authority, and to subordinate individual needs to the needs of the group. The school has the authority both to reward and to punish children based on their compliance with these expectations. Obviously, these requirements are in line with the children's developmental capabilities. Whereas a sixth-grade student is expected to complete and bring in homework daily, a first-grader might only be expected to leave her folder and pencil in the same place every day. In both cases, however, the child is being schooled in the kind of organizational skills that will eventually be called good work habits and will help ensure success as she tackles more complex and demanding tasks, first at school and eventually in the workplace.

Because school occupies such a large role in the life of middle-age children, both academic achievement and popularity become major contributors to a child's self-esteem. So it is most disturbing to have research conclude that intellectual accomplishment is differentially encouraged for boys and girls, with girls being subtly discouraged.[3] The classroom is a powerful transmitter of mainstream cultural values and norms. It would appear that girls are disadvantaged both at school and in their homes by the prevailing social notion that high achievement is not as desirable for girls as it is for boys.

MEDIA AND THE MIDDLE-AGE CHILD

The media tend to portray the middle-age child of six, seven, and eight as being precocious, spirited, inventive, and often "naughty." Most of the successful movies aimed at this age group focus on the youngster's awkward beginning moves away from the family and the trouble that ensues. Movies such as *Huckleberry Finn*, *Peter Pan*, and *The Secret Garden* document children's sense of both trepidation and exhilaration as they begin the journey (often literally) that will eventually lead them out of the family and into lives of their own.

Perhaps the most popular of all characters of this age is Kevin, played first by Macaulay Culkin in *Home Alone* (1990) and *Home Alone 2: Lost in New York* (1992) and then by Alex D. Linz in *Home Alone 3* (1997). *Home Alone* and *Home Alone 2* are among the fifty most profitable movies of all time. In the first two films, eight-year-old Kevin, who is tormented by his cousins and misunderstood by his overtaxed parents, is mistakenly forgotten by his family when they go on vacation. After briefly luxuriating in his freedom to do as he pleases, Kevin embarks on a series of misadventures, outwitting two bumbling criminals with a combination of imagination and cunning. It is worth noting that although *Home Alone 3* follows the same basic formula as its predecessors, at least Kevin's parents are no longer irresponsible and neglectful. Someone at Fox paid a bit of attention to the criticism directed at the first two movies. A bit, not a lot.

Overall, the movies are violent and disrespectful toward adults, who are portrayed as inattentive or foolish or both. Aside from his obviously neglectful parents, there are few adults who are capable of offering any protection to the abandoned Kevin. In fact, the first movie opens with a crook posing as a police officer in order to case the house. In the last *Home Alone*, the police are unsympathetic boobs who are annoyed and skeptical of Kevin's attempts to seek help when he spots intruders. "Don't put your money on the adults" is the clear message. These movies were enormously successful because they played to every youngster's fantasy that he is brighter, more sophisticated, and craftier than the grown-ups who loom over him. It takes a lot of courage for small people to begin tackling the world, and their insecurity is often made bearable by a healthy dose of bravado.

Nowhere is the use of bravado more clearly seen than in this age's fascination with superheroes. Superheroes allow children to borrow a sense of power and mastery as well as reassure them that good triumphs against evil. Superheroes reinforce the moral development of middle-age children with an emphasis on being good for its own sake. While the child struggles with the realization that his parents are not perfect, the superhero acts as a flawless surrogate parent.

Superhero shows, like fairy tales at an earlier age and horror movies in adolescence, serve important psychological functions for the growing child. Because they reflect the psychological realities of child development, all these genres are enormously successful. In one form or another, popular stories for children—whether *The Three Little Pigs* or *Teenage Mutant Ninja Turtles* or even *Buffy the Vampire Slayer*—tell a version of the same story. Children identify with the initial anxiety-producing situation (whether being chased by a wolf or by a murderer) and then find that resourcefulness and courage lead to eventual victory. Facing one bogeyman or another is a part of daily life for children, and it is no small wonder that they are anxious to hear over and over again that it turns out OK in the end.

Unfortunately, today's superheroes increasingly depend on violence and intimidation for their authority rather than courage and intelligence. Unlike the early superheroes—Superman, Green Lantern, and Spiderman—who battled criminals primarily with their wits and only occasionally with their hands, today's superheroes are equipped with an arsenal worthy of the Department of Defense. "It seems that kids look at karate chops and kicks as just another way of interacting," says a seasoned first-grade teacher. "If you tell them that such behavior is not OK on the playground, they just give you this kind of puzzled look and say, 'But the Turtles do it.'" Physical dominance, as portrayed by the current crop of superheroes, is a whole lot of fun. Here we see the seeds of violence as a form of humor, which will find full expression many years later as older children, adolescents, and adults laugh at carnage made playful in movies like The Terminator, Beverly Hills Cop, and Con Air.

Until children reach the end of this stage or the beginning of the next stage of development, they are not capable of understanding that the medium of television is a fabrication, that it is the workings of people's imaginations. Children at this stage are still prone to imitation. Many years ago, emergency room doctors coined the phrase "Evel Knievel syndrome" to describe children's injuries as they rode their bikes off rooftops and over cars.[4] Although the networks say they will not show things that children might imitate with disastrous results, this is simply not true. On an episode of the popular cartoon X-Men, one of the main characters stood on a railroad track, jumping aside at the last moment to avoid being killed. This neglect of even the most basic responsibility toward children indicts the industry. For most of this stage, children are often unable to make accurate judgments about the reality of the programs they watch. Children cannot distinguish a toy gun from a real one until age eight or nine. Hundreds of children have been accidentally killed because they failed to recognize the lethality of a real gun.

Children are more likely to be disturbed by violence on television when the violence appears realistic and when the child identifies with either the victim or the aggressor. In one study, children were exposed to dramatized events from popular television programs or movies involving either a fatal house fire or a drowning.[5] As expected, children viewing these scenes became more fearful than children viewing neutral scenes involving water and fire. More important, children who watched the frightening scenes overestimated the likelihood of such events, and their fear generalized to other related activities. "Specifically," the study noted, "children who had just seen a television drama about a fatal house fire were averse to building a fire in a fireplace."[6] Although children certainly need to be warned of dangers that pose a threat to their well-being, the continual exposure of young children to disturbing images does not increase their competency. On the contrary, it traumatizes them and ultimately makes them less capable.

Finally, it is important to note the differential treatment that girls and boys of this age receive in the media. In keeping with cultural stereotypes, boys are typically adventuresome, fearless, and bold. Girls, on the other hand, tend to be quiet, compliant, and fearful. Television programs on the Public Broadcasting Service work hard at dispelling stereotypes and tend to show girls more realistically. In addition, PBS shows do an admirable job of portraying cultural, physical, and ethnic diversity. Women, African Americans, Hispanic Americans, Native Americans, and physically and intellectually challenged individuals are portrayed regularly and realistically. Shows like this do attempt to provide children of this age with a "window on the world."

At its best, television offers children the opportunity to embark on a social and cultural journey that reaches far beyond their family and neighborhood. It has the potential to educate, to stimulate, to encourage prosocial behavior, and to advance an appreciation for diversity. Hate crimes in the United States are on the increase. *Sesame Street's* emphasis on black, white, and Hispanic American children sharing their crayons may one day make it easier for them to share other resources.

In marked distinction to PBS, the commercial television stations are negligent in their portrayal of women and minorities. Research done by Bradley Greenberg and Jeffrey Brand in 1992 showed that CBS did not include a single minority character in any regular role in their Saturday morning lineup (directed primarily at young children). These researchers conclude, "If you want to see racial diversity on Saturday morning television, watch the commercials and skip the programs."[7] Advertisers appear to have more sensitivity than programmers, undoubtedly because of greater marketing awareness. As any parent knows, kids in this age group have a significant say at the grocery store checkout counter about which brand of cereal, snack, and beverage to buy.

PSYCHOLOGICAL DEVELOPMENT AND THE MEDIA

It's Saturday morning, and seven-year-old Nicholas wants to play with his best friend, Tommy, who lives next door. As he walks out of the house, his mom reminds him that he forgot to make his bed and put away his pajamas.

"How are you going to get your room straightened up and still see your friend?" asks Mom.

"No sweat," says Nicholas. "I'll play with Tommy first, and I'll clean up later."

"No way," says Mom. "I'm tired of looking at your messy room. Clean up first, and then you can go out to play."

"You're always bossing me around," grumbles Nicholas, who nevertheless runs to his room, throws the quilt over his bed, and straightens his shelves. He then races out the door to play. Over his shoulder, in the general direction of his mother, he yells, "Meanie!"

Attachment

This example illustrates a major shift in attachment that takes place during middle childhood. No longer is Mom setting all the rules and Nicholas simply accepting or resisting her directions. Nicholas and his mother are beginning to negotiate.

Children and their parents are now involved in mutual problem solving, or what psychologist Eleanor Maccoby calls "co-regulation."[8] This more mutual relationship is possible because middle-age children are becoming increasingly competent and capable of self-control. Children at this age are very concerned with fairness. They are able to understand that their parents' requests are often reasonable and even in the child's best interest. This is not a smooth or easily accomplished process and, as the example with Nicholas illustrates, often involves a fair amount of resistance, complaining, and even the hurling of insults on the part of the child. "Gyp," "unfair," and even "liar" are common insults at this age. However, these beginning attempts at co-regulation are paving the way for what will eventually be true cooperation. Children and their parents are now constructing a relationship based not on biological necessity but on mutual needs and desires.

Children can now participate in their household in real and productive ways. Although many of their newly acquired skills are clearly fragile, children of this age can set the table, make their bed, and take out the trash. The gradual introduction of responsibility enhances the developing child's sense of accomplishment. The acquisition of skills, along with the child's natural drive toward autonomy, profoundly affects the nature of the attachment between child and parent.

At the beginning of this stage of development, around age six, children are straddling two worlds. Home and family, which have occupied center stage in the young child's life, must accommodate to the reality of school and the child's increasing interest in peers. By the age of eight, most children have become comfortable sharing themselves physically and emotionally with both their family and the outside world. This is not to say that family influence does not remain strong throughout this period of time. The family continues to exert tremendous power over the middle-age child, as it will in later childhood and on into adolescence. However, the child is also working very hard at constructing an identity of his own. "I'm a Girl Scout" or "I'm a baseball player," the middle-age child proclaims proudly. Although the family, particularly the mother, has been the center of the world for children, they now strive to make themselves the center of their own universe.

This change in balance in the parent-child relationship calls on parents to lessen their control and begin monitoring and guiding instead. This can be a difficult transition for parents who are used to being directive or who are overwhelmed. Statements like "Because I said so" or "Because I'm the Mom" may be expedient in clarifying who's in charge with small children, but such statements are generally ineffective and inappropriate with middle-age children. Just as peer relations among children are increasingly concerned with issues of fairness and equality, the parent-child relationship must also reflect this more sophisticated level of interaction.

Research has found that parents who are warm and who take a reasoning approach to discipline produce children who feel good about themselves, are cooperative and responsible, and have few behavior problems.[9] On the other hand, a lack of parental warmth, coupled with a strong reliance on power-assertive techniques, such as physical punishment and shouting, tends to produce children who are aggressive, noncompliant, and likely to project blame onto others.[10] In addition, the degree of control that a parent exerts, compared to the amount of autonomy that is encouraged, has very different effects on children. Domineering and restrictive parents are found to have children who are inhibited, shy, obedient, and overly dependent.[11] At the other extreme, parents who are excessively permissive tend to have children who are disobedient and irresponsible but also expressive and sociable.[12]

An extraordinary example of how the media can help children cope with distressing circumstances is *E.T.: The Extra-Terrestrial*, Steven Spielberg's classic film of childhood loss and reconnection. Spielberg reaches into the hearts of children who are experiencing loss and reassures them that their journey toward independence, though perhaps temporarily disrupted, need not be derailed. Elliot is the middle of three children, and his parents are in the midst of a divorce. Too young to be distracted by friends like his teenage brother, Michael, and too old to be oblivious like his young sister, Gertie, Elliot is sick at heart.

When E.T., a creature from outer space, is unwittingly abandoned by his people, he seeks out Elliot, knowing, with the wisdom of all good fairy tales, who can help him and who cannot. When Elliot tries to convince Michael of E.T.'s existence, Michael taunts Elliot, and Elliot can only reply to his brother, "Dad would believe me." Dad, of course, is nowhere to be found in the movie, and all three children struggle with their individual experiences of anger and abandonment. Finally, as the three children come to know E.T., they begin to feel both needed and reconnected. In one of the most touching scenes of the movie, Elliot and Michael are scavenging in their attic for things to help E.T. construct a telephone. Elliot finds an old shirt of his father's, and the two brothers, bound in a fraternity of longing and loss, debate whether their father's shirt smells of Old Spice or Sea Breeze.

Finally, the children are able to help E.T. return home, and they learn in the process that they can lighten their losses through compassion and the ability to internalize the people they love. Because children are able to hold within themselves images and positive feelings about their parents, they feel safe enough to spend the day at school, among peers, and eventually out in the world. I have seen many children in my practice who, in attempting to come to terms with some loss, have put to good use E.T.'s injunction that "I'll be right here" as he touches Elliot's forehead before returning to his spaceship. As is undoubtedly clear from the amount of space I've devoted to describing this movie, I feel it is an extraordinary piece of work. More important, it illustrates that the media can encourage, understand, teach, and elevate children and still turn out commercially successful products. As this book goes to press, *E.T.* is the third highest grossing film of all time (overshadowed only by *Star Wars*, another outstanding family movie, and *Titanic*).

Unfortunately, the media do not always reach middle-age children with such sensitivity. In particular, there are many movies that emphasize parental irresponsibility and incompetence. These movies detail ineffective parenting and children's resulting struggles to cope with a world that is beyond their capabilities. Here we tend to see children who have been forced to abandon their childhood and shoulder the burdens that rightfully belong to adults. Psychologists term children who are engaged in this reversal of role "parentified children." As was mentioned earlier, *Home Alone* is a prime example of a child who makes a virtue out of his parents' inattention. But unlike Kevin, most children who are neglected and forced to grow up too soon do so at great cost to their personal development and self-esteem.

Aggression

Children of six, seven, and eight are making significant strides in their ability to control aggression. The emerging ability to understand consequences helps the child predict that if he hits the child next to him, he is likely to end up in the principal's office. The socializing forces of society such as school, parents, and religion, combined with increased cognitive skills, help the middle-age child develop new strategies for dealing with angry feelings. This is not to say that children in this age group do not, with some regularity, indulge their angry feelings with aggressive displays of hitting or name calling; they certainly do. Rather, middle-age children are in a period of transition. They are beginning to understand the value of self-control both because it feels good and because of the social approval it brings.

Research confirms that middle childhood is a critical period during which children develop characteristic levels of aggression that tend to be maintained throughout life. The more aggressive child is likely to become the more aggressive adult.[13] Therefore the questions surrounding media violence and its long- and short-term effects on children are particularly relevant to this age group.

Children and Televised Violence. In one of the most comprehensive and significant studies on the effects of media violence on children, Huesmann and Eron followed hundreds of children over twenty-two years and assessed the effects of viewing violence on the child's level of aggression.[14] Their research found that *viewing violent television in the third grade correlated not just with aggression in the third grade but with predicting criminal behavior twenty-two years later at age thirty!* Although we may initially be skeptical of such grave findings, it should also be noted that these findings have been repeated in other studies and in other countries.[15]

Huesmann and Eron are blunt in their conclusions: "Aggressive habits seem to be learned early in life and, once established, are resistant to change and predictive of serious adult antisocial behavior. If a child's observation of media violence promotes the learning of aggressive habits, it can have harmful lifelong consequences."[16]

As a result of studies like Huesmann and Eron's, we have come to understand a great deal about the complex relationship between exposing children to media violence and actual aggression. Most studies have found that the relationship between aggression and television viewing is "bidirectional."[17] Aggressive kids watch more television, and more television leads to higher levels of aggression. Even children who are not particularly aggressive to begin with become more aggressive because of heavy television viewing. As a matter of fact, children who were not particularly aggressive to begin with and who watched a lot of violent television ultimately became more aggressive than children who were naturally aggressive but whose television viewing was restricted. *All children are made more aggressive by exposure to television violence.* This is such a discouraging finding because social scientists know that once aggression is adopted as a preferred way of handling conflict, it is very difficult to modify.[18]

Children and the Movies. Movies in which a young child is the victim of abuse and exploitation and in which adults cannot be counted on to fulfill their role as protector of the young are far more damaging at this age than movies that are clearly based in fantasy. *The Good Son* stars Macaulay Culkin as Henry, a seemingly engaging youngster who is gradually revealed to be a sadistic murderer. Unfortunately, many young children, accompanied by their parents, saw this movie despite its R rating. They were not expecting their *Home Alone* hero to be a serial killer. Parental responsibility and a rating system that makes clear the reasons for particular ratings would have spared many young children an extremely upsetting experience.

Henry's cousin Mark comes to stay with Henry's family following the death of Mark's mother. When it becomes increasingly apparent to Mark that Henry has killed his own baby brother and plans on killing his sister as well, he turns to adults to help him. Unfortunately, like so many movies involving children, adults are not available. Mark's father leaves on a business trip immediately after the death of his wife. When Mark tries to tell Henry's mother that Henry is trying to kill his sister, she becomes enraged and slaps Mark. Even Mark's psychiatrist is seduced by Henry's apparent goodwill.

I saw several children in my practice with recurring nightmares after viewing this film. Because there was so much to identify with in this movie (all the standard paraphernalia of middle-class childhood), children were easily drawn into a world that was familiar and ultimately terrifying. Although there is little in the way of graphic violence in this movie, middle-age children are past the point where all violence must be of the in-your-face variety to be frightening. By this age, children are becoming sensitive to the kind of psychological violence portrayed in *The Good Son*.

Movies such as *Star Trek*, although more violent, are less apt to be frightening than more realistic movies. This is because of the obvious fantasy element, which at this age can help children feel distance from what they are watching. The adventures of the *Starship Enterprise* have entertained generations because they combine action with the ever-popular theme of heroism in the face of danger. *Star Trek*'s roots lie in fairy tale and myth, and as a result its conclusions are typically optimistic. In addition, it is multicultural, multiethnic, and multispecies. It is not a bad choice for this age group, especially since older siblings and even parents are likely to enjoy watching it as well. Family entertainment has become increasingly difficult to find as studios aim for target audiences. Children's movies are for the most part intolerable to adults, as they focus on toilet humor and neglect even the appearance of a story or of character development. Adult movies are typically so perverse or blood soaked that they are completely inappropriate for young children.

Disney is attempting to revitalize family entertainment by providing us with movies like *The Little Mermaid*, *Anastasia*, and *Beauty and the Beast*. These are movies with enough wonder and action to please the youngest moviegoer, and enough plot, character development, and technical finesse to please adults. In this category are movies as diverse as *The Black Stallion*, *Willy Wonka and the Chocolate Factory*, and *Babe*. Although sometimes hard to discover, these kinds of movies provide an opportunity for parents and children to share some of the excitement of good moviemaking.

Children and the News. Graphic news reporting about violence, because of its factual nature, is likely to be particularly upsetting to children in middle childhood. Young children are exposed to ever more graphic images of death and destruction on the evening news. Several stations are attempting to deal with this problem by offering "family-sensitive" news programs that omit these disturbing images. This effort is to be applauded. Although we are encouraging children in this age group to become increasingly aware of the world outside their neighborhood, we still need to protect them from graphic images that can be traumatizing.

On October 1, 1993, twelve-year-old Polly Klass was enjoying a sleepover with two girlfriends when she was kidnaped from her suburban home in Petaluma, California. That she was abducted from her bedroom, while her mother slept in the next room, made this a particularly disturbing crime for children. The crime received an enormous amount of national news coverage. Polly's smiling face became a staple on posters and news programs. Unfortunately, she was found dead two months later, and images of her were again broadcast on television. Newscasts repeatedly juxtaposed a home video of Polly laughing and dancing with images of her covered, dead body found off a California highway.

A study conducted by psychiatrist Sara Stein and colleagues looked at the effects of such extensive media coverage on children. Over 1,100 children aged eight to eighteen in three different states were studied. Not surprisingly, the younger children (because of their inability to distance themselves) and girls (because of their identification) were particularly disturbed by these news stories. Although parents and the school attempted to help children feel safer, over 80 percent of the children reported that they were "sometimes" or "often" bothered by symptoms such as bad dreams or intrusive thoughts that they could not control. The researchers wrote: "Thus in viewing an event such as the news reporting of a child murder, many children will be unable to comprehend the significance of distance from the crime scene, for example, or that of random threat. As a result, children may not develop a reassuring sense of perspective on the crime, as adults do."[19]

In my own practice, which was not far from the kidnaping, I saw several young girls who exhibited symptoms of posttraumatic stress disorder following Polly's kidnaping. Previously healthy children reported sleep disturbances, concentration problems, and anxiety. One girl slept with a baseball bat next to her bed; another refused to sleep near a window. It is likely that parents underestimate the impact of disturbing images on their children. This is particularly true for real images that are seen on the nightly news.

Cognitive Development

> Mr. Jones went to a restaurant and ordered a whole pizza for dinner. When the waiter asked if he wanted it cut into six or eight pieces, Mr. Jones said: "You'd better make it six. I could never eat eight."[20]

This anecdote, which preschoolers find perfectly reasonable, is hilarious to the middle-age child. A great revolution in thinking is taking place. Somewhere around the age of seven, children stop thinking in terms of black and white and begin thinking logically. In the case of Mr. Jones and his pizza, the younger child believes that more slices mean more pizza; the older child, informed by logic, knows that the amount is the same no matter how you slice it.

This cognitive revolution, which Piaget termed the stage of "concrete operations," is characterized by increasingly efficient and logical thinking. Children at this stage are beginning to appreciate cause-and-effect relationships. All of this helps make living in the world more predictable and manageable.

Middle-age children are becoming rather effective problem solvers. Compared with younger children, children of six, seven, and eight are able to think more systematically about many different pieces of information. For example, an eight-year-old at a carnival who sees a very young child crying may walk over and ask if the little child is lost. The eight-year-old is able to use what he sees (an upset toddler), what he hears (crying), the context (young children at crowded events are generally with their parents), and his own experience (being lost once and being upset) to come to the logical conclusion that the young child is lost and needs help. Thinking is more logical and more sophisticated. Exactly because of this large developmental leap in cognitive skills, children are now expected to be, and are capable of being, full-time students.

Around age seven, parents have an opportunity to enhance their children's understanding of media in a new way. Although controlling the amount of time that children watch television is the most important variable for younger children, discussion and explanation now have greater influence over how much a child understands. A parenting style that filters and interprets the outside world supports the child's developing ability to understand and sympathize with others. Among children of equal intelligence, those whose parents are involved in explaining and discussing television programs with them learn more than those children who watch alone. It is not enough for a parent simply to be in the same room; discussion and explanation are the key factors.

One of the advances made during this stage in development is the child's increasing capacity to predict outcomes (what Piaget termed the ability to "reverse operations"). This has implications for how a child views media violence. The middle-age child is now able to understand that the man in custody at the end of the program is suffering the consequences for his violent acts at the beginning of the program. This newly developing ability to predict outcomes and to make connections between later and earlier events helps middle-age children to appreciate consequences.

However, middle-age children are still burdened by their egocentricity. Children at this age see things primarily from their own point of view and have difficulty taking another point of view. "Children who steal food should go to jail," proclaims the middle-class seven-year-old who has no experience in going to bed hungry and who has little capacity to put himself in the shoes of a child who must steal to survive. Although thinking skills are more sophisticated and allow a greater understanding of violence and its consequences, the egocentricity of the middle-age child prevents an appreciation of the broader social context of violence.

Early in this stage of development, children still do not have a firm and reliable grasp on the difference between reality and fantasy.

Professor Aimee Dorr's research, conducted at Harvard and UCLA, shows that the majority of first- and second-graders are unable to explain what is real on television.[21] For example, six- and seven-year-old children in her study believed that actors involved in shoot-outs must wear bulletproof vests "just in case the bullets are not fake." In addition, while some children this age understood that married couples on television were not necessarily married, they also thought "they must be very good friends." There is still a blurring of the lines between reality and fantasy at this age. Around the age of eight, there is a major jump in knowledge about the nature of television and a reliable understanding that what is seen on television is "made up."[22]

Children at this age still have substantial cognitive limitations that are easily exploited by the media. A child who repeatedly watches television characters attempting to solve their problems by the use of violence may be storing violent scripts that under certain conditions will encourage them to actually behave violently. Behavior does not have to be performed in order to be learned, and it is under conditions of stress that our more primitive responses find expression. Media executives are fond of invoking the concept of catharsis, the notion that watching violence somehow "bleeds off" our own feelings of aggression. Unfortunately, *catharsis has found no substantiation in any social science research*. In spite of this, the concept refuses to die and is regularly cited as a justification for violent programming, typically by those who are most likely to profit from such programming.

It is much more likely that watching violent television programming has a disinhibiting effect on the child's still tender control of aggression. Disinhibition is a physiological and psychological state in which defenses are lowered and behavior is more primitive. The person who has had too much to drink and is dancing the polka on his host's tabletop is said to be disinhibited. But you don't have to be a psychologist to understand disinhibition; just ask any mom whose six-year-old has pinned down his baby brother in imitation of a karate chokehold after watching *Teenage Mutant Ninja Turtles*.

Moral Development

- Rachel, age seven, comes home from school and is asked by her mom to take out the garbage. With a stricken look, Rachel responds, "I'm not your servant. Do it yourself!"

- Jacob, age eight, is lying on the sofa on Saturday morning watching cartoons. His mother, with impeccable tact, says, "You can watch another half-hour of cartoons, and then I want you to make your bed and straighten up your room." Without lifting his eyes from the television, Jacob replies, "Not today, Mom. It's Saturday. Dad doesn't have to work on Saturday, and neither should I. Kids have rights too, you know."

These two examples, familiar in one form or another to every parent with children in this age group, illustrate a new stage in moral reasoning for the child. Gone is the earlier childhood belief that parents are all-knowing. Just a year or two ago, children were typically cooperative and obedient. Authority was respected, and children generally believed they deserved whatever punishment was meted out. Beginning around age six or seven, this changes as the child enters a stage of moral reasoning in which everyone is entitled to his or her own point of view and adults no longer have moral authority over their children. As my middle son succinctly told me at this stage, "You're not the boss of me."

Children at this age also exhibit a tremendous interest in the concept of fairness. One of the constant lamentations of the middle-age child is "It's not fair." An exasperated father reports, "Every Sunday we would plan a family outing, and my seven-year-old daughter would spend the entire afternoon complaining, 'How come we always do what the parents want? How come we never do what the kid wants?'" This barrage would continue despite Mom and Dad's best efforts to come up with activities they thought would be appealing to their daughter, often activities the daughter had requested.

Children at this age are very preoccupied with fairness. With hawklike attention, they notice every compliment paid to a sibling

("How come you always pay attention to him and not to me?"), every piece of cake that is divided ("She got the bigger piece again"), and every privilege granted to a neighboring child ("Oh, sure, he's allowed to say up late. How come nothing special ever happens in my life?"). Children at this stage see fairness as being a tit-for-tat sharing of resources. Usually the child feels she has come up short.

The primary philosophy of this stage is "looking out for number one." Children at this stage of moral development often appear to be rigid, self-centered, and cruel. They subscribe to the philosophy "an eye for an eye, a tooth for a tooth." This rather chilling example from Dr. Lickona's *Raising Good Children* clearly illustrates the code of vengeance often subscribed to by the middle-age child. "A third-grade teacher asked her class what would be a fair punishment for a group of teenagers who broke into the zoo in Syracuse, New York, one summer night and killed more than a dozen animals. 'Shoot 'em,' said several children. 'Same as they did to the animals.'"[23]

With such a cold desire for retribution in kind, it's no wonder that this is a difficult time between siblings. No dirty look, no push, no sneer can go unpunished. Children this age may have to wait to exact their revenge, but at some point it will be payback time. Every exasperated parent knows what it feels like to say, "So what if he gave you a dirty look? Can't you just let it go?" For the most part, the answer to this question is no. The middle-age child has great difficulty letting go of real and imagined insults.

Although children at this stage can appear to be particularly cruel and selfish, parents should remember that this is actually an advance over the preschooler's level of moral thinking. Children now understand that fairness is not simply following the orders of those who are more powerful. Eventually, this broadening of the concept of fairness will allow children to understand that there may be many different points of view of what is fair and that fairness may depend on whether one is looking at benefits to the individual, the family, the society, or even the world.

Television programs and movies should reinforce the moral advances of this age group. Unfortunately, the opposite is often the case, particularly in movies and programs that emphasize justified retribution. The high body count in movies like *The Terminator* and *Die Hard* (which are seen by a surprisingly large number of children in this age group) suggests that murder and mayhem are justified when the hero is fighting against evil. This point of view is greeted with delight by middle-age children, who have a fierce but rigid sense of fairness and who believe in "every man for himself." Movies like these are a kind of moral poison for children this age because they reinforce a sense of morality that, left unchallenged, encourages a vigilante mentality. Like the children who suggested killing the youngsters who killed the zoo animals, children of this age have little empathy when it comes to others. Hyperviolent movies like *The Terminator* and *Die Hard* reinforce this lack of empathy by killing scores of people we never get a chance to know or identify with. They appeal to the moral weakness of children at this age.

Interestingly, commercial television does a good job of addressing many of the concerns of the middle-age child. Friendship and family relations are the themes of many popular shows. *Step by Step, Full House, Kenan & Kel, Home Improvement, Roseanne,* and *The Cosby Show* all deal with the kinds of real-life dilemmas that children face daily. Although the average twenty-two-minute situation comedy does not allow for an in-depth look at more serious problems such as child abuse, substance abuse by parents, racism, or public safety, it works well for problems like forgetting one's chores, lying to parents, petty theft, and loyalty to friends and family.

On one of the final episodes of the long-running situation comedy *Full House,* seven-year-old Michelle tells her father a secret that she had promised her friends she would not reveal. Her father lets the secret slip out, and when her friends find out, they are angry with her and banish her from the group. Michelle feels betrayed by her father and abandoned by her friends. The problem is resolved when Michelle and her dad talk about the importance of not betraying secrets. Her father encourages her to apologize and try to work it out with her friends. She does and is successful. The father has learned the importance of respecting his daughter's confidences, and Michelle has learned how to get help and use it effectively. Episodes like this are not trivial in the world of childhood. They are of utmost importance, and programs that address these concerns in an entertaining and useful way are extremely valuable to the middle-age child.

MIDDLE-AGE CHILD VIEWING CHECKLIST

Attachment

World is portrayed as reasonably secure   yes   no

Adults are reliable   yes   no

Children are encouraged to expand interests
and skills in ways that are safe and likely to
lead to success   yes   no

Aggression

Angry feelings are acknowledged   yes   no

Aggression is an unacceptable way of handling
conflict and frustration   yes   no

Provides alternate ways of handling aggression
that are both useful and appealing   yes   no

Children are not likely to identify with either
victims or perpetrators   yes   no

Cognitive Development

Makes it clear what is fantasy and what is
reality   yes   no

Cause and effect are highlighted   yes   no

Moral Development

Children are encouraged to think about the
consequences of action   yes   no

Children are encouraged to consider other
points of view   yes   no

TELEVISION HALL OF FAME

Reading Rainbow

Doug

Animaniacs

Full House

Home Improvement

Science Court

Ghostwriter

Beakman's World

Family Matters

Figure It Out

The Magic School Bus

Shelley Duvall's Bedtime Stories

MOVIES AND VIDEOS TO CHECK OUT

Star Wars

The Empire Strikes Back

The Wizard of Oz

Shelley Duvall's Faerie
   Tale Theatre

Toy Story

Any animated Disney
   movie

Return of the Jedi

E.T.: The Extra-Terrestrial

The Neverending Story

Willy Wonka and the Chocolate
   Factory

An American Tail

The Black Stallion

ADD YOUR OWN FAVORITES

_____

_____

_____

_____

6

Older Childhood

Ages Nine, Ten, and Eleven

It doesn't get much easier than this. Older children are enjoying a unique and delightful period of equilibrium. Friendly and accepting, this stage of development is a welcome breather for both parents and their children. In the words of two of the best-known developmental psychologists, Louise Bates and Francis Ilg, "There's nobody nicer than a ten-year-old."[1]

If you're having a hard day with your particular nine-, ten-, or eleven-year-old child, just think back to the "terrible twos" or think ahead to the rebellious teen years. For the most part, older children are enjoying a period of relative calm, good nature, and friendliness with peers, teachers, and family. Although eleven-year-olds may be starting to move toward the edginess of early adolescence, nine- and ten-year-olds express very high levels of satisfaction with their lives in general and their families in particular.

GENERAL DEVELOPMENT

Children at this stage of development are typically described as friendly, secure, outgoing, positive, and trusting. Although they certainly can be angry on occasion, these episodes usually blow over rather quickly. While the older child's spheres of interest are rapidly expanding, family is still home base. For the nine- and ten-year-old in particular, Mom and Dad (if not always siblings) are pretty great people. "I have the best family" is a typically exuberant comment at this age.

Instead of the dramatic changes of the preschool years and the explosive changes of adolescence, older children are changing in more subtle ways. Relative freedom from conflict allows children of nine, ten, and eleven to elaborate a sense of self, increase social and cognitive skills, develop empathy, and refine their sense of right and wrong. The nine-year-old who can now negotiate and resolve a conflict with a friend without calling in Mom to adjudicate has mastered a momentous task. She is learning to function independently as an autonomous social being in a world with other social beings. This accomplishment is no less historic than the toddler's first shaky steps or the teenager's sexual awakening.

Children at this stage of development are beginning in earnest the acquisition of adult skills. The range of tasks that older children confront is enormous: school, work, friendship, personal responsibility, and individual talents. The list of challenges is endless, and were it not for the natural enthusiasm of children this age, it might seem overwhelming to them. Instead, it is a golden opportunity, and the secure older child seeks opportunities to advance his sense of proficiency.

As was noted in Chapter Five, the major task of childhood is to gain experience and competence in the following three areas: consolidating a sense of self, forming close relationships with peers, and achieving success at school.

The emotional, social, and cognitive challenges that older children face are similar to those confronting the middle-age child. Much of what was written in Chapter Five about children of six, seven, and eight will be relevant to children of nine, ten, and eleven. Unlike the adolescent, who will be confronted with challenges quite different from anything previously encountered, the older child is expanding, developing, and refining skills and capacities already evident in middle childhood.

Consolidating a Sense of Self

Children of nine, ten, and eleven are working on expanding and refining their sense of self. At this stage, children understand that in addition to their physical selves, they possess a psychological self that is enduring across time. "I'm kind of quiet, but people seem to like me. I like doing nice things for other people" is one ten-year-old girl's self-description. It is a typical comment for this age because it acknowledges both her psychological self ("kind of quiet") and her relationship to other people ("people seem to like me"). This is a long way from this same girl's self-description in preschool, "I'm pretty tall. My hair is brown, and I hate broccoli."

The child now realizes that she is a single, unique person who is constantly evolving. She can consider various aspects of her experience and see them all as part of the same self. This ability to maintain a continuous sense of self despite the passage of time, differences in feelings, and physical change is critical to healthy emotional adjustment. As one child succinctly said, "No matter what, I've always got me."

As a child's private inner self develops, he becomes increasingly aware that other people also have internal thoughts and feelings, which may not be obvious. This awareness leads to a landmark understanding—that people can be motivated by things that are not readily apparent. At this stage children can begin to appreciate more complex story lines in the media.

As children move through elementary school, they become aware of themselves not only as individuals but also as group members. Researchers have found that at age nine or ten, children begin to evaluate their performance consistently and systematically by comparing themselves to others.[2] "I'm in the highest math group." "I'm the fastest runner in the class." These social comparisons help the child appreciate his uniqueness and differentiate himself from others. "My best friend and I are both really good athletes. But he's better at soccer and I'm better at basketball." Descriptions at this age frequently involve comparisons, not because children seek to crow over their abilities (many children at this age do not like to be singled out) but rather because comparisons help them know exactly where they stand.

Despite the dramatic changes in self-concept that take place during childhood, researchers have found that self-esteem tends to be consistent across time.[3] This is not surprising. We would expect the infant who was well nurtured to grow into a child who is confident and adaptable. In turn, the adolescent who is able to weather the demands of adolescence and still work on defining a healthy and stable sense of self will become a well-adjusted adult. This progression is partly the result of the child's inborn disposition, partly the result of good parenting, and partly the result of fortunate circumstances. High self-esteem is predictive of success in many areas, such as school, work, interpersonal relationships, and self-satisfaction. Although it is not written in stone, children who feel good about themselves are likely to be successful adults.

Erik Erikson proposed that the task facing children during the elementary school years is to confront increasingly difficult social and academic challenges. He labeled this stage "industry versus inferiority" and believed that children who worked hard and succeeded in meeting social and academic challenges developed a sense of mastery and self-assurance.[4] Conversely, children who are unable to master the tasks of childhood feel inferior and shun new activities. A vicious cycle begins when a child feels bad about one thing and then withdraws from other activities that might help him feel better.

Parents know that children of this age thrive when they are presented with new and challenging activities. This is the age of Little League and Brownies, Boy Scouts and 4–H Clubs, dance lessons, karate lessons, piano lessons, and any other activity the child finds appealing and the parent endorses.

Forming Close Relationships with Peers

As older children begin to see themselves as individuals, they are increasingly able to see their friends as complex people with unique characteristics as well. No longer are friends made because "we're in the same class" or "we live next door to each other." Older children describe their friendships as arising out of shared interests, attitudes, or admiration. "We both like being kind to animals" or "She's a great dancer, and that's what I want to be." Friends do not have to be exactly alike because the older child has developed a perspective that allows for different points of view. "We don't always agree, but he's a great friend anyway." Older children are able to engage in and communicate with friends in a broader and more meaningful way. Some remarkably enduring friendships are forged at this stage of development.

This newly emerging capacity to truly see things from another perspective has some rather peculiar manifestations in older children. "You're such a dweeb, Joshua," says ten-year-old Eric. "You're nothing but a princess, Laura," Chelsea says sarcastically. "Dweeb," "geek," "weirdo," or even "bitch" are common insults that children hurl intentionally to do psychological damage to each other. This is a big change from hitting, which was the younger child's typical response to frustration. It shows the shift toward the psychological and away from the physical as the arena for inflicting pain on others. Although insults appear cruel and childish, they actually represent a leap forward in the child's understanding of others. Eric and Chelsea use taunts to wound because they can stand in Joshua's and Laura's shoes and know how much the insult will hurt.

This is a particularly sensitive time in terms of teaching children about the value of prosocial solutions. Because of their increased capacity to see things from another point of view, as well as their more sophisticated psychological understanding, older children are capable of altruism. One study of children in fifth grade demonstrated that parents who value altruism and provide good models of helpful and considerate behavior have children who are also altruistic. Children at this age are likely to identify with the parent of their own sex. Altruistic fathers strongly influence their sons; altruistic mothers strongly influence their daughters.[5] Research has shown that a child's prosocial behavior can be increased when exposed to adults who behave compassionately. This is particularly true when the adult is warm, nurturing, and powerful.[6] Just as we saw that children tend to model themselves after powerful aggressive people, children will also model themselves after powerful altruistic people.

School Achievement

Although family is still the major agent of socialization, it competes with school and peers for influence on the child. School continues to be a major factor in the lives of older children, and children at this stage often spend more time with peers than with family members. As usual, development in these areas is interrelated. Children who feel good about themselves are apt to do well at school and to enjoy popularity among their peers.

Older children are comparing their performance with the performance of other children. This is encouraged by the school, which tests, grades, and places children in different groups depending on their ability. Most adults have clear memories of the delight or the mortification of having their grades called out in class or posted in a public place. One grandmother told her grandson about missing a spelling word and being forced to sit with a dunce cap on her head in the row labeled "dunce alley." Although such insensitive episodes are thankfully rare now, children are still very aware of their position in the social and academic hierarchy. The teacher may not call a student a "dunce," but other children will not hesitate to say, "Are you in the stupid group again?" The school experience has the potential to either enhance or destroy self-esteem. Research studies have repeatedly shown that classroom adjustment and academic success at this age predict mental health in adulthood.[7]

School has an enormous impact on the child's current development, as well as her eventual level of adjustment. It is disheartening to have research show that girls are still discriminated against in the classroom. In a study of fifth-graders, high-achieving girls received the most criticism and the least praise *from their teachers* than any other group of students. Boys, when they are criticized, are reproached for misbehavior or lack of neatness. Poor performance in boys is typically attributed to a lack of effort, whereas poor performance in girls is seen as a sign of low aptitude. This difference in attribution is very important because it suggests to girls that their poor performance can't be helped and is beyond their control. Boys, on the other hand, are encouraged to believe that effort can help them become higher achievers.[8]

Carol Gilligan and her colleagues at Harvard University have been studying the psychology of girls and women for close to thirty years. Their research shows that preadolescent girls are experiencing a crisis in their lives that may be heightened by school. They have observed that at about age eleven, girls reach a watershed in their development. If forced to choose between their natural exuberance and society's demands to be quiet and deferential, young girls often begin a process of distancing themselves from their natural exuberance. "Don't beat the boys," "Don't talk too loud," and "Try to be a little more feminine" are typical exhortations. Girls face an endless number of prohibitions that can dampen their enthusiasm and sense of authenticity.[9] Couple this with the consistent, if subtle, discouragement they receive in the classroom, and it is little wonder that preadolescent girls often show a lessening of interest in academic success and an increased incidence of depression. It is important that mothers defend their daughters and encourage them to remain spirited, connected, true to themselves, and academically challenged. In particular, girls this age should be allowed to express their full range of feelings. Mothers can both model and encourage their daughters to be independent, honest, and outspoken.

MEDIA AND THE OLDER CHILD

Like the middle-age child, the older child is intrigued by movies and programs that emphasize increasing separation from family and provide the first tantalizing look at adolescence. In the coming-of-age classic *Stand by Me*, four preadolescent boys sit around their clubhouse, smoking, swearing, and insulting each other. Treated with contempt by the older adolescents in the movie, these four boys clearly have nothing but admiration for the teenagers who despise them.

Particularly toward the latter part of this stage, children are anxious to peer into the world of adolescence and to observe its rituals of dress, language, and social behavior. They tend to view media offerings that focus on their own age group as "babyish" and beg to be allowed to watch programs such as *Beverly Hills 90210*.

Peer pressure is becoming strong, and children this age are loath to admit that they still enjoy PG-rated movies or even Saturday morning cartoons. When he was eleven, my oldest son used to say he was watching cartoons "to chill," thus invoking the language of adolescence to ward off his feelings of childishness. Children at this age need a break from the pressures of growing up and should not be ridiculed when they allow themselves to return to the entertainment they enjoyed when younger.

Developmental tasks are formidable at any age, and we all need a respite from the demands of life. Disney has had enormous success in the past few years recognizing "the child in all of us" and producing movies such as *Aladdin*, *The Hunchback of Notre Dame*, and *The Little Mermaid*, which manage to engage adults as well as children. Development does not proceed in a lockstep manner. The older child who one day begs to see *Face/Off* or *Scream* may be found watching *Bugs Bunny* the next day. This is normal behavior.

The impact of the media on this age group is very significant. Eleven-year-olds watch more television than any other age group, averaging twenty-eight hours per week.[10] Twenty-three research studies, conducted over twenty-six years in the United States and abroad, have consistently shown that this much television viewing has a small negative effect on school achievement. Interestingly, watching up to ten hours of television per week enhances achievement slightly, but as we have seen, most children watch far more than this. After ten hours per week of television viewing, achievement scores begin to decline. There are several possible explanations for this finding. It may be that parents whose children only watch ten hours per week or less are particularly active in providing other more challenging activities for their children. They may be using the television to expand their child's world rather than as a baby-sitter. It may also be that it is only beyond ten hours a week that television begins to replace more intellectually stimulating activities such as homework or reading. This negative relationship between television viewing and academic achievement is stronger for girls than it is for boys and stronger for children of high intelligence.[11] Interestingly, girls with low IQs show some small benefit from more television viewing.[12]

Although boys' academic performance may be slightly less affected by the media, some studies show that their aggressive behavior is affected more.[13] Young girls and boys seem to be equally affected by media aggression, but after age six, as social norms become more clearly differentiated, boys seem to be more affected. We can only speculate as to why boys may be more vulnerable, but part of the explanation seems to come from the content of popular media. Childhood is in large measure about the adventure of separating from one's family and becoming one's own person. Adventure movies and television programs are particularly appealing to children because they address these concerns. "What's it like to be on my own?" "How will I manage out in the world?" The real answers to these questions are complex and, ideally, involve a growing appreciation for cooperation and sensitivity in relationships. Boys in particular are frequently presented with dangerous and thoughtless answers to these questions.

When Kevin in *Home Alone* is frightened at being abandoned by his family, he dives under his bed. He coaxes himself out by saying, "Only a wimp would be hiding under the bed. I can't be a wimp—I'm the man of the house." In fact he is not the man of the house; he is only a child. Under normal circumstances, any child would be most distressed to be in Kevin's shoes. However, Kevin never cries or tries to enlist adult help, even when burglars attempt to break into his house. Instead he devises a series of tortures (hot irons falling on people's heads, paint cans knocking them down the stairs) to protect himself. Kevin is victorious, and the message seems to be that if you are a crafty, aggressive, unfeeling little thug, then you'll be OK.

More sinister are movies that feature men of robotlike proportions who are avenging something or other. These movies need to be divided into two different categories because I believe their effects on children are substantially different. The first category includes movies such as *Terminator 2: Judgment Day*, which are beloved by this age group and are clearly fantastical. Whether the hero is literally a robot, as in *Robocop*, or only figuratively, as in any Arnold Schwarzenegger movie (no, I'm not talking about his acting, only his larger-than-life physical self), the child of this age has the cognitive capacity to understand that this is fiction, and that knowledge lessens the likelihood of identification and imitation. Although I believe that these movies are not particularly in the best interest of children because they reinforce the attitude that becoming a man is in large measure about becoming sadistic, aggressive, and unfeeling, they are less disturbing and less likely to encourage imitation and identification than more realistic films.

The second category of violent movies should be of greater concern to parents. These are movies such as Charles Bronson's *Death Wish*, Steven Seagal's *Hard to Kill*, and Brandon Lee's *The Crow*, in which the hero is a regular guy caught in extraordinary circumstances. Many of the heroes in this genre become killers in order to avenge women who are raped or murdered. In these movies, every unfortunate cultural myth has been rolled into one dreadful saga. The messages conveyed are "It's OK to be violent as long as you're the good guy," "Women can't take care of themselves and need men to protect them," and "Violence in the pursuit of justice is noble." Movies such as these reflect and magnify the worst aspects of our cultural stereotypes. They exploit many young men's budding machismo with messages that are dangerous both to themselves and to society.

One reason boys are differentially affected by the media may be that the role models they are given are so deficient yet very stimulating at the same time. Steven Seagal in *Out for Justice* is sexy, strong, macho, and, of course, a police officer. Seagal is a dazzling master of the martial arts, and his charisma is palpable. Unfortunately, he has trouble putting together a complete sentence, and the majority of his social interactions consist of breaking some part of the human body. To confuse the issue further, he says things like "Don't be a bad guy, be a good guy" as he breaks someone's arms. At a time when boys need clear models about who are the good guys and who are the bad guys, movies like *Out for Justice* muddy the moral waters.

Both movies and television programming directed at boys draw them into a world dominated by conflict, which is then resolved through the use of guns, swords, martial arts, and torture. Although there is very little research on video games, it is likely that the kinds of video games so loved by boys this age are only adding to their repertoire of aggressive solutions. In games like "Mortal Kombat," brutality is rewarded: "Rip her spine out and advance to the next level!"

Good guys do a great deal of the killing. Over and over again, young boys are presented with powerful male role models who choose force over cooperation, intimidation over mutuality, and impulsivity over thoughtfulness. Certainly boys grapple with the issues of power and submission and dominance; gun play, sword play, and fighting are normal expressions of this conflict. They have probably always been part of boys' play. But when the media provide so much support for violent resolutions, they cease to be simply components of fantasy and are too often seen as viable ways to conduct one's life. There are few movies that instruct young men about how to deal with rage, loss, and desperation without blowing someone's head off. In a country where young men are murdering and being murdered in record numbers, learning how to handle powerful feelings effectively becomes a matter of life and death.

Research has shown that there are several factors that foster aggression in children once they have been exposed to television violence. These include

- Violent behavior that is seen as justified[14]
- Violent behavior that is rewarded[15]
- Cues in the portrayed violence that have a similarity to those in real life[16]
- Violence that is portrayed without consequence, such as no discernable pain, sorrow, or remorse[17]
- Violence that is realistically portrayed or seen as a real event[18]

It is exactly because vigilante movies are frequently presented in a context of ordinary life that they are potentially damaging to children. The ordinary backgrounds of many of these movies makes it easy to identify with the hero. The suburban bedroom in the movie may have the same sheets as the ones on your child's bed, and the adolescent actress may look more or less like your daughter or the girl next door. Who wouldn't be outraged if their wife or mother or sister were raped or murdered? Though these movies encourage children to identify with the hero, children repeatedly come to a savage and unacceptable conclusion: that the appropriate response to violence is more violence. Unfortunately, too many young men in our society have taken this advice to heart. Just as girls are so poorly served by media that reinforce passivity, dependence, and lowered expectations for achievement, boys are poorly served by media that reinforce insensitivity, competition, and aggression.

PSYCHOLOGICAL DEVELOPMENT AND THE MEDIA

Peter and his group of ten-year-old friends are hanging out in the schoolyard during recess. They want to be out of earshot of the teachers on patrol because Peter is recounting a juicy story. The night before, Peter slipped downstairs and watched his older brother "making out" with his new girlfriend. Peter's friends are wide-eyed and eager as he describes how his brother slipped a hand under his girlfriend's blouse. "No way!" says one of the boys as Peter describes catching a glimpse of skin as his brother lifted the girl's blouse. Just then a group of girls passes by, and one of them, Julie, makes eye contact with Peter. All of a sudden Peter's friends start taunting, "She likes you, she likes you" and push Peter into Julie's path. Peter looks abashed and quickly retreats to the safety of his group of friends. "Girls are geeks," he says with disgust. Later that afternoon in class, Peter finds himself thinking about Julie and has trouble concentrating on his math problems.

Although the family is still very important to the older child, other strong ties are being forged. Interest in the opposite sex, though rarely acknowledged openly, is beginning. The older child spends more time with friends than with family. School takes up a large portion of the day. The older child is no longer interested only in being a "good kid." He now wants to be a good student, a good friend, a good athlete, a good dancer, and so on. Accomplishment does not revolve only around furthering one's success in the family but involves furthering one's personal success as well. Of course, these domains overlap. For instance, the child who is successful at school is generally appreciated at home for academic achievement.

Attachment

Children at this developmental stage are increasingly capable of taking care of themselves, both physically and psychologically. They frequently resent baby-sitters and feel quite capable of taking care of themselves for a couple of hours. Toward the end of this stage, some children are even beginning to do some baby-sitting of their own outside the home.

Parents need to shift their parenting styles as their youngster becomes increasingly capable and independent. Children of this age need to be allowed greater freedom to explore their developing capacities; they also need protection and supervision to make sure they don't get in over their heads. Parents at this stage should be guiding more and directing less. Older children have a point of view, and it is important that parents communicate respect for their child's developing perspective, even if they don't always agree with it.

Older children are forming opinions and prejudices, which often last a lifetime. The media are powerful communicators of cultural values. As noted in Chapter Three in connection with George Gerbner's work, television cultivates attitudes that are not only at variance with reality but also actually contribute to violence and victimization.[19] Parents who have fallen victim to what Gerbner calls a "mean world syndrome" undoubtedly convey their insecurities and apprehensions to their children. Singer and Singer described a "mean and scary world" viewpoint found in children. Their research supports Gerbner's findings that heavy viewers of television violence experience the world as a particularly frightening and unfriendly place. "Our data provide some indication that, even when various controls are taken into account, heavy TV viewing is significantly associated with elementary school children's later aggressive behavior, restlessness, and belief in a 'mean and scary world.'"[20] Parents need to cultivate optimism, not anxiety, in their children.

A wonderful movie called *The Secret Garden* captures with great delicacy the anxiety and excitement of moving beyond a world controlled by adults into one elaborated by the child's own inventiveness and courage. In this gorgeously photographed movie, a young girl named Mary Lennox is orphaned in India and sent home to England to live in a large and gloomy estate with her uncle. She uncovers the secret of the estate: that her aunt died in childbirth, and the son she had given birth to has been confined to his bed, unable to walk for years. Like Mary, the boy is nine or ten, but unlike her, he has had no access to the world, most particularly the magical garden that his mother had created before her death. The movie contains so many elements of interest to this age group—venturing out into the world on one's own, the forming of intense friendships, the beginning of affection for the opposite sex, and the attraction of adventure. Best of all, this is a movie that has the power to enchant both children and adults, making it an experience to be shared by parent and child. As film critic Roger Ebert noted about *The Secret Garden*, "The summer of 1993 will be remembered as the time when every child in the world wanted to see *Jurassic Park*. The lucky ones saw this one, too."[21] Parents may have to do some digging to find entertainment that supports their child's healthy moves toward autonomy. However, such movies and television shows do exist and are particularly valuable in providing instruction on how to begin living one's life with enthusiasm and integrity.

Aggression

Older children are exposed to extremely high levels of media violence. Current estimates are that 15 percent of all television material is violent. With the average child this age watching close to four hours of television per day, this translates into some thirty-six minutes a day during which children witness violent crimes such as rape and murder. The child who is a moderate viewer of prime time television is entertained by about fifteen murders a week, not counting cartoons or the news.[22] All of this seems temperate compared to the 81 violent deaths in *Robocop* or the 264 violent deaths in *Die Hard*. Scientists have come to understand a great deal about how this steady diet of media violence affects older children.

In many ways, the television has become personified. Increasingly, it is taking over the role of society's storyteller. It is frequently referred to as the "third parent" or an "uncertified teacher." It is not "just entertainment," as people in the media are fond of saying, because it creates and elaborates attitudes just as much as it reflects them. As George Gerbner points out, "For the first time in human history, most of the stories about people, life and values are told not by parents, schools, churches, or others in the community who have something to tell but by a group of distant conglomerates that have something to sell."[23]

The number of hours that children spend watching television ensures its status as a communicator of the social order. As one of my sons said, "If they can say 'it sucks' on television, why can't I say it at home? It's just an ordinary word now." The media in large measure have come to define what is appropriate and acceptable in our society.

There are differences between boys and girls in their readiness to fashion their own behavior after the aggression that they see in the media. Since we know that one of the factors that encourage aggression is identification, it is not surprising that boys are more likely to exhibit aggressive behavior. Men outnumber women three to one in prime time television and six to one in action movies and programs—a genre aimed at this age group. Same-sex modeling is stronger than cross-sex modeling. In addition, girls generally see television as less realistic than boys do.[24] As we have seen, believing that the violence is realistic and justified is one of the conditions most likely to encourage aggression.

Although girls may be less likely to model aggressive behavior after movie and television characters, they are also learning something about aggression from the screen. Unfortunately, what they often learn is that girls and women are the frequent recipients of male abuse. Boys learn how to be aggressors. Girls learn how to be victims.

In the movie *Dirty Harry*, one of the original male-vigilante-as-hero movies, there are only five extremely brief scenes that include women—one wife, one secretary, two sexually promiscuous naked women, and one dead naked teenage girl. Although this movie was made over twenty-five years ago, its view of girls and women is remarkably similar to today's MTV videos. Women and girls are sexual accessories to the real action, which is about men showing their power in various ways, typically aggressive, sadistic, and narcissistic. Women have very limited roles in the action movies that children of this age find so appealing, and when they appear, they are frequently portrayed as victims.

In reality, most victims of male aggression are other men. The media's persistent distortion of this social reality adds to the young girl's sense of vulnerability. Excellent movies such as *Flirting* and *A Little Princess* attempt to present more realistic models to girls and encourage their strivings toward independence and competency. Even Disney, with *Pocahontas*, has finally made a movie in which the heroine honors other commitments besides falling in love with some handsome prince. However, even movies that portray spirited women, such as *Thelma and Louise*, often have a subtle but poisonous subtext: independent females end up dead.

Should parents restrict viewing of aggressive programs and movies for children of this age? Yes, of course. At this age, as throughout childhood, parents are in large measure responsible for what kinds of experiences their children are exposed to. In the best of all possible worlds, television is an activity with a purpose. Although there is a certain fondness for saying that television should not be a baby-sitter, there are good baby-sitters who take our kids out, show them the world, and help them develop, and there are bad baby-sitters who are passive and do not engage our kids. We want television to be the former kind, and when it is, calling it a baby-sitter is no insult. Children and their parents should look over television listings at the beginning of the week and make decisions about specific programs. Not all programs and movies that children watch must be educational or elevating. As Roger Ebert has said, "Most movies are not for any one thing, of course. Some are to make us think, some to make us feel, some to take us away from our problems, some to help us examine them."[25] However, we should ensure that our children are not consistently exposed to messages that are at odds with our values.

Jerry Mander, in his popular book *Four Arguments for the Elimination of Television*, argues that television is such a hopeless enterprise that it should be eliminated.[26] I disagree. Television and the movies still provide significant experiences for children this age that are both entertaining and informative. *Home Improvement*, *Step by Step*, *The Cosby Show*, and even *Roseanne* reinforce family values in the truest sense; that is, an open, loving, and cooperative family is the surest launching pad out into the world. *Star Wars* and *Star Trek* took kids to outer space; *E.T.* and *Huckleberry Finn* took them to inner space and the territory of loneliness, divorce, and friendship. *Aladdin* took them to Arabia; *White Fang*, to the Yukon. *Mister Rogers' Neighborhood* has taken them to the symphony, and *Sesame Street* has taken them to Israel, Spain, and China. When successful, the media expand the child's world bringing rich experiences into his living room and life. At best, the media encourage curiosity and an appreciation of diversity. The potential of the media to enrich children's lives should not be underestimated.

Television has its greatest negative effects on those children whose parents are not involved in their viewing and who have few friends.[27] To lessen television's influence, parents can use the opportunity of watching with their children as a jumping-off point to discuss issues such as conflict resolution, the use and misuse of power, and the cultural stereotypes embedded in the media. Open-ended questions such as "Did that story make sense to you?" "What made you care about the characters?" "Can you think of other solutions to the problem?" encourage the older child to put to use expanded social and cognitive skills and begin thinking about a variety of solutions and consequences.

Cognitive Development

Jennifer, age eleven, comes home from school preoccupied and downcast. Her mother asks if anything is wrong. "I had a fight with Emma," Jennifer says and retreats to her room. Lying on her bed, Jennifer goes over the day's events. Her birthday is next week, and Emma was going to take her to the mall after school to shop for a present. At the last minute, Emma backed out, saying, "I gotta do my homework; my parents are really on my back." Hurt, Jennifer took off in a huff, saying, "You never keep your word." All the way home, Jennifer felt bad. She realized she was disappointed because last year none of her friends remembered her birthday. Besides, her own English grades weren't so hot lately, and her parents were giving her a hard time. She telephoned Emma. "Can we go shopping on Saturday instead?"

This everyday example illustrates the tremendous progress in thinking that has been made by the older child. Whereas the preschooler would have called her friend a "poo-poo head" and the younger elementary school child would have looked around for another friend, the older child has the capacity to think about her situation with insight and empathy. Despite her disappointment, Jennifer is able to reflect on her feelings and to see that they have several causes. She is angry at her friend, but she's also been disappointed in the past and understands that this adds to her current feelings of betrayal. She is also experiencing parental pressure and knows that it can be stressful. Jennifer is able to empathize with her friend in spite of being disappointed. This lessening of egocentricity is one of the great accomplishments of this stage of development. As a result, Jennifer is better able to feel for her friend even when her own wishes are being thwarted. Jennifer is able to stand in Emma's shoes.

Children at this stage of development may be most vulnerable to the effects of media violence because although their ability to think and empathize is great, their store of experience is still relatively limited. Also, don't forget, it is during this stage that watching television is at an all-time high, with the average child watching some twenty-eight hours of television per week. Though cognitive advances are significant, children at this stage still take much of what they see quite literally. Whereas the very young child may not be frightened by a hijacking recounted on the news because he is too young to understand what is being said, and the teenager may be concerned but still knows that hijackings are rare, the child of nine, ten, or eleven knows just enough to be frightened but not enough to have much perspective.

Television is exerting a particularly potent effect on children during these years. They are watching a great deal of television with less or no parental supervision. During this stage of development, long-term interests are emerging, and lifelong attitudes as well as patterns of behavior are being cultivated. What are children watching?

For one thing, too many children of this stage are watching slasher movies. These movies, which include the likes of Freddy

Krueger in *Nightmare on Elm Street* and Jason in *Friday the 13th*, are often referred to as "splatter fests" by the critics. These movies will be discussed in greater detail in Chapter Seven, but they deserve mention here because they are seen so frequently by children in this age group. In a poll conducted by *TV Guide*, an astounding 89 percent of eleven-year-olds have seen the R-rated *Nightmare on Elm Street*. (Unbelievably, this same poll found that 20 percent of children under the age of five have seen this movie).[28] Slasher movies are among the most disturbing and inappropriate movies available for consumption by children. In my clinical experience, Freddy Krueger is the single greatest media-created source of nightmares for young children. He is a child molester and murderer; he is disfigured and cruel; and worst of all, he inhabits the dreams of children. A slew of child psychologists could not have come up with a more terrifying character if they tried (except maybe Chucky in *Child's Play*, where a youngster's favorite toy, in the safety of his own home, turns out to be a serial killer).

Older children, however, seem able to get away from Freddy and his likes all too easily. Ask any eleven-year-old if he is frightened by Freddy Krueger, and the response is likely to be an indulgent and jaded, "What's the matter with you? It's a movie!" By the age of eleven or so, the unremitting barrage of violent images that children have been exposed to for the past decade has done its job. Children have become so desensitized, so accustomed to fictionalized, violent imagery, that they no longer find it disturbing.

It is frightening enough to understand that media violence is encouraging some children to incorporate violent solutions into their everyday behavior. It is perhaps even more frightening to confront the fact that even larger numbers of children are becoming tolerant of these solutions. Ronald Drabman, in a series of experiments on media violence and desensitization, tested the hypothesis that "viewing violence under the guise of entertainment many increase one's tolerance of aggression that occurs in the real world and thus make one less willing to aid when he witnesses such behavior in his own life."[29]

Drabman divided children into three groups: one group was exposed to a violent program, one saw a neutral program, and one saw no program at all. He found that older children who had seen the violent program were more likely to ignore the distress of children in trouble, and if they did respond, they responded more slowly than those who had seen the neutral program or no program.

Unfortunately, much of what children this age are exposed to by the media works at cross-purposes to their developmental advances, such as an increased ability to think critically and with empathy. Parents would do well to look for media offerings that encourage newly emerging critical skills and help develop an understanding of different perspectives. True prosocial behavior is emerging during this stage of development and deserves to be encouraged. Often this can be done through comedy, as children this age watch more situation comedies than any other form of television. *The Mask* and *Liar Liar* were both funny movies and also showcased the kind of hero that children could identify with—sometimes uncertain, often bumbling, but always with his heart in the right place. Comedies can be good alternatives to the mind-numbing excesses of violence often targeted for this age group.

Moral Development

Moral development is accelerating at this stage because of the child's newly emerging capacity for true and ongoing empathy. Children at this developmental stage tend to be nice. A deepening sensitivity to other people, coupled with an increasingly well developed conscience, helps the child of nine, ten, and eleven want to please others.

However, children at this age also have a strong commitment to their own values. "I was going to cheat on the math test, but my conscience would have bothered me," says a ten-year-old boy. "Nobody saw me take the blouse, but inside of me I knew it was wrong, so I put it back," says an eleven-year-old girl. These children are giving evidence of a conscience that needs no external enforcement in order to be felt. Conscience is no longer only the fear of a punishing parent but has become a voice deep inside. Psychologists and psychiatrists talk about superego development, and parents notice that "he really seems to know right from wrong for himself now." It is a landmark in moral development.

Parents and the media have a special opportunity during this stage to help children further their moral development. Children are particularly accommodating at this age, and many are interested in the idea of what makes a good person. They are curious about moral values such as responsibility and honesty. All parents want to see their children enter adolescence with a sense of independence and an honest and responsible conscience.

Many outstanding movies and television programs encourage moral development as well as provide wonderful entertainment for children. George Lucas's *Star Wars*, *The Empire Strikes Back*, and *Return of the Jedi* were all blockbusters and are among the highest grossing movies of all time. These films continue to be avidly consumed in their technologically altered and enhanced form by a new generation of children. Although hardly breaking thematic ground, these movies have enthralled both children and adults for over twenty years.

These movies are so beloved by children for several reasons. Like all good fairy tales, they take place "long ago, in a galaxy far, far away." This device allows children to both participate in the story and watch it from afar. *Star Wars* is the archetypal journey story, and as this chapter makes clear, this journey out of the family and into one's own life is the major task of childhood. Luke Skywalker, with his ordinary demeanor and air of confusion and insecurity, is easy for children to identify with. He is an ordinary young man called on to perform extraordinary feats as he confronts the Forces of the Evil Empire led by Darth Vader. Instructed by archetypal wise man Obi-Wan Kenobi (Luke's own parents are dead, as is the tradition in fairy tales), Luke learns to draw on his own moral and intuitive strength. "May the force be with you" has now reassured two generations of young children that somewhere inside of them is the ability to go out into the world, survive, and even triumph.

These are movies that for all their spectacular fight scenes contain a minimum of violence and virtually no bloodshed. Despite the battleships, lasers, and assorted extraordinary hardware, it is the people who concern us most. At the theater kids "oohed and aahed" over the fight scenes, but in my office they were most concerned with Luke's struggles. Would he be able to lead the Rebel forces? Was Darth Vader his father, and if he was, how could Luke kill him? Could Yoda really teach him to use the "force"? Despite thrilling intergalactic fights, fantastic aliens, and spectacular special effects, Star Wars is a very psychological movie. It defines issues (how to face the dangers of the world) and presents solutions (develop internal strength and moral conviction) in a format that is breathtaking and compelling for children in this age group. It is moviemaking for children at its finest.

OLDER CHILD VIEWING CHECKLIST

Attachment

Dangers of the world are portrayed realistically   yes   no

Tone of the movie is not particularly anxious or
apprehensive   yes   no

Children are encouraged to develop their
capacities in ways that are realistic and
likely to bring success   yes   no

Aggression

If violence is part of this program or movie,
is it necessary to the plot?   yes   no

The price of violence is portrayed realistically   yes   no

Cognitive Development

Encourages use of critical thinking   yes   no

Helps children see that there are many
different ways to look at things   yes   no

Consequences of actions are realistic   yes   no

Moral Development

Empathy is encouraged   yes   no

Social and individual problems are presented
as complex and in need of thought and
reflection before action   yes   no

TELEVISION HALL OF FAME

Nick News

Bill Nye the Science Guy

The Cosby Show

Dr. Quinn, Medicine Woman

The Secret World of
   Alex Mack

Gargoyles

Boy Meets World

The New Ghostwriter Mysteries

Pepper Ann

MOVIES AND VIDEOS TO CHECK OUT

The first six are most likely to appeal to girls.

Little Women

The Secret Garden

Fly Away Home

Harriet the Spy

The Baby-Sitters Club

Secret Adventures
   (a video series)

Any Star Trek movie

The Star Wars trilogy

The Nutty Professor

Lucas

Angus

Big

ADD YOUR OWN FAVORITES

_____

_____

_____

_____

7

Early Adolescence

Ages Twelve, Thirteen, and Fourteen

Being a young teenager is not easy. Neither, for that matter, is living with a young teenager. No other period of development generates as much fear and anxiety in parents as early adolescence. Surly, confused, oppositional, and often withdrawn, the early adolescent seems an unfortunate replacement for the easygoing and cooperative child of the previous developmental stage. Erik Erikson observed that "in their search for a new sense of continuity and sameness, adolescents have to refight many of the battles of earlier years, even though to do so they must artificially appoint perfectly well-meaning people to play the roles of adversaries."[1]

GENERAL DEVELOPMENT

Adolescence is demanding and difficult. It is a time of accelerated physical, sexual, social, cognitive, and emotional development. Adolescents are navigating one of life's greatest challenges—the transition from childhood to adulthood.

Physical and hormonal changes are noticeable, often painfully so. Early pubertal changes—pubic hair, breasts, and menarche for girls; increased genital size and facial and body hair for boys—are both anticipated and dreaded. Adults often forget the confusion they felt as they shed their childhood bodies. A twelve-year-old girl is unable to complete her homework because she spends two hours

in the bathroom trying to figure out how to insert a tampon. A thirteen-year-old boy finds himself unable to concentrate in school,
fearful that his erection will be noticed if he is called to the black-
board. While physical changes are the most conspicuous, they are
really only the tip of the adolescent iceberg. Changes in peer relationships, family relationships, cognitive abilities, self-concept, and
social roles all conspire to keep the young adolescent off-center and
preoccupied.

Coupled with the unrelenting physical changes of early adolescence is the need for remarkable emotional adjustment. Perhaps the
most noticeable shift occurs around issues of autonomy and self-
determination. The anthem of adolescence has many variations,
but essentially it is some form of "Leave me alone," "Don't tell me
what to do," or "You can't run my life anymore." Children who just
a few months ago were cheerful and compliant are suddenly resent-
ful and provocative. The notion that adolescence must include extremely high levels of parent-child conflict in order for the child to
become fully independent has been discredited. However, mild to
moderate levels of parent-child conflict, particularly in early adolescence, are typical.[2] Parents are forced to step aside and are frequently replaced by the adolescent's peers.

For many parents, this conflict and withdrawal is painful, coming at a time when middle age is imposing its own developmental
challenges. In a knowing moment on My So-Called Life, fifteen-year-
old Angela is out with her attractive, middle-aged mother. A good-
looking man smiles at them and her mother brightens, thinking the
attention was meant for her. Her face collapses imperceptibly as she
realizes that he is actually admiring her daughter. Mothers who
enjoyed shopping trips with their daughters now find those same
daughters stricken at the thought of being seen together in the same
mall. One thirteen-year-old boy instructed his father to only use his
first name when introducing himself, lest someone suspect that they
were related. These can be powerful blows to parents who previously
enjoyed a close and friendly relationship with their children. Al-

though painful for both parents and teens, such poignant displays of self-doubt are reasonably short-lived.

Although the young adolescent experiences periods of increased conflict, the cultural commonplace that "teenagers are crazy" has been shown to be an inaccurate and potentially dangerous misconception. Both professional and popular perspectives have encouraged the view that adolescence is a period of disequilibrium unmatched in the human life cycle. The German expression *Sturm und Drang*, meaning "storm and stress," was popularized in 1904 by G. Stanley Hall, the father of American psychology, to describe adolescence. No less an authority than Anna Freud asserted that it was often difficult to differentiate between adolescent behavior and pathology.

Research over the past three decades has helped clarify what is and what is not expectable adolescent behavior. Although early adolescence is a time of particular sensitivity and rather characteristic behaviors (withdrawal, moodiness, self-absorption), the vast majority of young teenagers pass through this stage of development without exhibiting major psychological or emotional disorders. As a group, adolescents have no more or no less emotional illness than any other age group. Approximately 20 percent of all teenagers suffer from clinical symptoms—that is, symptoms such as anxiety or depression that are of significant severity and duration to warrant a diagnosis and treatment.[3] This rate is comparable to adult rates of emotional illness.[4]

Teenagers can be moody, anxious, and depressed. They tend to suffer from feelings of self-doubt and inferiority. However, should these feelings be intense and unremitting, it is likely that the teenager needs psychological help. Teenagers do not "grow out" of true depression or anxiety disorders any more than adults do.

Although not emotionally ill, adolescents can appear idiosyncratic to adults in their constant attempts to define and refine their identities. Low-riding "skater pants" and dark, hooded sweatshirts can seem foreign and a bit forbidding to parents. However, adults need to be cautious and not overinterpret these superficial signs of nonconformity. Although certain aspects of dress or appearance, such as "wearing colors" to show gang affiliation, can signal real danger, the vast majority of adolescent indulgences in dress and appearance are harmless and short-lived. This does not mean that parents have to like or sanction all adolescent excesses. One of the major developmental tasks of adolescence is to develop a new and enduring identity. Many hats must be tried on before the teenager finds one that fits. Parents should pick their battles carefully. Save the showdown for the body piercing; skip the haircut.

MEDIA AND YOUNG ADOLESCENTS

Teenagers have been given a bad rap by the media. They are portrayed alternately as sullen, withdrawn misanthropes or as violent, testosterone-driven deviants. The rebellious, alienated teenager has become a cinematic icon ever since James Dean perfected adolescent angst in *Rebel Without a Cause* some forty-five years ago. Why have we chosen to see adolescents as more troubled (and troubling) than they actually are? When Marlon Brando was asked in *The Wild One*, "What are you rebelling against?" and replied, "Whadda ya got?" he set the standard for teenagers as alienated, rebellious individuals in constant conflict with family and society. This theme has been repeatedly elaborated in some of the most popular films of the past four decades, beginning with *The Wild One* (1953) and *Rebel Without a Cause* (1955), continuing through *West Side Story* (1961), *A Clockwork Orange* (1971), *Saturday Night Fever* (1977), *Purple Rain* (1984), and *Sid and Nancy* (1986), and ending with more recent films such as *My Own Private Idaho* (1991) and *Kids* (1995).

Whereas movies have tended to focus on adolescents as wild, troubled, and alienated, television has presented them as one-dimensional and sanitized. From Wally and the Beaver on *Leave It to Beaver* through David and Ricky Nelson on *Ozzie and Harriet* to Samantha on *Who's the Boss?* and D.J. on *Full House*, television teenagers have been primarily concerned with their looks, shopping, and borrowing the family car. Only recently have television programs such as *The Wonder Years*, *Beverly Hills 90210*, *My So-Called Life*, and *Party of Five* looked at the more serious and pressing issues that adolescents face: drug abuse, teen pregnancy, and violence, as well as the less dramatic but equally important issues of self-esteem, school performance, and peer acceptance.

By neglecting to present varied, appropriate, and relevant role models for teens, both society as a whole and the media in particular have failed miserably in their responsibility to this age group. Without healthy and clearly defined roles and expectations, young adolescents are extremely vulnerable to the media, which tend to provide clear but undesirable roles and standards. In the long tradition of vigilante-as-hero movies, Jean-Claude Van Damme in *Cyborg*, Sylvester Stallone in *Rambo*, and Arnold Schwarzenegger in *The Terminator* present romanticized versions of mass murderers who suffer neither remorse nor doubt. Equally troubling is the affectionate treatment of cannibalism, sadism, and psychopathy in movies like *The Silence of the Lambs*, *Demolition Man*, and *Natural Born Killers*. Clearer yet more antisocial role models are hard to imagine. In a particularly confusing movie, *Heat*, starring two of our most popular actors, Al Pacino and Robert De Niro, the boundary between good and evil is completely dissolved. Cops and killers are one and the same, and De Niro makes being a mass murderer look appealing, even heroic. In the best of all possible worlds, young adolescents would not be exposed to these mostly R-rated movies. But in fact their advertising is heavily targeted toward teenagers, there are few appealing alternatives, and parents too frequently feel that they have little control over what their teenagers watch.

The task of adolescence is to begin creating a new adult. There are periods of intense exhilaration as well as abiding anxiety and depression both for teenagers and their families. Power relationships that were carefully forged over the past twelve years are obsolete. Parents are often at a loss as to how to relate to this "new" family member. Unfortunately, parents frequently fall back on trying to reassert their previous authority and as a result become overly restrictive. Typically, this parenting approach backfires. Authoritarian households are found to have higher rates of delinquency than more democratic households.[5] The adolescent's task is to develop an emerging identity; the parents' task is to allow increasing degrees of freedom without sacrificing their child's physical safety or mental health.

One of the most common ways that adolescents work on their emerging identity is by spending a significant amount of time daydreaming. Teenagers of twelve, thirteen, and fourteen spend inordinate amounts of time in their rooms. Intrusion is discouraged by a variety of signs, locks, and offensive posters. While staring into space, teenagers are crafting the individuals they are about to become. "How do I look?" "Will I make a fool of myself?" "What will I be when I'm older?" "Am I any good?" and so on. Early adolescence is a period of intense self-doubt. By addressing these commonplace concerns of young adolescents and offering them creative, healthy solutions, the media can become allies in their development.

Teenagers are avid media consumers. Ninety-eight percent of all households in the United States have at least one television (the average home has 2.25 TVs), and young teenagers spend, on average, twenty-six hours per week watching television. Seventy-five percent of American homes have VCRs, and teenagers make up a disproportionately large audience for the six million videos that are rented daily. Sixty percent of American homes have CD players, and teenagers make up 25 percent of all music sales. This translates into adolescents spending over $3 billion a year on music. Teenagers obviously represent an enormous potential audience for advertisers. With teenagers spending $89 billion per year, some $3 billion on athletic shoes alone, they become a significant and (unfortunately) vulnerable consumer group.[6] Their value to advertisers is, of course, enhanced by the many years ahead of them in which to be loyal consumers.

The potential magnitude of the adolescent's buying power is a fact not lost on companies in the business of selling addiction. Name recognition and product identification take place at younger and younger ages, as even small children come to recognize cartoon characters and animals like Joe Camel and Spuds Mackenzie. Much of the advertising in the cigarette and alcohol industry targets issues to which adolescents are most vulnerable: peer pressure, independence, rebellion, and personal acceptability.

The Marlboro Man, one of the most successful campaigns in advertising history, reflects Americans' romance with the cowboy, the rugged individualist who answers to no one. In *Breaking Away*, an angry young Dennis Quaid points to a Marlboro advertisement and says, "That's where to be. Wyoming. Prairie, mountains, nobody around." The pitch here is to the adolescent's desire to be free, particularly free of parental demands. The product itself, of course, brings addiction and therefore a decrease rather than an increase in freedom.

Virginia Slims runs a particularly damaging advertising campaign that ties female liberation to not just cigarette smoking but to weight loss as well. Liberation in this case appears to be the right to give yourself a life-threatening illness. Adolescent girls are the only group who show an increase in cigarette consumption. An estimated 20 percent of young women suffer from a serious eating disorder. Dr. Lorraine Morgan, when director of internships at Stanford's Program in Human Biology, called the prevalence of eating disorders among adolescent girls and young women a "health crisis."[7]

While the overselling of consumer goods to American adolescents may be inappropriate and troubling, the selling of addiction is potentially lethal. In an article titled "The Selling of Addiction to Women," Carol Moog writes:

> It's one thing for a woman to purchase too many cosmetics or jeans in a convoluted effort to gain love and acceptance by measuring up to Madison Avenue. At that point she's buying into the cultural myth brought to us through the wonders of advertising, that women must be young, ingenuous, gorgeous and innocuous. But what about when she's being lured with

products which are dangerous, even lethal, and addictive? The stakes are much higher, and the trade-off for a woman isn't just a genuine sense of self, it may be her life.[8]

As a clinical psychologist, I must add that "a genuine sense of self" is critical to leading a healthy and productive life. Though perhaps not as immediately life-threatening as cigarette and alcohol abuse, a poor self-image can be just as dangerous, potentially leading to anorexia, bulimia, unnecessary cosmetic surgery, and depression.

There have been some gains in raising the awareness of adolescents about the dangers of smoking and alcohol abuse. Not surprisingly, these gains have come as a result of efforts outside the tobacco and alcohol industry. In 1988 Harvard University's School of Public Health launched a major campaign to educate the public, via the media, about substance abuse. This program received strong support from the entertainment industry. In response to Harvard's program, ABC's popular sitcom *Growing Pains* aired an episode titled "Second Chance." In this episode, a close friend of the show's teenage lead character was seriously injured in a car accident after having "just a few drinks." The young adolescent vowed to take full advantage of his second chance and lead his life more carefully and thoughtfully. Unexpectedly, he dies. According to *Daily Variety*, the show's producers had decided to have the character die in order to "break the typical sense of denial by young people that they're anything but immortal."[9]

Cigarettes are the most heavily advertised product in the United States; alcohol is second. One out of every six deaths in the United States is attributable to cigarette smoking. Nearly half of all violent deaths—automobile accidents, suicides, and homicides—are alcohol related. Alcohol problems cost our nation over $70 billion per year.[10] A large percentage of people begin smoking and drinking in early adolescence, encouraged by the seductive and deceptive images of advertisers. Our society's tolerance of drug peddling to adolescents is unconscionable. Targeting our youth for addiction should not be tolerated any more than billboards encouraging heroin or advertisements for crack cocaine on the sides of buses. Parents need to make it known that they will not support programming that puts their children at risk by encouraging or glamorizing addiction. Parents, along with schools, must help teenagers recognize the ways in which the media's appealing portrayals of cigarettes, drugs, and alcohol is designed to manipulate young people into a lifetime of drug use and abuse.

PSYCHOLOGICAL DEVELOPMENT AND THE MEDIA

"Would you like to go to the movies with Dad and me?"

"No!" (said with the kind of emphasis usually reserved for the unthinkable).

"Why not?"

"I'm not that kind of person."

"What kind of person?"

"The kind of dweeb who would spend Saturday night with his parents."

In this typical interchange, the young adolescent can make it perfectly clear what kind of person he isn't; the much more difficult task is knowing what kind of person he is. Adolescents know that they are shedding their childhood, but they haven't yet evolved into the person they will ultimately become. They have not had the time or the experience to generate a new self. The creation of this new self is the task of the teenage years.

The young adolescent's moves toward independence are often erratic and tumultuous. While there is great striving toward becoming an individual, there is also a great sense of loss for the security of childhood. The day my eighth-grade son had to fill out a schedule for high school, I found him in tears on his bed. "I feel like it's too soon for my childhood to be over," he said in a moment of rare vulnerability. Although it is exactly this process of separation, of growing up, that is the hallmark of having successfully parented a child, it is often met with both joy and sadness by parent and child alike.

Attachment

Becoming an adult demands becoming independent of one's parents. This demand is at the heart of much of the conflict between young adolescents and their parents. To some degree, adolescents need to reject their families in order to forge their own identities. Parents are challenged, ignored, and endlessly criticized during early adolescence. Parents who understand the reasons and the temporary nature of this disruption in family relations are in a much better position to help their child (and themselves) pass through this demanding and often difficult period.

It is important that parents not take their young adolescents' squawking too personally. "You're so uncool." "What do you know?" "I refuse to be seen with such weird-looking people" (said by a teenager wearing pants with the crotch around his knees and green dye in his hair). No matter how good and close a relationship you have had with your child, no matter how liberal or conservative or apolitical your point of view, no matter how well you dress or how much you know, your adolescent is driven to find fault with you. It helps teenagers to know that grown-ups have faults. Painfully aware of their own shortcomings, adolescents find solace in not having to be perfect in order to be an adult.

Being critical of one's parents also allows the adolescent to consider other adult points of view. "My coach said . . ." "My teacher said . . ." Although parents may feel displaced by their teenagers' sudden reliance on other sources of authority, it is an important advance for this age group. It allows the adolescent to expand his horizons and draw from other role models.

Teenagers, like the toddlers they were some ten years earlier, are essentially explorers. The media make available new places, different people, other points of view, and fresh experiences. Nothing is so foreign or so remote that it cannot be brought into the teenager's world via the television or the movie screen. Early adolescence is a watershed in development; attitudes that will be carried into adulthood are being formed and consolidated. The media become a large source of information for this age group, as they rely less on parents and more on outside information for developing a worldview. Therefore the media's potential for encouraging prosocial attitudes, as well as for cultivating and enhancing antisocial attitudes, continues to be significant at this age.

Young adolescents need not be shielded from conflict and violence. On the contrary, these issues are relevant to this age group. What specific kinds of effects do the media have on adolescents? In what ways are their behaviors and attitudes being influenced? How can the media help young teenagers in their struggle to separate from family and forge a healthy and prosocial identity? Where have the media been successful in their attempts? Where have they failed? How can parents help adolescents become thoughtful consumers of the media?

Certainly coming-of-age movies such as *The Breakfast Club*, *Stand by Me*, and *This Boy's Life* have been successful both in entertaining young adolescents and in addressing their concerns. Movies that realistically portray the young adolescent's struggle with attachment and separation from family are particularly useful to this age group. Adolescents benefit from being exposed to the consequences of different courses of action. Movies and television provide an opportunity to witness, from a safe distance, the results of different life choices. It is not realistic, or even desirable, for adolescents always to make good choices. Often just as much can be learned from making a poor choice as from making the right choice. What matters is that adolescents increasingly appreciate the fact that choices carry consequences.

Personal Best is a movie about two young women runners who are competing for a spot on the U.S. Olympic Team. The movie tackles the question of intimacy versus personal excellence. The two women fall in love with each other but find that their intense competition precludes a completely open heart. This moving and natural movie was enjoyed by many adolescent girls. While dealing with complex issues such as identity and homosexuality, it poses questions, provokes thought, and suggests answers. It does not preach or demean. It is a movie that takes seriously the issues of adolescence and young adulthood, does not trivialize these concerns, and encourages reflection—hallmarks of good moviemaking for this age. It is just one of many fine movies, including *Ordinary People*, *Dead Poets Society*, *School Ties*, and *What's Eating Gilbert Grape?* that prove that adolescents can be successfully engaged, entertained, and instructed all at once.

Parents frequently feel that they have little control over their young teenager's viewing choices. Certainly their authority is different than it was when their child was small. Parents now need to appreciate the power of influence as opposed to control. Influence takes more time and more tact than "Because I say so." However, the judicious use of influence provides young adolescents with a model for a more respectful and adult way of dealing with others. Contrary to popular belief, study after study has shown that adolescents crave more, not less, discussion with their parents.[11]

Watch what your teenager watches and then encourage discussion. Listen.

Aggression

Adolescents make up a disproportionately large percentage of both the victims of aggression and the perpetrators of aggression. Firearms are the leading cause of death of black teenagers and the second leading cause of death of white teenagers. One out of every four teenage deaths is caused by a gun.[12] The issue of how young adolescents experience and deal with their aggression takes on an added sense of urgency given these distressing statistics. The easy availability of firearms ensures a shockingly high rate of adolescent homicide, suicide, and accidental death.

In a suburb of San Francisco, two boys' desire to handle a gun was so strong that one child climbed through a bathroom window to get to his father's gun, kept in a locked bedroom. While fooling around with the gun, the thirteen-year-old boy accidentally shot and killed his nine-year-old friend. The tragic consequences for the families of both youngsters are inestimable. A relative of the dead child plaintively said, "With guns being glamorized so much on TV, kids will do anything just to hold a gun."[13]

These were not emotionally disturbed, psychopathic youngsters. They were a couple of kids whose parents took responsible precautions with their guns. The allure of handling the same kind of weapon seen nightly in the hands of their favorite entertainers proved fatally irresistible. The media's insistence on glamorizing guns makes a significant contribution to the high levels of homicide in this country. Although the United States is not the most violent country in the world (that distinction goes to war-torn third world countries), we are far and away the most violent among industrialized countries. Children at younger and younger ages are murdering and being murdered. From 1985 to 1995 there was a 116 percent increase in the number of twelve- to seventeen-year-olds who were murdered.[14] These numbers are expected to increase as larger numbers of children enter adolescence in the next few years.

In April 1998, the country was once again rocked by the spectacle of children mowing down classmates. In Jonesboro, Arkansas, two boys, aged eleven and thirteen, dressed in camouflage and lay in wait as their school emptied out during a false fire alarm. Heavily armed with an assortment of high-powered rifles and handguns, they killed four young girls and a teacher. Six months earlier, a fourteen-year-old boy opened fire on a prayer circle at his school in West Paducah, Kentucky, killing three students and wounding many others. Only months before that, a sixteen-year-old boy in Pearl, Mississippi, killed his mother and then, at school, his ex-girlfriend and another student. More incidents could be added to this list. It sickens me to write any more.

We are in the midst of a crisis. We are losing an insupportable number of young lives because too many teenagers are incapable of working out the interpersonal conflicts that are an inevitable part of everyday life. The media, because they bear responsibility for glamorizing violence and offering easy solutions to difficult problems and because they have the power to shape both individual and social perspectives, should begin to use their influence to preserve this country's youth.

One of the greatest concerns that parents have about their young adolescents is the youngsters' tendency to act impulsively. Young adolescents are under the influence of many new and powerful feelings. The emergence of sexual feelings is both exciting and confusing. Adolescents can find themselves in trouble if they feel overwhelmed by these new feelings. Many agencies of society recognize this developmental challenge and try to aid adolescents in their efforts to think before they act.

Sex education classes teach the wisdom of waiting for a degree of emotional as well as physical maturity before becoming sexually active. Driver's education classes teach the need for responsibility and the necessity of following the law if one is to be accorded the adult privilege of driving. Drug education classes teach that seemingly minor decisions of the moment can have far-reaching consequences. Over and over, adolescents are reminded that decisions such as "I'll smoke just this one cigarette" can have consequences that the young teenager does not yet have the experience to envision. This doesn't mean that most young adolescents will never try that cigarette. What is of importance is that adults and major agencies of society are clear that they expect adolescents to think about the consequences of their actions.

If the media have failed in their responsibility to young adolescents, and I believe they have, it is precisely because of their lack of emphasis on consequences. Killings may be everywhere, but funerals are hardly ever seen, and the mind-numbing grief of real-life loss is rarely acknowledged. In *Total Recall*, Arnold Schwarzenegger puts a gun to his wife's forehead, pulls the trigger, and deadpans, "Consider that a divorce." In the movie she is an agent who has double-crossed him, and so his retaliation is "justified." The audience, composed largely of teenagers, is left laughing at murder and one of the most serious of our social problems, spousal abuse.

Similarly, hugely popular television programs such as *Cops* blur the boundaries between violence as real-life tragedy and violence as entertainment. The program opens with the infectious popular song "Bad Boys." We are still tapping our feet as the first incident of child abuse, spousal abuse, or drug abuse unfolds on our screen. The police and the judicial system work to protect people from the same experiences that we choose to have pour into our living rooms nightly. Jerry Springer and other talk show hosts work hard at setting up situations that are so incendiary that fistfights are inevitable. Violence is no longer something to be avoided; it is now turned to for entertainment and for relaxation.

One of the greatest tasks of adolescence is learning to be able to control impulses. This allows the process of planning for the future to begin in earnest. When President Clinton was on MTV in the spring of 1994, he exhorted millions of teenagers and young adults to begin thinking about the future in terms of years, not days or weeks. His emphasis was well placed. The media can be a powerful ally in helping young adolescents appreciate the wisdom of delaying gratification. Over and over, in ways that are sensible and appealing, the young adolescent needs to be taught the skills that will help him work out differences of opinion verbally rather than with a weapon and to anticipate that today's actions may affect his future. Without this ability, the young teenager in our society is all too often finding that he does not have a future at all.

One of the most disturbing trends to emerge from Hollywood is what are popularly termed "slasher movies." Spectacles of exceptional gore and gruesomeness, these R-rated movies are disproportionately consumed by young teenagers. This illustrates the limited value of a rating system that is only marginally enforced in theaters and not enforced at all in most video stores. Of course, these movies eventually show up, pretty much intact, on our television screens via cable.

Typically, teenagers in slasher movies are murdered with unprecedented sadism by an unstoppable male psychopath. Affectionately called "slice and dice" movies by film critics, the best known of this genre include the *Nightmare on Elm Street* series and the *Friday the 13th* series. Extraordinary only for the amount of graphic violence shown, slasher movies invariably link sexuality and aggression and pander to the adolescent's desire for stimulation. As any parent who has yelled, "Lower that music!" can attest, adolescents seem to crave mind-numbing levels of stimulation. This overstimulation probably provides a welcome relief from the young adolescent's self-rumination. Slasher movies exploit this vulnerability without offering solutions that adolescents can actually use to lessen their preoccupations. They teach adolescents nothing about how to live in the world and are morbidly pessimistic.

The most disturbing aspect of these teen exploitation films is the merging of violence and sex. For many young adolescents, Freddy Krueger is their first experience with soft-core erotica. It is a most unwelcome introduction to sex. For instance, in *Nightmare on Elm Street,* a young girl is killed right after having sex with her boyfriend. Her flimsy nightgown is shredded by Freddy's knifelike fingers until she is soaked in blood. Moments later, Freddy returns to another naked teenage girl, lying in the bathtub, where his hand rises between her spread legs before she too is murdered. And on and on it goes, with young women being mutilated, decapitated, exsanguinated, and disemboweled. I urge every parent to watch one of these movies. Sickening as the experience is, it will introduce you to what many children—perhaps even your child—can watch without batting an eyelash.

Although most teenagers do not engage in sexual intercourse until later in adolescence, attitudes about sexual intercourse, as well as the opposite sex in general, are being formed in early adolescence. Parents, schools, and the media are in positions of influence if they can reach young adolescents before they begin acting on their sexual desires. The schools have long recognized this and begin sex education years before teenagers become sexually active.

One of the most critical aspects of this education is to help adolescents become aware of potential risks once they become sexually active. Since we live in an age where lack of communication about sexual matters can have deadly consequences (at least 20 percent of all AIDS patients contracted the disease in their adolescence), adolescents need to truly understand the responsibility they assume when they become sexually active.[15]

Movies and television programs that do not emphasize the serious consequences of unprotected sex or abusive relationships (sexual or not) are acting irresponsibly. MTV, which shows videos ad nauseam in which women are portrayed as nothing more than sexual objects, is irresponsible in a way that no amount of brief public service messages can counter. Although MTV insists that it has "standards" to determine what videos are allowed on television, repeated calls to its offices for a copy of these standards were ignored.

In his provocative analysis of MTV videos, Professor Sut Jhally points out that the essential role of women in many rock videos is simply to be looked at as objects.[16] To that end, women are often presented as body parts—breasts or legs. This refusal to take women seriously (women in rock videos never seem to have jobs, and if they do, it usually involves taking their clothes off), along with the focus on women as mere body parts rather than as full human beings, represents the first step toward dehumanization. Research tells us that it is exactly this capacity to dehumanize women, to see them as nothing more than sexual objects, that leads men to hold increasingly tolerant attitudes toward rape.[17]

When physical or sexual abuse are glamorized, we are putting our children at risk. In the United States today, a child is abused every thirteen seconds, born to a teenage mother every fifty-nine seconds, arrested for a violent crime every five minutes, and killed every two hours.[18] It is estimated that some form of violence takes place in one out of every three households. One out of every four women is subject to some form of sexual attack during her life.[19] The epidemic of violence among American youth has become so severe and so threatening that the Surgeon General has declared violence one of our most serious public health problems.

It is our responsibility as parents to protect our children, but it is also important for teenagers to see that having strong values is an integral part of living one's life well. We can do this by not allowing our children to view things that we find patently offensive and by refusing to give economic support to sexist, racist, and other unacceptable media offerings. My young adolescent fought long and hard against my Guns N' Roses prohibition, whose hit album *Use Your Illusion I* had multiple references to "faggots" and "bitches." As parents, we all make decisions about which lines can be crossed and which cannot. Clearly, these lines change along with the development of our children. Parents should clearly communicate the values that are particularly important to them. Everything may be open for discussion, but not everything is open to compromise.

Cognitive Development

Young adolescents are in the middle of the second great revolution in thinking—the ability to think abstractly. Thinking at this stage approaches the level of adult thinking. Teenagers are long past seeing things only in black and white. They are able to understand symbols and to see that people may have motives that are not readily apparent. They can think about the past, the present, and the future. Their thinking is no longer limited to their own point of view. They can begin to make formal, logical arguments. This is what Piaget termed the stage of "formal operations." Young adolescents are sophisticated thinkers, a fact that their teachers (although not always their parents) can vouch for.

Rather than appearing to be capable of complex, adult thinking at home, young teenagers often appear to their parents to be ornery, hypercritical, and rigid in their thinking:

"Do you think it was right of Lauren to leave her girlfriend at the mall and go off with James instead?"

"How should I know? Besides, what do you know about friends?"

"Well, I was just wondering what you thought."

"That's the trouble with you—you're always trying to figure out what I'm thinking. Sometimes your girlfriends are the most important thing, but sometimes they're not."

Here we have some hallmarks of a typical early adolescent conversation. Mom ends up feeling criticized,while her daughter feels intruded on. But if some of the crankiness of the adolescent can be ignored, this example shows that the real issues being struggled with are competing allegiance and moral judgment. The younger child would have had a simple yes or no answer. The adolescent struggles with more complicated realities.

Adolescents are great debaters. They argue about their clothes, their allowance, their homework, their curfew, their responsibilities, and just about anything else that can possibly be argued about. Although this can certainly become irksome for parents who are tired and harried, it is a testimony to the young adolescent's growing intellectual prowess.

The adolescent mind takes nothing for granted, a necessary precursor to the ability to think clearly and scientifically. Allow your adolescent to flex her intellectual muscles. Young teenagers are full of ideas, and to the extent that they are free to indulge and expand their thinking at home, parents are in a better position to monitor and encourage intellectual development.

Adolescents are manufacturing their future selves. In the arena of thought, this means crafting a position on everything from their homework schedule to land mines. Parents need to control their shock when their thirteen-year-old announces at the dinner table, "I don't understand why they don't legalize marijuana; everyone knows pot can't really hurt you," or "I wish they would hand out condoms at school; lots of kids are 'doing it' anyway." First of all, adolescents at this age are given to hyperbole. Think for a moment about what "everyone is doing it" or "I'm the only one" means. In my house, these phrases usually mean it's possible that a handful of kids in our county are being allowed to do something one of my sons would like to do. Do not prematurely cut off communication with your teenager; learn to take adolescent exaggeration with a grain of salt.

Teenagers need a safe place in which to practice their burgeoning intellectual skills. A healthy home provides young adolescents with a laboratory and a launching pad from which to securely catapult themselves into adulthood. Home becomes a training ground in which young adolescents can develop positions, resist coercion, and become independent thinkers. Encouraging debate and discussion at home lays the groundwork for a young adult who thinks independently, can resist the pressure of the crowd, and is able to stand by moral decisions even if they are unpopular. Few parents would quarrel with these goals for their children.

One aspect of adolescent thinking that parents often find irritating is that although their young philosopher may have all kinds of lofty ideas about how to solve the world's problems, these ideas seem to find little application in daily life. "It is disgusting that we don't recycle. You guys are probably the only people in the world who don't care that our planet is being destroyed by garbage and consumerism." Could this be the same child who leaves a trail of litter at the fast-food restaurant or is insulted when you suggest that she walk or ride her bike rather than be driven someplace? Young adolescents are new to the world of ideas. The connection between theory and practice is fragile and will take many years to solidify. The idealism of adolescence is a precursor to social action. Don't expect too much of your teenager yet, but encourage thinking about social issues. Teach action through your own involvement in good causes.

Adolescents generally like television programs and movies that make them think about physical danger, separation and individuation, identity, commitment, and success. The movie *Wild Hearts Can't Be Broken* tells the story of Sonora, a strong-willed orphaned young adolescent girl who runs away from an unsympathetic aunt rather than become a ward of the state. Through the force of her persistence and her love of horses, she realizes her ambition of becoming a "diving lady." She joins a traveling circus and rides horses off a forty-foot tower into a pool of water. Sonora is blinded in an accident when her horse stumbles, sending her crashing into the pool. Driven by determination and love for her work, she eventually returns to performing even though she has been repeatedly cautioned that she can never ride again.

This movie addresses many of the themes of adolescence: separation from family, finding one's own identity, and overcoming physical danger. This film teaches more about real courage than all the macho posturing of a movie like *Cliffhanger*, which purports to be about courage but is really about the mindless myth that links masculinity and violence. Although we would prefer our young teenagers to view the more realistic and prosocial films, it is not likely that this will always be the case. There is an element of rebellion in adolescent tastes, and as one of my teenage patients pointed out, "If grown-ups all hated *Bambi*, that's probably what I'd want to see."

Though young teenagers can be encouraged to see movies that are more instructional and optimistic and can be prohibited from seeing movies that are at complete variance with family values, a wide swath of movies are neither. Taken individually, perennial teenage favorites such as *Beverly Hills Cop*, *Lethal Weapon*, *Die Hard*, and *The Terminator* probably do little to either advance or inhibit adolescent thinking. As a steady diet, however, I would argue that they present adolescents with a worldview that is pessimistic and cynical and that endorses violence and impulsivity. They appeal to the young adolescent's lowest level of thinking rather than encouraging newly emerging abilities to think abstractly and to tackle and understand complex problems.

What these movies can provide is an opportunity for parents to discuss violent solutions as a way of resolving interpersonal differences. Talk with your teenagers about what they see. Encourage your adolescents to challenge the point of view of the movie. Explore how it is that the audience has become so sympathetic to a murderer. In what ways has the movie or program manipulated its audience, and how does it accomplish this? It's an opportunity for adolescents to actively think about what they are viewing instead of simply being passive recipients, and it's an opportunity for you to help guide their newly emerging abilities to think and analyze. It may seem like they're not listening but, more often than not, they are.

Moral Development

Along with the revolution in thinking that young adolescents are experiencing is a revolution in moral development. Young adolescents are able to appreciate that people and their motives are complicated. They understand that morality can be relative and endlessly ponder questions such as "If your life depended on it, could you eat human flesh?" or "If you knew you could save the lives of many innocent people, would you kill one evil person?" These questions are alluring to young adolescents because they go beyond the kind of black-and-white answers that were previously so satisfying to them as children.

The hallmark of this stage of moral development is an increased capacity for caring and cooperation. Young adolescents are able to consider the point of view of the group, be it their peer group, parents, school, or society at large. Unlike younger children, adolescents want to be good, not only to please people in authority or because they have something to gain, but also because they now have an internalized image of a good person and strive to live up to it. They benefit from living up to this image in two ways: they think well of themselves (self-approval), and others think well of them (social approval). Together, these two types of approval can boost self-esteem and help the young adolescent create a more altruistic and responsible sense of self.

Just as we saw the decrease of black-and-white thinking in young adolescence, we also see the decline of severe moral judgment. At this stage, teenagers are more forgiving and flexible in their moral judgment because they are able to consider extenuating circumstances and to understand that people's motivations can be quite complex. As opposed to the philosophy of "every man for himself," young adolescents can embrace a more benevolent and unselfish "all for one and one for all" attitude. Mercy begins to temper justice. "Mike is smoking pot. It's a tough time for him because his mom is sick." "I gave Susan a dollar. She was crying because she lost her allowance. You know how forgetful little kids can be."

Given this significant shift in moral reasoning, why do young adolescents seem so hideously critical of their families? Reading about the compassion of the young adolescent in the preceding paragraph may make some parents think I am writing about a totally different creature than the one they have living in their home. Compassion? Mercy? Often it seems like the young adolescent is engaged in full-blown, take-no-prisoners verbal warfare with the family. "You guys are just hopeless" or "Please wait outside so no one sees you" is hardly the height of tolerance or charity. What is this crazy dichotomy that allows young adolescents to empathize with friends' major flaws while at the same time being so hypervigilant and critical of their own family's minor or imagined flaws?

During the childhood years, it is primarily parents who supply the role models for appropriate, caring behavior. This changes in adolescence, when the drive to create an individual identity separate from the family forces a temporary withdrawal and even a renunciation of family attitudes, behaviors, and values. The peer group often replaces the family as the most important transmitter of attitudes and behavior. At this stage, being accepted by other kids becomes a full-time job and often a preoccupation. Kids give up lifelong interests if a friend declares them "uncool." Most young adolescents are desperately unhappy with their looks, their personality, their family, and often their life in general. Projecting some of their hypercritical self-evaluation out onto the family helps maintain a level of equilibrium. The assaultive, critical comments and questions adolescents pose to their families, such as "What do you know?" "I can't believe how dorky you look!" "Please don't let anyone see you," are all reflections of the insecurity they feel. Rephrased, these comments might be "What do I know?" "Am I really a dork?" and "These horrible pimples on my face—I wish I was invisible."

Even though there may be much conflict between parents and new teenagers, this does not reflect an undoing of the previous twelve years of child rearing. If parents have been successful in laying the foundation of clear moral values for their children, their young adolescent is better able to benefit from exposure to different values and to withstand the pressure of their peers whose values conflict with their own. For many of the reasons that have been discussed in this chapter—the need to break away from family, the development of a new sense of self, the reliance on friends—adolescence is a period of marked vulnerability to peer pressure and conformist thinking. "Everyone's doing it" is a remarkably powerful justification for most young adolescents. Social approval often takes precedence over conscience

Parents need to help their young adolescent feel good about themselves by maintaining a healthy and positive relationship with the family and by providing acceptance and love in the face of adolescent insecurity. These can be trying times for parents, but it is critical that they remain involved. They need to further their young adolescents' moral development by actively modeling what they believe to be moral behavior. This is no time for "do as I say, not as I do." Adolescents are very critical of hypocrisy. Finally, parents need to balance their teenagers' need for control and independence with parental experience and judgment. A good rule of thumb is to say yes when you can and no when you must.

Movies and television programs that deal with common adolescent issues, such as autonomy, separation and individuation, commitment, and career, and that emphasize the often painful process of self-evaluation are helpful to young adolescents. Although *Beverly Hills 90210* depicts older teens and young adults, it tends to be watched by younger adolescents who are looking for clues as to "what's next." Although this program overemphasizes some of the dramatic elements of adolescence, such as sex and drugs, and underemphasizes the more ordinary dilemmas, such as grades and self-esteem, it does portray the adolescent's struggle to consider consequences and forge a personal sense of right and wrong. The issue of going against the crowd is repeatedly considered, and support is largely given to those who are able to "march to their own drummer." This perspective is very helpful and probably of greater significance than the actual content of each episode. It communicates that a major task of adolescence is to be one's own person and to consider and feel comfortable with one's point of view, one's judgment, and sense of morality, whether or not this is the popular point of view. Programs like this appeal to the young adolescent's higher level of reasoning and recognize the complexity of this stage of development.

Many excellent movies have attempted to deal with the complex moral issues and dilemmas that adolescents face without trivializing their struggles. In *This Boy's Life*, Ellen Barkin and Leonardo Di Caprio play a mother and young adolescent son down on their luck. In an effort to provide stability for herself and a male role model for her son, she marries an unhappy and abusive man. As he is increasingly tormented by his sadistic stepfather, the boy begins to plan his escape from both his family and the leaden town they live in (appropriately named Concrete). He edges toward juvenile delinquency, changes his grades, and writes fake letters of recommendation in order to get into an eastern prep school. Though some of his behavior is wrong, it is understandable. Dilemmas like the ones presented in the movie—Is it ever OK to hit a parent? Are there situations in which lying and cheating are reasonable responses?—help the young adolescent think about moral issues as being complicated and situational rather than simple and absolute.

MTV and Moral Development: An Oxymoron

While young adolescents are busily engaged in developing attitudes and behaviors toward the opposite sex, every effort should be made to communicate that respect is the underpinning of all successful relationships. Gangsta rap lyrics that demean women and encourage violence against them promote the idea that abuse of women is admirable and commonplace. Although a superficial reading of this kind of music suggests that only black gangsta rappers hold such reactionary beliefs, many adolescents are well aware that records are produced and distributed by large corporate machines. It is this complicity of the adult world in packaging and popularizing abuse of women, as well as violence in general, that is ultimately most damaging. Rich, powerful, mostly white men in suits tolerate and promote the dehumanization of women. Though these facts may not be clear to adolescents, they should be acknowledged by adults. Large corporations, such as Time Warner, have been involved in financing some of gangsta rap's most hateful messengers.

MTV, the most conspicuous purveyor of adolescent stupefaction, insists on reducing the complexities of life to banal, misogynistic, and myopic music videos. Without a hint of irony, MTV airs brief public service announcements decrying drugs or guns or violence when only moments before it showed videos glamorizing these same problems. Rather than encouraging the adolescent's more advanced level of cognitive and moral development, MTV plays to the remnant of the child in every teenager who demands stimulation at the expense of reflection. Tom Freston, chief executive officer of MTV, when asked to describe what qualities it takes to run MTV, revealingly said, "Shallowness and the ability to fake sincerity." In another part of this interview, Mr. Freston suggested that "not thinking too much seems to have worked so far."[20]

The cornerstone of moral development is the ability to empathize with someone else's point of view. Movies and television programs that dehumanize individuals or groups of people work against the evolution of moral development. For all its brief public service messages on rape, MTV cannot undo the hours of propaganda provided by showing women in dog collars, on leashes, and as sexual objects in its music videos. Poignant poems about violence as part of the channel's "Enough Is Enough" campaign are not likely to reduce the impact of the hours of glamorization of violence in gangsta rap. To take a moral position against these various infringements on human rights and either censor or censure them would send a powerful statement to the primarily young adolescent audience. But then again, Mr. Freston might have to think.

YOUNG ADOLESCENT VIEWING CHECKLIST

Attachment

Encourages adolescents to consider a wide range of viewpoints	yes	no
Supports family and community	yes	no
Emphasizes respect as the foundation of all successful relationships	yes	no

Aggression

Emphasizes complex individual and social factors that lead to aggression	yes	no
Is clear about long-term consequences of acting impulsively	yes	no
Provides healthy, positive role models who choose alternatives to acting aggressively and impulsively	yes	no

Cognitive Development

Encourages adolescents' new ability to acknowledge and be curious about other points of view	yes	no
Emphasizes complexity of most problems	yes	no
Models reflection, compromise, and consideration of others as effective problem-solving skills	yes	no

Moral Development

Encourages a social as well as an individual perspective	yes	no

Is relevant to the day-to-day problems faced
  by young adolescents   yes   no

TELEVISION HALL OF FAME

My So-Called Life   Party of Five

Beverly Hills 90210   Star Trek: Deep Space Nine

Boy Meets World   The Fresh Prince of Bel-Air

The Cosby Show   Moesha

Dr. Quinn, Medicine   The Wonder Years
  Woman

MOVIES AND VIDEOS TO CHECK OUT

This Boy's Life   Wild Hearts Can't Be Broken

Seven Years in Tibet   Mister Holland's Opus

The Breakfast Club   Contact

Dead Poets Society   The Man in the Moon

Pretty in Pink   Ordinary People

Breaking Away   The Fugitive

ADD YOUR OWN FAVORITES

_____

_____

_____

_____

8

Adolescence

Ages Fifteen, Sixteen, Seventeen, and Eighteen

If early adolescence is a time for distinguishing oneself from one's parents, middle and later adolescence is a time for distinguishing oneself from the crowd. As we saw in Chapter Seven, early adolescence is marked by turmoil, overidentification with peers, and high levels of conformity. The young teenager fights mightily against her parents in an effort to begin forging an identity of her own. As the teenager moves along in adolescence and begins to feel less vulnerable to the pull of childhood, she begins a process of experimentation and exploration that will eventually lead to a new and stable sense of self. In order to do this, teenagers invent and reinvent themselves on a regular basis.

GENERAL DEVELOPMENT

Fifteen-year-old Katie had been involved in gymnastics since she was seven. She attended class twice a week for almost eight years and consistently ranked high in the competitions she insisted on attending. At times her parents worried that gymnastics was consuming her life and suggested that she might find other activities interesting as well. These suggestions were always met with vehement denial and tears.

"There is nothing in the world I like better than gymnastics" was Katie's unequivocal response.

Three weeks after her fifteenth birthday, Katie announced that she was no longer interested in pursuing gymnastics and criticized her parents for "making it my whole life."

Clean-cut, sixteen-year-old Seth was captain of the junior varsity football team. He was an outstanding and aggressive athlete who had participated in team sports for many years. He had always aspired to be on the varsity team, and his excellent performance in his sophomore year assured him a place on the varsity team the following year. Over the summer, his parents noticed that he began growing his hair out and even wore a small earring in his newly pierced ear. While he continued to play football, his parents often heard him criticizing the aggressive nature of his teammates. He signed up for elective courses in poetry and journalism. He did, however, eagerly accept the college football scholarship that was offered to him in his senior year.

Parents of younger adolescents often feel that they are living in a war zone with their new teenager. Parents of older teenagers often feel more bewildered than attacked. Erik Erikson coined the phrase "identity crisis" to help clarify and define this period of development.[1] Although crisis may be misunderstood to mean catastrophe or emergency, Erikson did not see this as a pathological state. He understood that adolescents who are experiencing an identity crisis are in a normal stage of development but one that is of singular importance. Out of this "crisis" a coherent and stable adult identity will emerge.

The development of an identity, of a sense of self, is a process that takes place over decades. Throughout childhood and early adolescence, the child is forging a sense of self that undergoes continual and radical change. These changes take place as the child gets feedback from himself and his environment. My athletic oldest son "knew" he was going to play for the NBA when he was in elementary school, "thought" he would play for them in junior high school, and in high school he started thinking about law school "just in case" he didn't make it to the NBA. Interests, competencies, and opportunities wax and wane over many years.

The challenge of adolescence is to assemble different pieces of the self into a working whole that serves both the individual and society. Inquiry and experimentation are critical to this period of development, as they allow teenagers to try on many different identities before settling on one that is consistent with their abilities, nature, and opportunities. While parents may be baffled by the fact that fastidious, conservative, fashion-conscious Suzy suddenly lives in a room that resembles a garbage dump, buys her clothes at the Salvation Army, and is out protesting animal rights violations, Suzy is in fact "taking care of business." Without this period of exploration, Suzy would face significant psychological risk.

Erikson identified two unfortunate outcomes that can result when teenagers are not able to go through this normal process of exploration. The first of these he called "identity foreclosure." This refers to what can happen to the teenager who continues to see things only through the eyes of others. Most typically, this would be the eyes of his parents, but it could also be the eyes of other important peers or adults, such as gang members or religious leaders. He goes to church every week because that's what his parents expect, he plans on being a lawyer because "all the men in this family are lawyers," and his criterion for dating is whether or not his parents would approve of his choice in girls. Instead of developing an identity of his own, he has adopted the identity provided him by others.

In effect, this child has completely bypassed adolescence. He has sidestepped the developmental task of identity formation, and it is likely that this strategy will ultimately produce an individual who suffers from deep feelings of emptiness and depression. Although it is essential that parental and community values be communicated to adolescents, the teenager must also have an active and vigorous role in forging his own identity. We cannot simply lift our identities from those around us, no matter how well intentioned they are.

The second and more generally recognized consequence of a poorly navigated adolescence is what Erikson termed "negative identity." As in identity foreclosure, parental overinvolvement plays a major role in the formation of a negative identity. The family that is considered a pillar of the community finds itself with a provocative, "druggie" adolescent. An upper-middle-class family finds that their teenager has renounced materialism and is joining a cult. Of course, many adolescents go through periods of opposing their parents' point of view. It is only when adolescents feel they have no choice but to solidify their opposition in the face of parental overinvolvement that true negative identity takes place. Once again, this is a poor conclusion to the process of developing a unique identity. Teenagers often need to "de-identify" with their families for a period of time. However, the task of identity formation is aided when teenagers feel free to explore their options in the context of family support. *Ideally, a supportive and respectful family is the critical context in which teenagers can work on the major task of identity formation.*

Adolescents are solidifying the gains they made in middle childhood when they worked hard at mastering different and increasingly complex tasks. Teenagers have to connect the abilities and talents they developed in childhood to realistic adult goals. Here we see the importance of the middle years, when much effort went into developing skills and learning information. The adolescent now has to reconcile her private image of herself with how the world views her, and she knows the world is larger and often less gentle than her family has been. While her parents have only admired her crabbed piano playing, she has heard others play who are more talented and is better able to see where she stands in the world. It is not enough that she's a good athlete or a good listener. The teenager wants to know how to translate abilities into skills that will serve her in the real world. The good English student could be an advertising executive or a journalist. The good listener could be a psychiatrist or a sound technician for a movie studio. Adolescence is a time to experiment with how one's abilities will be of service in adulthood.

As we saw earlier in this chapter with Katie and Seth, adolescence is not necessarily a period when skills that were evident in youth are polished and accepted. Although some teenagers may continue to pursue long-standing interests, others seem eager to disassociate themselves from earlier interests. Identities are embraced and discarded with equal zeal. One day the teenager is a Democrat and the next a Republican. Jocks become poets and poets become jocks. Good girls become fast girls and fast girls become nuns. Great passions well up and just as frequently dry up. Parents often tell their teenagers to "play the field" when it comes to dating because they recognize the hazards of cutting off social options too early. Likewise, teenagers need to play the field when it comes to political ideas, moral choices, academic interests, and other outside activities.

Parents need to keep in mind that adolescence is often a period in which there is actually less, rather than more, than meets the eye. Although teenagers like to think of themselves as outrageously different from their parents and from each other, there is an almost comic quality to the similarities of their differences. Erikson called this a "uniformity of differing." Teenagers who abhor the conformity of their blue-jean-and-blazer-clad suburban parents all wear their baseball caps backward and their flannel shirts covering their uniformly sagging pants. By the end of adolescence, however, individual differences in dress, manner, interests, and activities are clearly visible.

There's a final point that I would like to make in this section on general adolescent development. In my practice, parents have often come to see me wanting to know exactly "how much rope" to give their adolescents. My answer has always been "enough so they don't hang themselves." The issue of setting limits with teenagers runs through this chapter and through Chapter Seven. Give your teenager enough opportunity to try out different identities, different ideas, and different activities. Don't be overly involved or critical of your teenager's changes of heart lest you interfere with his ability to craft a healthy sense of self. But as parents, we also want to be sure that our children are protected from real danger. It's one thing to allow your teenage son to hang out with a couple of kids who smoke; it's quite another if he starts selling drugs. Your daughter's dressing like Madonna is one thing; her sleeping with half the football team is something else. How are parents to gauge when their adolescent's exploration is healthy, when it is flirting with danger, and when it demands intervention? The following is a brief list of what I consider to be the most frequent adolescent danger signs.

- *Regular drug or alcohol use*. Approximately 90 percent of all high school seniors say that they have had some experience with alcohol. This number has been constant for quite some time.[2] Although it is very difficult to say where experimentation stops and abuse begins, it is likely that teenagers who use drugs or alcohol over time and more than occasionally are at risk. In addition, the frequent use of these substances is generally tied to other problems such as depression, low self-esteem, and risk-taking behaviors. If parental injunctions prove useless, professional intervention is mandatory. Alcohol is involved in an extremely high percentage of adolescent deaths.

- *Promiscuity*. Sexual intercourse among adolescents is prevalent. By age fifteen, approximately 25 percent of adolescents are sexually active. By age seventeen, approximately half of all teenagers are sexually active. By age nineteen, 70 percent of girls and 80 percent of boys are sexually active. In general, boys become active about one year earlier than girls, and black youth are more sexually active at younger ages than their white or Hispanic counterparts.[3] Sexual activity among adolescents is surprisingly monogamous, with 50 percent of sexually experienced adolescent girls having sex with only one partner and another 35 percent having had sex with two or three partners. These statistics make clear the distinction between being sexually active and sexually promiscuous. Most teenagers, at some point during their adolescence, will become sexually active, but the vast majority do not become promiscuous. Sexual promiscuity, like drug and alcohol abuse, is correlated with an array of psychological problems such as low self-esteem, depression, and a prior history of being sexually abused. Because adolescents have become one of the fastest growing groups of HIV-infected individuals, responsible sex has become a matter of life and death.

• *Teenage depression and suicide.* Whereas the suicide rate for adults has remained relatively constant for the past thirty years, it has quadrupled for adolescents aged fifteen to nineteen. The suicide rate for adolescent boys is twice as high as it is for girls. White adolescents are twice as likely to commit suicide as black or Hispanic adolescents. The increased availability of firearms is believed to contribute dramatically to the increase in successful suicide attempts, since youthful suicide is often an impulsive gesture made possible by the lethality of readily available guns. In one epidemiological study, researchers found that although people keep guns in their homes for self-protection, these guns are actually used for suicide almost forty times more often than they are used for killing an intruder.[4]

In my experience, adolescent depression is one of the most overlooked and misdiagnosed psychiatric illnesses. Too often, the clinical symptoms of depression—apathy, withdrawal, hopelessness, and often aggression—are considered part of the normal *Sturm und Drang* of adolescence and are not taken seriously enough. Teenagers who exhibit these kinds of behavior for more than brief periods of time should be evaluated for depression. Untreated depression places the adolescent at risk for early death whether by suicide or by an increased likelihood of engaging in risk-taking behaviors such as drinking and driving.

MEDIA AND ADOLESCENTS

"I wouldn't mind thinking I was somebody."

Mike, in *Breaking Away*

This simple statement, spoken by an adolescent who feels his future options are limited, illustrates the longing and hopefulness of all teenagers. If at the end of adolescence, teenagers feel like they are "somebody," the developmental tasks of adolescence have been successfully resolved. These young people will carry an enduring sense of self into adulthood. On the other hand, those adolescents who enter adulthood feeling like "nobody" are at risk for leading lives that are unproductive, unsatisfying, and frequently antisocial.

This is not a book about the sociology of adolescence, but it is impossible to write about teenagers and ignore the crisis that American youth are experiencing. The role of the media's effects on adolescents can be understood only if we realize that our teenagers are confronting unprecedented social problems. Although the reasons for these problems are complex and not easily solved, the media's contribution to the problems of teenage violence, pregnancy, drug and alcohol abuse, and hopelessness are well documented and substantial.

To claim that all these social ills are caused by the media would be preposterous. However, to ignore the role of the media in contributing to these dreadful statistics is to ignore one of the most potent influences in the lives of teenagers. Children who watch *Sesame Street* can increase their cognitive skills; those who watch *Mister Rogers' Neighborhood* have been shown to exhibit more compassionate behavior. Adults have learned to buckle up, quit smoking, and begin exercising, largely from massive public health campaigns presented through the media. Advertisers spend millions of dollars each year to "educate" us about the virtues of their various soaps, detergents, and deodorants, knowing that a successful advertising campaign can change the way we think and what we buy. So certainly adolescents, with their thirst for information and taste for experimentation, are also likely to learn from the media. Don Roberts, chairman of the Department of Communication at Stanford University, aptly summarized the hard reality of media influence on adolescents: "The issue is not whether mass media affect adolescent perceptions, beliefs, behaviors. Rather, it is one of society's judging how many adolescents need to be put at risk, in what way, before various corrective actions are viewed as necessary and justified."[5]

Adolescents turn to the media for many different reasons. They are plagued by concerns about identity, actively seek information about the adult world they will soon enter, and need significant amounts of time to do nothing in order to work on their internal preoccupations. The media can provide relief, information, and distraction. Are the media honestly meeting these needs, or are they in large measure exploiting a vulnerable market?

The media have glamorized the portrayal of guns so completely that adolescents brought into emergency rooms with gunshot wounds are amazed to find that they are in pain. Guns have become as ubiquitous a symbol of adult power as packs of cigarettes in previous decades. The throwaway lines of casual violence, such as "Make my day" or "Are you feeling lucky, punk?" have become part of the common lexicon. There is not a single studio head in this country who is not aware of the exploding homicide rate for adolescents. These captains of industry have all been shown the connection between media portrayals of violence and real-world violence. Their continued dismissal of these facts is unconscionable.

Teenagers, for the most part, do not need protection from the realities of life. On the contrary, they need as much information and education as possible. *Dead Poets Society* deals with suicide, *Boyz N the Hood* with homicide, *Philadelphia* with AIDS; *Schindler's List* documents genocide, and *Amistad* chronicles slavery. Responsible movies such as these do not hesitate to confront and explore the kinds of difficult topics that interest adolescents. But they provide a historical context, emphasize complexity, explore alternatives, and show teenagers the consequences of actions that may limit or even destroy future opportunities. Although certainly difficult and painful to watch, these are all outstanding movies for older teens, and I do not hesitate to recommend them.

Of course, one of the purposes of the media is to provide distraction, a way of "kicking back" and forgetting about one's problems. We all need downtime. Action movies are exciting and engrossing, allowing us to turn our attention away from our own difficulties. This is a perfectly reasonable use of entertainment. Horror movies can also serve a psychological function for adolescents. They are a rite of passage that allows the teenager, at a safe distance, to dare to be unafraid and capable of confronting anxiety. They hold the same attraction that fairy tales held for younger children. They help prepare their adolescent viewers for going out into a world that contains many frightening unknowns. They also help adolescent males, the major consumers of such movies, lessen the psychological grip of mother by proving that they are "man enough" to manage on their own.

Evil has its attractions—from fire-breathing dragons to evil stepmothers to serial killers—and people of all ages are interested in the darker aspects of humanity. This is because we all carry within ourselves thoughts and fantasies that are cruel and violent. It is naïve and dangerous to deny the duality of human nature. But the socializing agents of society—family, school, religious institutions, and the mass media—are charged with the responsibility of helping children and adolescents understand and control their aggression.

At the risk of being repetitious, I will say again that no one movie or television program, no matter how violent, is likely to be damaging to reasonably healthy adolescents. The problem lies in violence that is the rule rather than the exception. Although boys do benefit from the man-as-dragon-slayer story, it is only one of many stories they need to hear. They also need man-as-father, man-as-nurturer, man-as-healer, and man-as-peacemaker stories if they are to enter adulthood truly equipped for the varied responsibilities they will find there. Unfortunately, outstanding television programs, such as My So-Called Life, which dealt with serious and common adolescent problems, are often short-lived. Teenagers have become so habituated to extreme violence that they lack the patience and insight needed to appreciate even marginally more demanding programs.

Despite the entertainment industry's claim that it is only giving the public what it wants, research shows that it is action, not gratuitous violence, that appeals most to audiences. The surprise summer hit of 1994, Speed, with Keanu Reeves, though not an intellectually demanding movie, managed to be thrilling while maintaining a minimal body count. *Apollo 13* was a gripping and fascinating history lesson, loudly applauded by the group of teenagers sitting next to me in the theater. *Crimson Tide* provided a good dose of action and suspense and still managed to pose questions particularly appealing to adolescents: Where does one's greatest responsibility lie? What constitutes betrayal? How does one decide between one's conscience and the dictates of society? All of these movie were popular with adolescents, and good examples of how audiences can be entertained and riveted without being soaked in blood. Entertainment executives might consider these types of action movies as absorbing, responsible, and profitable alternatives to movies featuring gratuitous violence.

I had an interesting experience while rewriting this chapter for the paperback edition. I realized that with a few exceptions, almost every television show or movie I mentioned in both adolescent chapters featured male characters. Many of the "picks" at the end of the chapters were movies or television shows featuring male characters. Great art, of course, transcends gender, and there is much for adolescent girls to learn from *Quiz Show* or *Seven Years in Tibet*. Until I watched Jodie Foster in *Contact*, however, I did not realize how significant the lack of female heroes is.

Contact is a modestly good movie based on the novel by Carl Sagan. Although filled with Hollywood contrivances, it does manage to convey the sense of wonder and awe that were characteristic of Carl Sagan's presentation of the universe. Dr. Ellie Arroway, played by Jodie Foster, is an astronomer who has dedicated her life to trying to make contact with intelligent life beyond earth. Fighting the sense of loneliness born of early losses (Mom died giving birth, and Dad is around just long enough to nurture Ellie's childhood curiosity about space), Ellie is fiercely dedicated to the idea that we are not alone. "Do you think there are people on other planets?" young Ellie asks her dad. "I don't know, but if it's just us, it would be an awful waste of space," he chides her. This movie is about outer space, but it is also about inner space and Ellie's quest to understand the meaning of life. This movie is actually willing to grapple with questions of theology. Ultimately, Ellie is willing to risk her life in order to have a chance to have her questions answered.

What was so profoundly affecting to me as I watched this movie was the fact that Ellie is bright, young, attractive, curious, and determined. Something started clicking as I watched her. There is a scene in which she is about to enter the space capsule that will catapult her out of our universe. She has waited all her life for this moment, and she trembles with anticipation and terror. As she walks alone across the bridge that leads her to the capsule, I had to remind myself to breathe. And then it hit me: I was watching a woman, a woman I could identify with, confronting her capacity to reach beyond fear toward maturity and wisdom. I have felt that way stepping over the airplane threshold as I tried to conquer my fear of flying; I have felt it being wheeled into the operating room to give birth to each of my three sons. I had never seen a woman on the screen confronting that moment.

This is not to say that such moments do not exist in film. They do. But not often and typically not by women who are alone. Rose chops the handcuffs off Jack in *Titanic* as the ship sinks, but she is capable of such selflessness and bravery only in relationship to the man she loves. Ellie, on the other hand, resists a romantic entanglement with a very appealing man, the better to pursue her quest without compromise. Women in general, but adolescent girls in particular, are in desperate need of role models who encourage independence, autonomy, and character development. Young girls who learn that they can depend on themselves, that they have within themselves the resources to grow and to contribute, are much more likely to lead fulfilling lives as well as to ultimately contribute to their families and communities.

Interestingly, we do seem to have such role models for young girls. Movies as profoundly different as *Pocahontas* and *A Little Princess* both present girls who are navigating difficult situations aided by their strength of character. How odd that adolescent girls, disproportionately large consumers of movies, find so few young women role models who encourage them to retain their curiosity and honesty and, most important, their commitment to self-development as a precursor to commitment to others. Carol Gilligan has rightfully pointed out that girls, as they approach adolescence, are discouraged from retaining their natural "voice," curiosity, enthusiasm, and forthrightness.[6] Nowhere is this more apparent than in our lack of imaginative stories for adolescent girls.

PSYCHOLOGICAL DEVELOPMENT AND THE MEDIA

Whenever I speak to a group of parents with high school kids, I'm asked the same question: "At this age, what can a parent possibly do to restrict a teenager's viewing choices?" The question is unfortunate on two counts. First, restriction is not the major issue. It is unrealistic to suggest that a teenager's viewing can be restricted in the same way as a younger child's. Second, the question has a kind of implied despair about being able to control adolescents at all. Both of these misunderstandings stem from popular misconceptions about attachment between parents and teenagers.

Attachment

There is no question that the tie between parents and adolescents is markedly different from the tie between parents and younger children. Parents are no longer repositories of wisdom, filling up eager young vessels with their knowledge, life experience, and sense of morality. Teenagers are eager to construct an identity of their own, one far less dependent on their parents and more in line with each particular teenager's strengths and weaknesses. As we have seen, this means several years of exploration and experimentation with everything from clothes and mannerisms to ideas and identities. Attachment continues, although its quality changes. Studies show that most teenagers crave more time with their parents. Equally surprising, once adolescence is over, most children grow up to be more or less like their parents.

How can parents construct a relationship with their adolescents that includes advice and guidance but is not seen as intrusive or controlling? First, parents need to call on the natural curiosity and intellectual expansion that teenagers are experiencing. Rather than repeated admonitions of "what garbage" kids are watching, parents serve their teenagers well by asking open-ended questions such as "What do you think about men treating women that way?" "Was there another way he could have settled that fight?" and "Why did she allow herself to be beaten?" The media present a myriad of opportunities for parents to help their adolescents think about and formulate opinions on different issues.

The O. J. Simpson trial, which took place during much of the original writing of this book, provided numerous opportunities to talk with my two older sons about violence, spousal abuse, sports, hero worship, and friendship. Parental pronouncements such as "What a jerk!" may make parents' values known, but they do not expand the teenager's own thought processes. Teenagers need to know where their parents stand and have opportunities to think through a problem and come to their own conclusions. Model enthusiasm for the world of ideas. Ask questions, discuss, be thoughtful. Talk to your teenager!

One of the extraordinary events taking place at this time in a teenager's life is the discovery of love and sex. While emotional reliance on parents is diminishing, the adolescent is finding new support and nurturance in intimate relationships with peers. These relationships can be sexual or not, heterosexual or homosexual. They become part of the process by which adolescents come to define their own identity. Erik Erikson describes this stage with great insight: "This initiates the stage of 'falling in love,' which is by no means entirely, or even primarily, a sexual matter—except where the mores demand it. To a considerable extent, adolescent love is an attempt to arrive at a definition of one's identity by projecting one's diffused ego image on another and by seeing it thus reflected and gradually clarified. This is why so much of young love is conversation."[7]

Unfortunately, the media choose to ignore this reality of adolescent development. Conversation, discussion, and endless thinking are large components of adolescent life, but they are virtually ignored by the media in favor of sexual adventure. Although sexual issues are critical as never before and will be discussed at length in this chapter, let's focus for a moment on the equally compelling emotional aspect of adolescent love. As parents, we know that it can be hard to remember parts of our adolescence, but we all remember our first broken heart. The emotional investment that teenagers make in each other can be unparalleled. Although couples break up frequently and seem to treat each other with apparent indifference, the truth is that these failed relationships can be excruciatingly painful to the adolescent.

One reason *My So-Called Life* was so well liked by adolescents was that it acknowledged the primacy of adolescent emotional connection, not just sexual activity. The producers of that program made a sound decision by having their fifteen-year-old central character, Angela, remain a virgin. This device allowed the show to circumvent many of the mandatory sexual escapades of television characters and instead focus on psychological development. Though sex certainly came up as a subject on *My So-Called Life*, sex was mainly talked about and not carried out. Characters were given the opportunity to plumb some of the conflict and ambivalence characteristic of adolescents. Similarly, *Party of Five*, while not ignoring sexual issues, addresses itself primarily to the myriad issues of growing up—friendship, school, and career plans, as well as drug and alcohol problems. A particularly engaging cast makes this a well-deserved favorite among adolescents.

A wonderful movie called *The Man in the Moon* beautifully portrays two sisters, one on the verge of adolescence and the other closer to adulthood. The movie chronicles their shifting intimacy with each other as well as their passionate love for a local boy. This movie provided a particularly telling opportunity for me to witness the power of treating adolescents with respect. Moments after I began watching, my teenage son wandered in to the room. I was certain that this movie, about two girls, set in some dusty small town in the 1950s, would provoke disinterest at best, sarcasm at worst. But he sat and began watching with me, pulled in by the honest portrayal of adolescent hope, longing, and confusion. This is a movie totally devoid of any of the usual devices to grab and hold our attention. Its drama takes place entirely in the dialogue and body language of its characters. My son and I sat spellbound on the couch, immersed in this family whose lives were so different from our own. But we each recognize the language of the heart when it is spoken clearly and directly. When the movie was over, my fifteen-year-old, *Rambo*-loving son said, "That was the best movie I ever saw." We frequently underestimate our teenagers. They deserve to be spoken to—and profit from being spoken to—directly, honestly, and with dignity.

The video store often provides a wider and more interesting selection of movies than the current crop of movies featured at the local cinema. Bring home movies that look appealing. Invite your teenager to watch with you.

Teenagers and Sex in the Media

The basis of all successful human relationships is respect and affection. Teenagers should be encouraged to see programs and movies that acknowledge that fact. Unfortunately, teenagers frequently feel pushed into sexual activity before they have a firm grasp on the emotional underpinnings of human connection. The media have failed to show that real human connection comes out of emotional intimacy, not just sexual intimacy. Overall, the media portray sex as glamorous, spontaneous, and, most dangerously, risk-free.

Learning about sex is different for teens than any other kind of social learning because much of the information comes not through participation and observation but from each other—and much of it turns out to be false. Teenagers watch each other skateboard and then try it themselves. Even such things as "how to talk to girls" is something that the teenage boy watches in a variety of contexts (how Dad talks to Mom, how his big brother talks to his girlfriend) and then gradually participates in at the level he finds comfortable. Sex, however, is not something that teenagers learn through observation.

When it comes to disseminating sexual information, parents and educational and religious institutions vary greatly in their willingness and comfort level. Parental denial plays a large part in limiting access to sexual information as teenagers have sex at younger and younger ages. This trend has potentially devastating implications for our society, as it is well documented that younger teenagers are less likely than older teens to be well informed about birth control and disease prevention and are more likely to engage in unprotected sex than older teens.

Because adolescence is a time of lessened parental control, greater access to the media, and few competing sources of information about sex, it comes as no surprise that the media play a very important role in the sexual socialization of teenagers. Unfortunately, little of what teenagers see about sex in the media is thoughtful or respectful. Instead, teenagers are exposed to a sexual world heavy on violence and other assertions of power and low on love and commitment. MTV has immersed adolescents in a world where sexual activity is primarily the province of hormonally flooded males with little concern for their female partners. Consequences of sexual activity are virtually nonexistent, and the few mentions of contraception are often paired with emotional indifference. Snoop Doggy Dogg, one of rap's most popular mainstream performers, may have a "pocketful of rubbers" for the "bitches in the living room,"[8] but he has nothing meaningful to teach adolescents about the joys and responsibilities of human love.

The media have been grossly negligent in portrayals of sex and its consequences. Approximately 85 percent of all sexual relationships on television are between unmarried or uncommitted couples.[9] Typically, the media are content to stick with the subject of casual sex rather than struggle with the far more complex issue of human intimacy. Watching television and the movies, one would think that sex stops at the altar.

While preparing this book, I watched many dozens of the most popular teenage movies, and I never saw a reasoned and intelligent discussion of birth control. According to most stories told by the media, intercourse and pregnancy are unrelated events. Can we measure the percentage of the million babies born to teenagers this year who in some measure owe their existence to such repeated irresponsible portrayals of teenage sex? Not likely. Like violence, teenage pregnancy is the end point of many individual and social factors. But there is no doubt that media portrayals, on the whole, have been derelict in informing teenagers about the consequences of sexual activity.

Aggression

As we saw earlier in this book, aggression as a style of dealing with conflict is something that is learned early in childhood and learned well. In fact, it is quite difficult to modify aggression once it is the preferred way of handling problems. In this respect, parents may be able to relax a bit over what their teenager is watching. By adolescence, most children have a reasonably consistent way of handling interpersonal conflict. It is unlikely that media violence can turn a previously cooperative and peaceful child into a mid-adolescent criminal. That kind of damage is done earlier in life by any number of social and individual factors.

Although crimes are being committed by younger and younger individuals, adolescents still make up a disproportionate number of both perpetrators and victims. With very few exceptions, seven-year-olds don't rape and murder, but seventeen-year-olds do. In her powerful book *Boys Will Be Boys*, Myriam Miedzian looks at the many factors in our society that contribute to boys' developing a sense of self that relies heavily on aggressive posturing. "Many of the values of the masculine mystique, such as toughness, dominance, repression of empathy, and extreme competitiveness, play a major role in criminal and domestic violence and underlie the thinking and policy decisions of many of our political leaders."[10]

This book forces the realization that it is not simply "aggression" being studied, but male aggression. The vast majority of crimes are committed by men, and so we need to pay particular attention to the messages that the media send to boys.

There is little question that the media have failed to provide teenage boys with role models that are worthy of imitation. The unremitting use of violence as a solution to interpersonal conflict serves the adolescent boy particularly poorly. Suppose an adolescent finds himself confronted by a mugger demanding his wallet. The knee-jerk aggressive script that television all too frequently presents for this type of situation is not likely to make the adolescent a hero; it is more likely to land him in the hospital, if not the morgue.

Why is it that males seem particularly attracted to media messages that stress intimidation and the abuse of power as ways to navigate the world? Boys are far more affected by male role models than by female role models, whereas girls are equally affected by both. Women in the media are typically portrayed as being less aggressive and more socially conscious than men. Perhaps it is the acceptance of female role models that confers a protective factor on girls, making them less vulnerable to the aggressive, macho images that suffuse popular culture. Boys desperately need a wider range of male role models, some of whom incorporate the more traditional female values of cooperation and sensitivity. It would be of great benefit for adolescent boys to see male characters who are appealing without being violent. Unfortunately, male characters who are gentle and sensitive are also frequently portrayed as defective or crazy, as in *Edward Scissorhands* or *Don Juan DeMarco*.

A peculiarity of our culture is that exposure to sexual material is considered more damaging to children than exposure to violence. The Puritan aversion to sex still evident in our culture results in some truly extraordinary contradictions. In 1993 *NYPD Blue* caused a stir by breaking the nudity code on television. For the first time, a major television program allowed one of its stars to bare his buttocks. No matter that we had seen decades of shootings, knifings, rapes, and mutilations; David Caruso was shown bare-assed. I personally would rather have my children see someone's butt hanging out than someone's brains hanging out. Call me a romantic.

We have decided, against all scientific evidence, that we need to shield our youth from sex but not violence. Tom Cruise's saying "fuck" twice in *Rain Man* is not the equivalent of Woody Harrelson's bloodbath in *Natural Born Killers* (both R-rated movies). The effects of these two movies on children are considerably different, and that difference is not adequately acknowledged under the current rating system. Although there is a value to ratings that reflect what the hypothetical "average American parent" would consider appropriate for their child, there is also value in considering what research has to tell us about what is damaging to children. The rating system would be far more useful to parents if it acknowledged different developmental stages and gave additional information about why films received their particular rating.

Many of our most popular movies directed at a teenage audience— *The Terminator, Die Hard, Out for Justice, Tomorrow Never Dies, Scream*—feature gratuitous violence and often combine sexual and aggressive messages. Is it true that the sexual content is what is most damaging? After all, adolescent boys are having their first sexual experiences and are formulating attitudes toward women that they will carry for a lifetime. Edward Donnerstein, one of this country's leading authorities on pornography, has spent decades studying the effects of pornography and violence. In 1987 Donnerstein and his colleagues published *The Question of Pornography: Research Findings and Policy Implications*. They write in their preface:

> It is perhaps ironic, but we did not write this book because of our concern about the prevalence of sexually explicit materials in American society. Rather, we were concerned that so much attention was being paid to the possibly damaging consequences of exposure to pornography, that more pervasive and more troubling combinations of sex and aggression in the media were being ignored. We contend that the violence against women in some types of R-rated films shown in

neighborhood theaters and on cable TV far exceeds that portrayed in even the most graphic pornography.[11]

One of the chapters in the book, titled "Is It the Sex or Is It the
Violence?" attempts to bring decades of scientific research to bear
on answering this question. A series of studies by Donnerstein and
colleagues show that violence, or a combination of sex and violence
(but not sex alone), tends to encourage callous sexual attitudes
toward women.[12] For example, in one of the experiments, a group
of college-age males were shown one of four different movies. The
first film featured aggressive pornography, with themes of rape and
violence. The second film was X-rated but contained no aggression
or sexual coercion. Viewers judged these two films equally sexually
arousing. The third film contained scenes of aggression against
women but lacked any sexual content. The fourth film had neutral
content.

After viewing the movie, the men were asked to complete ques-
tionnaires measuring their attitudes toward rape. Among the men
who saw a sex-only film, only 11 percent indicated some likelihood
that they would commit rape. Among those who saw the sex-and-
violence film, 25 percent indicated some likelihood that they would
commit rape. And among the men who saw the violence-only film,
*fully 50 percent of the men indicated some likelihood that they would rape
a woman* (italics mine). The authors conclude, "We risk the possibility that many members of our society, particularly young viewers,
will evolve into less sensitive and responsive individuals as a result,
at least partly, of repeated exposure to violent media, particularly
sexually violent media. Such a possibility should be alarming, if not
to law makers, at least to policy makers responsible for rating
motion pictures and thus to limiting young people's access to sexually violent depictions."[13]

Although the results of studies like these are generally not known
by the public, they are well known to academics and to media executives. Bringing this information into the debate about media and
responsibility is imperative. Parents have their work cut out for

them. At the very least, we must work to ensure that our teenage boys understand that such attitudes and behavior are reprehensible. Mothers need to command respect from their sons, and fathers need to be involved in lessening the impact of these degrading messages by discussing the realities of love, sex, and aggression with their sons. More than 20 percent of college-age women report sexual abuse, often in the form of date rape.[14] The devastating problem of sexual violence will not go away without active intervention. The high levels of sexual abuse in our society suggest that sexual violence is not committed by a few deviant men. Rather, it is a common and too frequently acceptable way of exercising control over women.

Cognitive Development

Adolescents continue to undergo a revolution in thinking that began at about age eleven. Younger children can appreciate different points of view as long as they are familiar and testable. Middle adolescents, on the other hand, can entertain multiple perspectives about things that are hypothetical and outside their realm of experience. Piaget called this "formal operations." For example, a sixteen-year-old can think about what it would be like to stay out late and have fun, and at the same time she can appreciate that her parents might worry and even eventually call the police. Based on this ability to foresee consequences, adolescents are capable of making more informed choices than younger children. Not all fifteen-year-olds think like adults, and not all adults reach the stage of formal operations. In general, however, adolescence is a period of time in which reasoning shifts from being based on the obvious to being based on an awareness of complexity.

This more advanced appreciation of life has an important bearing on how adolescents understand the media. Ideally, the media would aid teens in the development of a more sophisticated worldview. Adolescents like to think. They relish the opportunity to flex intellectual muscles. Schools acknowledge the adolescent's more advanced way of thinking and substitute essay questions for true-or-false or multiple-choice questions. Students are encouraged to present arguments, often at odds with their own point of view, because they can now make a cogent case from someone else's viewpoint. The feminist may have to argue against abortion; the school liberal may have to outline why social programs should be eliminated.

Television as a medium is ill suited to advancing the kind of intellectual growth necessary to produce reflective adults. Neil Postman, in his classic book *The Disappearance of Childhood*, points out that electronic media, by their very nature, encourage a childish worldview.[15] Just as childhood is characterized by a desire for instant gratification and minimal thoughtfulness, so does television lure us into a world that is fast, vapid, and without consequences. Television that jumps from *Roseanne* to a Calvin Klein sexual fantasy to genocide in Croatia with equal enthusiasm and emphasis does not allow for the kinds of distinctions necessary to develop a sense of context and meaning.

One of the tasks of adolescence is to develop a sense of historical continuity and context. Adolescents need to feel that they are part of the ongoing human process. The isolation of adolescence is lessened when the teenager can glimpse himself at work, with a family, as part of a community. This is why teenagers are so interested in movies and television programs that deal with issues of career, relationships, and social issues. Popular movies such as *Reality Bites* or *Good Will Hunting* help muddled adolescents feel that eventually they will be able to figure out how to work and how to love.

Although movies can take the time to tackle complex problems, television usually cannot. This is most evident on the news. Adolescents watch the news more frequently than younger children. Although they often feel that they are watching a more "grown-up" form of television, the fact is that the news is just another way of packaging entertainment. Murder, missing whales, and special reports on hair loss alternate with commercials. The adolescent's newly acquired cognitive skills are never called on.

There is nothing in the news that is not understood, and all too often seen, by the average ten-year-old. Although some thoughtful news programs, such as the *Newshour with Jim Lehrer,* suggest the complexity of domestic and world problems, these programs are rarely watched by adolescents. Postman uses the news, probably because it is often considered the most "serious" of television offerings, to illustrate how little illumination is generally found on television.

> This way of defining the "news" achieves two interesting effects. First, it makes it difficult to think about an event, and second, it makes it difficult to feel about an event. By thinking, I mean having the time and motivation to ask oneself: What is the meaning of such an event? What is its history? What are the reasons for it? How does it fit into what I know about the world? By feeling, I mean the normal human responses to murder, rape, fire, bribery and general mayhem. . . . The point is, of course, that all events on TV come completely devoid of historical continuity or any other context, and in such fragmented and rapid succession that they wash over our minds in an undifferentiated stream. This is television as narcosis, dulling to both sense and sensibility.[16]

In effect, the media, and particularly television, fail to provide adolescents with experiences that would help develop their thinking and aid their sense of coming into a reasonable world. Once again, this presents greater problems for some adolescents than for others. Teenagers whose parents encourage careful thinking, both by modeling reflective thought and encouraging their teenagers to do likewise, are encouraging intellectual development. The problem is not that teenagers are exposed to occasional doses of tasteless, overstimulating, anti-intellectual junk. The problem is that too often, that's pretty much *all* they're exposed to.

Moral Development

Six neighborhood boys decided to indulge in the teenage ritual of drinking a beer in the bushes before the school dance. Three of the boys were caught by the school's vice principal, and three escaped. The police were called, and although none of the three were charged, they were suspended from school for a week. I was asked by the high school to talk with the boys and their families. The next week provided a crash course for me in the vicissitudes of teenage morality.

The three boys who were caught were uniformly remorseful. However, their reasons for being remorseful were different. Two were extremely concerned that they would be punished and might lose their "good kid" status. One of the boys was distressed because "it was stupid to break the rules. I know better than that." More interesting was that two of the boys who weren't caught showed no remorse at all. They were quite articulate and insisted the school couldn't "prove" anything once they had left the campus. The third felt that he had "broken his parents' trust" and should be punished. These different responses are interesting in that they illustrate both the strength and the weakness of Kohlberg's theories of moral reasoning.

Clearly these six teenagers experienced a moral dilemma and showed very different ways of thinking about their predicament. All six of these students were honored at an assembly the following week for outstanding academic achievement, so the issue of intelligence is insignificant here. In fact, the example does a good job of illustrating Kohlberg's contention that moral reasoning lags behind cognitive advances. These six kids, who showed the highest levels of academic achievement, varied in their moral reasoning across all of Kohlberg's stages.

The boys who felt vindicated because they weren't caught could be considered to be at Kohlberg's earliest stage of moral reasoning, what he called "preconventional morality." In this stage all that matters is whether you get caught or not. This kind of reasoning is seen typically in toddlers and young children. Those boys who worried that they would lose their "good kid" status exhibited "conventional morality"; that is, their reasoning focused on what others would think of them. This reasoning is typical of childhood but is also probably the highest level of moral reasoning for many, if not most, adults. Finally, the two boys who were concerned about the more abstract principles of broken trust and social obligation exhibited Kohlberg's highest level of moral reasoning, "postconventional" or "principled morality." In this stage moral reasoning focuses on abstract principles underlying right and wrong. Though Kohlberg's stages are descriptively useful, my own experience tells me that they are far more fluid and situational than Kohlberg suggests.

What is critically important for teenagers is that they are exposed to the process by which people make moral judgments and decisions. To some degree, the content of what is seen in the movies and on TV is less important than the modeling of moral reasoning. Retribution movies of the Van Damme, Seagal, Schwarzenegger, or Stallone genre are damaging for adolescents less for the violence they show than for the kind of primitive eye-for-an-eye philosophy that lies behind the heroes' decisions. Typically, the male hero in these movies does not struggle with issues of principled morality. The teenager's beginning ability to make moral decisions based on social rather than individual needs is sorely tested by vigilante movies.

There are movies that engage the adolescent's newly emerging level of moral reasoning. A movie like *Quiz Show* is not only entertaining but also forces the viewer to grapple with the fact that moral decisions are difficult and corruptible. It is a particularly appealing movie for adolescents because it concedes that temptation is not easily turned away (a fact that adolescents are all too familiar with), while at the same time fully exploring the consequences of submitting to seduction. This outstanding movie, directed by Robert Redford, chronicles the quiz show scandal of the 1950s. Audiences believed that they were watching contestants on shows like *Twenty-One* and *The $64,000 Question* struggle to answer difficult questions in order to win money. In fact they were watching a carefully choreographed deception. Contestants who were likely to boost advertisers' products were fed correct answers. Charles Van Doren, an engaging English professor, is seduced by the opportunity but eventually finds himself in the middle of congressional hearings.

Though the toll on the individuals involved in this scandal is high and Van Doren never teaches again, the machinery behind the duplicity, the advertisers and the network, remain untouched. This movie provides a wonderful opportunity to discuss with adolescents what goes on behind the scenes of the programs and movies they watch. Though Van Doren's charade in the 1950s seems more pathetic than criminal, it sowed the seeds for today's pocketbook journalism and propaganda passing for documentary. In the movie, Richard Goodwin, the congressional investigator who uncovered the scandal, says, "I thought I was going to get television. The truth is television is going to get us." This is real meat for the adolescent to chew on. Although cheating on quiz show questions might seem puerile to adolescents whose media heroes are tried for murder, assault, and sexual molestation, Quiz Show never seems outdated. Movies like this, which don't rely on violence and formula, are often overlooked by adolescents. This is unfortunate because, although most adolescents will never be involved in real violence, all will face the kinds of moral decisions that Quiz Show so carefully considers.

Unfortunately, television and cinema aimed at this age group rarely take the time to engage the adolescent's new reflective capacities. Instead, adolescents are portrayed struggling with the most dramatic and highly charged aspects of life. Inner-city teens struggle to stay alive and arm themselves adequately; suburban teens deal with cutthroat competition, peer pressure, and existential angst. Themes tend to focus on the delinquent, the tragic, and the dramatic. Some of these films do teenagers a service by highlighting the most difficult aspects of adolescence. But it is not enough to draw attention to a problem; the media must also present solutions that are viable, attractive, and safe.

Teenagers certainly need to consider issues that affect their lives, both the dramatic and the mundane. Media that encourage adolescents to consider their future as well as their present and that support the integration of individual principles with social demands are of great service. They act as allies of those other powerful agents of socialization—family, school, religion—that strive toward producing men and women of conscience.

ADOLESCENT VIEWING CHECKLIST

Attachment

Emphasis on responsible treatment of more
adult themes

yes   no

Focus on issues that are relevant to teens
(school, career, friendship, love, sex,
alcohol, drugs, and so on)

yes   no

Complexity of human attachment is
acknowledged

yes   no

Practical solutions to common problems
are offered

yes   no

Aggression

The cost of giving in to deadly compulsions
is clear

yes   no

Perpetrators are not attractive

yes   no

Violence is clearly portrayed as both an
individual and a social problem

yes   no

Role models provide clear alternatives to
aggression as a style of handling conflict
and frustration

yes   no

Cognitive Development

Calls on more complex and sophisticated
thinking skills

yes   no

Role models are reflective and thoughtful
(a good clue for evaluating this is whether
there is more dialogue or more action)

yes   no

Moral Development

Temptation to act immorally is openly
acknowledged   yes   no

Consequences approximate what teens are
likely to encounter in real life   yes   no

TELEVISION HALL OF FAME

Party of Five   *The Fresh Prince of Bel-Air*

My So-Called Life   *Dr. Quinn, Medicine Woman*

Biography

MOVIES AND VIDEOS TO CHECK OUT

Boyz N the Hood   *Philadelphia*

Schindler's List   *Amistad*

Quiz Show   *Malcolm X*

In the Name of the Father   *Good Will Hunting*

Jerry Maguire   *Field of Dreams*

Hoop Dreams   *Gandhi*

Chariots of Fire   *Crimson Tide*

Dead Man Walking

ADD YOUR OWN FAVORITES

_____

_____

_____

_____

PART THREE

Where Do We Go from Here?

9

What Parents Can Do

It is easy to identify the problem of media violence and its effects on youth. It is even reasonably easy to describe the problem, evaluate existing research, draw from personal and professional experience, and consult the experts. But it is extraordinarily difficult to come up with suggestions and solutions that have any "teeth" in them. The usual platitudes of "reducing violence" and "safeguarding our children" are sentiments that are unlikely to be challenged, but they are also sentiments that have produced little measurable change. This chapter will look at the opportunities available to parents for effecting meaningful change in how media teach, persuade, and seduce our children.

There is no question that children learn from the television shows and movies they watch. Children are continuously learning from their environment. Much of this learning is incidental, things our kids "just pick up" rather than things they are intentionally taught. They learn from parents, teachers, peers, siblings, and from the general culture as well. But the media send their messages to our children for many more hours each week than any other institution. Children spend thirty and sometimes even forty or fifty hours a week with different forms of electronic media—television, movies, video games, computer games, and music. Reading that is not school related clocks in at less than ten minutes a day. Compared to the few minutes a day spent with their fathers, the forty or so minutes spent with their mothers, and the six hours of school (which is in session only nine months of the year), it becomes clear that media, and television in particular, are accounting for disproportionate amounts of children's time. The electronic media's emphasis on the fast, the flashy, and the nonreflective is squeezing out more important experiences of relatedness, communication skills, and thoughtfulness.

Those in the entertainment industry who maintain that they are "only entertainers" insult our intelligence. Although they are entertainers, the power of their medium has made them much more. They are storytellers in a culture so fragmented that the traditional communicators of cultural values are often absent. Commercials not only hawk deodorants, soap powders, cars, and sneakers but also a set of values compatible with consumption. Much as a pharmacist dispenses prescriptions, the media dispense perceptions. Drinking will make you relaxed, fun, and sexy. Cigarettes will make you "kool." Nike sneakers will make you "like Mike." As long as the media's main job is to sell, they can never truly be free to entertain, let alone educate or elevate.

In talking with dozens of media executives while preparing this book, the most common response to criticism was, "If you don't like it, turn it off." Repeatedly the point was made that parents are in charge of their children, not media executives. Certainly, parents are a child's first line of defense against corrupting influences. But eventually I began to feel that telling parents to shut off the TV is as irresponsible as telling them not to use seat belts. As parents, we of course have the responsibility to drive carefully, and if everyone drove carefully, perhaps we wouldn't need seat belts. But we know that we cannot control the drunken driver who is barreling down on the wrong side of the road, and so we demand reasonable protection from the those who profit from the cars we buy. We do our best to protect our children by buckling them in, even if we have impeccable driving records.

Similarly, our children are exposed to media that we cannot reasonably be expected to control. Our kids go to other kids' houses, rent videos with no questions asked, and see R-rated movies on cable in the middle of the day. Although we may be absolutely responsible about what our children see, the fact is that few parents have absolute control over what their children are exposed to. Hillary Clinton and many others believe that "it takes a village" to raise a child. Economic pressures and job insecurity ensure that harried, overtaxed families have less time to spend with their children. Whether it takes a village or not, it certainly does take a whole lot of people concerned with child welfare to make sure that our children are reasonably protected.

Evidence tells us that the media bear some responsibility for this country's increase in violence and particularly for the glamorization of guns. Just as consumers have demanded that automobile manufacturers take some responsibility for the potential lethality of their product, so should we demand that those in the entertainment industry provide safeguards for their youngest consumers. We do not ask that cars be banned, despite their enormous contribution to premature death. Although it has become de rigueur for anyone suggesting restrictions to be called a censor, the fact is that few people are advocating censorship. Parents want, need, and are entitled to as much help and information as possible about the programs their children are watching.

There is no question that the media send moral messages to our children. The media are continuously telling stories that suggest what are "good" ways to lead one's life and what are "bad" ways, which choices are likely to be rewarded and which to fail. One of the main functions of art is to describe and illuminate the human condition. We are most drawn to experiences that not only recognize our struggles but also in some way point us toward solutions. I would assume that anyone who is reading this book is doing so in the hope of having suggestions or solutions revealed. The messages of the media, both obvious and often embedded, significantly affect how children come to understand right and wrong.

Extended families, which previously spread the hard task of child rearing among a group of adults, no longer live in the same house. Often they do not live in the same town or even the same state. Matriarchs, patriarchs, shamans, and religious leaders, all those previously charged with the responsibility of handing down a set of values from one generation to the next, never considered themselves "just entertainers." They understood the grave responsibility of their task, and if they were clever and entertaining in the telling of their tales, so much the better. Responsibility comes with power, and unlike Charles Barkley's "I am not a role model" commercial for Nike, people who were in positions of authority were expected to accept their responsibility.

As long as entertainment executives continue to ignore the scientific research that shows, clearly and unequivocally, that they are a major socializing force on American youth, we are unlikely to see much change in what our children are exposed to. Entertainment is "show *business*," not "show culture," "show art," or "show education." As one major network executive remarked to me, "My allegiance is to my corporation, my sponsors, my characters, and then to the children." This listing of priorities is not accidental. Television is a business, and its product is the audience it delivers to advertisers. Children, of necessity, are the last priority in a business that, as it is currently constituted, owes allegiance to corporate America, not to America's children. David Walsh, in his thought-provoking book *Selling Out America's Children*, argues that we are a country that has put profits before values, with disastrous effects.[1] Nowhere is this more evident than in the media. The point is not to put the entertainment industry out of business by insisting on commercially unattractive programming but to draw attention to the fact that there is an audience for commercial ventures that have a conscience as well as make money.

Overall, the media do a very poor job of representing the complex, diverse nature of various groups in this country. Most white suburban children who have little contact with black children see blacks typically depicted as either sports heroes or criminals. Alternatively, black children with little real-life experience with white children see a world of affluence and trivial concerns that is not representative of the lives of any group of children, regardless of race or gender. A study carried out by Children Now, a nonpartisan policy and advocacy organization, looked at the ways in which television depicts children. They found that only 10 percent of television shows featured children dealing with major social issues such as racism or safety, and a mere 2 percent featured children dealing with major family issues such as child abuse.[2] In a country where one child in three lives in a single-parent home and where murder is the leading cause of death of large segments of our youth population, the media are in a position to teach children more effective ways of coping with a host of social problems. Certainly, a major function of television is to entertain, but programs as varied as *Mister Rogers' Neighborhood, Party of Five*, and *My So-Called Life* and movies as diverse as *The Hunchback of Notre Dame, Breaking Away*, and *Hoop Dreams* have tackled difficult social and personal issues with great success. In the words of Walt Disney, it is possible "to educate entertainingly, and entertain educationally."[3]

The Children Now Conference at Stanford University in March 1995 was an important gathering of media executives, writers, academics, and child advocacy groups. There I had the opportunity to talk at length with Dick Wolf, who is currently the president of Wolf Films in association with Universal Television. Mr. Wolf began his television career writing for *Hill Street Blues*, which earned him an Emmy nomination. He has been the executive producer of several of our most popular television shows, including *Miami Vice, Law and Order, New York Undercover*, and *Players* (which elevates rap singer Ice-T, of "Cop Killer" fame, to prime time hero). He is a man at the top of his profession who was brave enough to face a rather hostile audience. I was determined to get his perspective on whether the media were fulfilling their moral obligations to this country's children. Mr. Wolf was generous with his time and cordial in answering my questions.

One of the comments that Mr. Wolf had made during his talk was that he did not allow his own children to watch many of the shows he produced. He said this without hesitation, and I was stunned that such an articulate person could miss the irony in his statement. If he didn't consider these shows appropriate for his own children, how did he feel about the fact that many children, for a variety of reasons, are regularly exposed to his programs? When we talked about this in some detail, Mr. Wolf took the position that parents are responsible for monitoring their child's activities. "I know this can make me sound like a jerk, but it's just not my responsibility."

Now I hardly believe that we should have twenty-four hours a day of *Barney & Friends* or *Mister Rogers' Neighborhood*. Certainly, I'm interested in having good quality programming for people at all ages. *Law and Order* is as good as it gets, a dramatic, responsible, well-written adult program. But Mr. Wolf's disowning of responsibility, the knee-jerk "tell parents to shut it off" response, bothered me. Television is ubiquitous and has been quite successful in circumventing parental disapproval. My four-year-old is not allowed to watch *Power Rangers*, but half his preschool class comes to school wearing various forms of licensed *Power Ranger* clothing. McDonald's features them on its place mats. The morning I began writing this chapter, I noticed them cavorting up the side of my Quaker oatmeal box. This is no simple matter of turning off the television and being done with the problem. The commercial enterprises associated with our most popular programming make it naïve to suggest that parental supervision is all that is required.

Mr. Wolf said, "My responsibility is to be an entertainer." He felt a great deal of accountability toward the sponsors of his program. He felt that his job is "to tell the truth" but felt no accountability toward the overarching problems of our society. Just as I was internally polishing my position that the captains of this industry are either profoundly dishonest about the impact of their work or singularly allergic to self-reflection, Mr. Wolf happened to mention that he had written the screenplays for two movies that he felt dealt with some of the moral questions I was raising. Neither movie was a particular financial success. One, *School Ties*, a movie about anti-semitism, was mentioned in Chapter Seven as an example of movie-making at its best—entertaining, reflective, socially conscious, and honest. My jaw dropped, and with some pleasure Mr. Wolf chided, "What are you going to do with that?"

What I did with "that" was to spend many weeks thinking. How was it possible that Mr. Wolf, who clearly could speak in a language that I found redeeming and valuable to youth, could also fail to acknowledge his unique responsibility for the images and stories shown to those same young people? It would be easier to come up with a group of damning quotes from executives who produce irresponsible programs. But over and over I heard from some of the producers whose work I had come to respect most—Dick Wolf from *Law and Order*, Charles Rosin from *Beverly Hills 90210*, and Greg Weisman from *Gargoyles*—that they were just trying to tell a good story.

My conversations with all these producers were revealing and instructional. I came to have a greater appreciation of the complexity of the industry and the competing demands on those who work in broadcasting. I easily fell into a trap when Mr. Wolf suggested that we block all violent images from the air between 3:00 and 6:00 P.M. Anticipating my approval, he pointed out that CNN only has a single transponder, meaning that it broadcasts simultaneously to the East and West Coasts, and therefore the blackout time would be six hours, not three. How could CNN possibly change the nature of its programming (which is largely devoted to world affairs with a heavy dose of violent images) for such a long period of time? Who would support the network for the services that are deemed so critical at other times—coverage of wars, disasters, and the like? As Mr. Wolf succinctly said, "Can we cut to the chase? There are no easy answers."

People who work in the entertainment industry have multiple allegiances: to their craft, their corporation, their conscience, their advertisers, and their audiences. Parents, however, have a simpler agenda: they want to protect their children from unhealthy influences. We want to make sure that our children don't believe that aggression is a useful way of settling interpersonal conflict. We want all the help we can get in educating our children about the responsibilities that go along with sexual activity and drug and alcohol use. We want our children to grow up to be good people. We care less about whether our children are entertained and more about their character, the choices they make in life, and most important, their safety.

As the statistics throughout this book make clear, there is a crisis going on in the United States, and violence is only one symptom of a deeper and more pervasive problem. We have become a country of many rights and few responsibilities. Parents charge the media with irresponsibility while the media charge back that parents are the ones who are being irresponsible.

In the following section I would like to offer suggestions for change that parents can make. In the final analysis, it is parents, not media executives, not Madison Avenue, and not corporate America, who are most concerned with the welfare of our children. The job of raising, protecting, and educating children has always been the family's. Obviously, the family has never functioned alone but is set within a larger context of both a particular social group and society at large.

We can effect change by working together, not by working at odds with each other. Even if we protect our children, monitor what they watch, and instill what we believe to be good values, they are still at substantial risk in a world that deifies affluence and glorifies violence. A stray bullet fired by a hopeless adolescent whose desire for a product outweighs his appreciation of life can find my child or yours. We are not only parents; we are also citizens of the world. This message is rarely shown on television, which focuses on individual achievement and personal happiness. It is a message we must fully appreciate ourselves before we can communicate it to our children.

SUGGESTIONS FOR PARENTS

It would be wonderful if parents could all march to Hollywood and demand better programming for their children. Galvanizing the entertainment industry would seem to be the most efficient way of making sweeping changes in the nature of children's television. However, it seems unlikely that we will be seeing "television violence can be hazardous to your health" warnings on our screens any time in the near future.

How can we encourage programming that meets the developmental needs of most children and is in accordance with most parents' values? Surveys show that despite the diversity of opinion in this country, there is actually a great deal of consensus on what "good values" are.[4] Loyalty, responsibility, family, integrity, and courage are all high on the list of values that parents say they want to see in their children. There are few who would quibble with these values. In 1992 top leaders of youth and education groups, under the guidance of the Josephson Institute, met to formulate a character-education program. They named six values that they believed to define good character. Called the Six Pillars of Character, they are trustworthiness, respect, responsibility, fairness, caring, and citizenship.[5] Parents, educators, youth leaders, and ethics scholars all pretty much agree on the character traits that produce good human beings and therefore a more vital and resilient society. How are we failing to communicate those values to our children? And how can we use the media to reinforce the values we consider important rather than supplant them with confusing and often antisocial messages?

The following list of suggestions, all supported by research as well as by common sense, is intended as a guide for parents who would like to lessen the negative effects and encourage the positive effects of media on their children.

Watch Television with Your Kids

Research studies have repeatedly shown that parents are not particularly interested in what their children watch. Less than half of all parents monitor their child's television viewing. The most frequent interventions parents make with regard to television are rules about how late their child can stay up and watch. Television, it seems, has become entrenched in the lives of children, and parents are reluctant to change that.

It is unrealistic to expect parents to watch everything their child watches. However, in order to take a stand about television viewing or movies, we have to see enough to have a leg to stand on. I suggest that parents spend a week or two getting an idea of what their children are watching. Are your children channel-surfing out of boredom? Is their viewing more selective? What kinds of selections are being made? A steady diet of situation comedies is not the same as a steady diet of adventure and action shows. And even within these genres there are substantial differences. Situation comedies are by far the most frequently watched programs by children of all ages. However, *Home Improvement* is a far cry from *Married . . . with Children*. Children need help discriminating between humor that entertains and teaches and humor that insults and humiliates.

Daytime talk shows have become a favorite with junior high school kids. Spend a couple of hours with Geraldo or Jerry or Ricki. What exactly are adolescents gaining from this procession of perversity? Do we want our children to be exposed, in remarkable detail, to the kinds of pathology usually reserved for a psychotherapist's office? How does the child or adolescent incorporate the parade of pathetically deficient adults portrayed on these programs with an optimistic worldview in which adults are capable and in charge?

What children watch depends on many factors, including age, gender, interest, and what's available. Unlike almost any other form of entertainment, television tends to be a nonselective ritual. Kids with spare time tend to turn it on, not to view a particular program, but to kill time. This is a particularly poor use of television because it encourages indiscriminate viewing.

Once parents are familiar with what their children are watching, at what times, and under what circumstances (boredom? relaxation? background noise?), they can develop a plan to help their child avoid the worst of what TV offers and enjoy the best.

Aside from arming us with information about what our kids see, watching with our children serves a number of well-documented aspects of child development.

Watching with Children Increases Comprehension. Several researchers studied children over a two-year period and found that when parents watch with their children, *and actively discuss and explain* what is seen, the youngsters' understanding of television content improves.[6] Parental involvement also improves children's judgment about reality and fantasy, increases prosocial behavior, and lessens the desire to watch television altogether. Their findings were particularly compelling for boys. This may be because girls' verbal abilities are evident earlier, and so they may need less explanation to understand the programs they watch.

Simply sitting in the same room with a child while she watches is not likely to be beneficial. Parents need to comment, explain, and interpret in an active process of interaction with their children. The media, and television in particular, pour into our homes and into the minds of our children. Without parents helping children sort out and understand the many messages that are delivered, children are vulnerable to misunderstanding much of what they see.

Watching with Children Decreases Stereotypical Thinking. The power of television to provide children with stereotypes is greatest when children have few other sources of information. Stereotypes, like aggression, are learned early and are difficult to correct.[7] When my nine-year-old son saw the movie *Dances with Wolves*, he was fascinated by hearing the language of the Sioux. "I never really thought about it. I guess I thought they just spoke English." The message most of us grew up with was that cowboys are good guys and Indians are bad guys. This movie was the first time that many children in this country had any exposure to a sympathetic but relatively unsentimental view of Native American life. Parents watching this movie with their children were given a tremendous opportunity to talk about the ways in which the media promote ideas about groups of people and how often these ideas are inaccurate. Movies like this can be a wonderful jumping-off place for discussions, for trips to the library or a museum, and for further reading on the subject.

Watching with Children Increases Prosocial Behavior. A number of studies have shown that watching television programs with prosocial messages increases cooperation, sensitivity, and caring among children. *Mister Rogers' Neighborhood* is a program that has been scrupulously studied by social scientists, who find that watching this program for as little as two weeks helps preschoolers be more cooperative, more nurturing, and better able to express their feelings.[8] It also helps children follow rules, stick with a task, and tolerate frustration. *Barney & Friends*, written by a team of early childhood educational specialists, has been shown to enhance not only cognitive development but emotional and social development as well.[9] With the show's attention to safety issues, *Barney* has enabled children as young as two to warn family members about house fires. Other studies have shown that even older children and adolescents are positively influenced by prosocial portrayals.[10]

Researchers have found that although kids tend to learn aggression by simply watching it, prosocial behavior is learned far more effectively when combined with additional reinforcements such as role-playing and discussion.[11] Rivers of ink have been used to write about the effects of media violence on children, but there has been barely a trickle of interest on the effects of prosocial television. This is unfortunate because several researchers have found that *prosocial portrayals have a potentially larger effect on children than antisocial portrayals.*[12]

Parents need to choose more prosocial programming and encourage their children to adopt the prosocial behaviors they see. As has been noted many times in this book, aggressive behavior is learned early, learned well, and is very resistant to change. Exposing children to prosocial programs, and helping them interpret what they see, is one way to diminish the enduring power of early aggressive television messages.

Shut It Off

A colleague of mine who researches children's reactions to traumatic news reports relates this telling story. She received a phone call from a woman, agitated and tearful. The sobbing woman said that she and her daughter were watching news coverage showing the recently found body of a murdered young girl. They tried switching channels, but the image of the young girl's body was everywhere. Her daughter was terribly upset, and the two of them were crying. What should she do? "Shut it off," my colleague said gently.

Television is not a permanent part of our environment. It comes by invitation into our homes and should be shut off when it is not serving a useful purpose.

Put Children on a Television Diet

Watch a few hours of children's television, either on Saturday morning or after school. Don't pay attention to the programs (an easy task), but do pay attention to the commercials. Strikingly, it seems that there are only two things that children buy. (Or more accurately, two things that children can nag their parents to buy for them.) One is toys, which have been discussed at length in Chapter Four. The second is sugar-coated cereal or some closely related type of junk food. According to children's commercials, American youth somehow subsist on a diet of Froot Loops, soda pop, bubble gum, Hostess cupcakes, and Cheetos. The connection between heavy viewing of television and obesity has been well documented.[13]

Dr. Milton Chen, a leading advocate for quality children's programming, suggests that one way to limit the amount of television that children watch is to put them on a television diet, modeled after a food diet. The analogy allows us to recognize that choosing what to watch is more complex than simply turning off the bad stuff and only watching good stuff. Diets make us aware that we have different kinds of needs. We eat for nutrition, but sometimes we eat for pleasure, and sometimes we eat for comfort.

Similarly, our children ought to be using television primarily to educate and inform. This doesn't mean watching only "educational TV" with its connotation of one too many animal specials; rather, it means watching programs that stimulate a child's thinking. There are many amusing, informative programs for kids to watch, and parents need to become familiar with them.

I was pleasantly surprised to find a half dozen remarkable new programs for my preschool son, many of them on PBS and Nickelodeon. *Mr. Rogers' Neighborhood* and *Sesame Street* are perennial favorites, as well they should be. Shows such as *Rugrats*, *The Magic School Bus*, *Reading Rainbow*, *Lambchop's Play-Along*, *Bear in the Big Blue House*, and *Wimzie's House* give young kids a wider choice of wholesome entertainment than ever before. For elementary school kids, there's *Beakman's World*, *Nick News*, *Carmen Sandiego*, *Animaniacs*, *Pepper Ann*, *Doug*, *Full House*, and *Family Matters*. Older kids and teens can be entertained and occasionally even educated by shows like *Home Improvement*, *Star Trek: Deep Space Nine*, *Beverly Hills 90210*, *The Secret World of Alex Mack*, *Dr. Quinn: Medicine Woman*, *Boy Meets World*, and *Party of Five*. This list is not exhaustive; it just points out that there are many good programs available to kids of all ages.

A couple of years ago my whole family was stuck in a miserable hotel during a rainstorm over Christmas vacation. The local theater was showing the movie *Dumb and Dumber*, and all five of us, aged four to forty-nine, went to see it. We all laughed a lot. Was this a great movie? Not at all, although being able to entertain such a diverse group of people is an impressive accomplishment. Mostly, seeing this movie was a kind of mindless adventure that was fun and pleasant for the whole family—a jelly doughnut for the mind. Sometimes kids (and adults) want to kick back, put their minds in neutral, and watch entertaining but uninspiring pap. We don't always want to read serious literature; there are times when *People* magazine hits the spot. An occasional candy bar is fine; a steady diet of junk food isn't. As parents, we don't hesitate to see that our children are eating properly; we need to be equally attentive to their media diet.

Teach Children to Watch with a Purpose

Television is a vehicle and a means to an end; it is not a way of life. Many children sit for hours on end, mindlessly channel-surfing their way through life, as opposed to living it. Children need to be taught that the television, just like every other appliance in the house, has a specific function. We do not leave the hair dryer on once our hair is dry or the toaster on once the toast has popped up. We recognize the specific uses of these appliances and know when to shut them off. Our kids need to be similarly educated about television.

One way to begin teaching this is to sit with our children and go over the programs they are interested in seeing. Look at *TV Guide* or your local television listings and make decisions about what your child's television week will look like. Some parents are quite successful at holding their children to a number of choices that they agree on. Others find that some accommodations and changes can be made over the course of the week. Either way, the exercise of sitting down together and making decisions about what will be watched teaches a very valuable lesson. It teaches children that television viewing is a directed activity. Allowing even young children to participate in this exercise makes it clear from the beginning of their relationship with television that *television is not a device that we passively allow to fill up dead space; rather, it is a source of entertainment and education that we actively pursue*. Parents need to help their children become consumers of media, making thoughtful and economical choices about programs that are of real interest to them. Often that means thinking about our own choices as well.

Many parents find it hard to keep their children to a set number of television shows. While this certainly can be accomplished, some parents may find it easier to dispense with the whole issue. When I found it hard to keep my youngest from watching too much, we spent endless hours negotiating. I became irritated and annoyed; he seemed to always whine for more. After following all of my own suggestions, with somewhat limited success, I realized that for this particular child, clear and nonnegotiable rules were going to be most effective. TV was banned during the week and available on weekends. After some significant initial complaining, he quickly adjusted to the routine, and I spared myself the daily squabble. Contrary to my expectations, after a few weeks he watched far less television on the weekends than previously as he became increasingly interested in other activities. Each child is different. Find a routine that works in your particular house. Stick with it.

Provide Other Cultural Opportunities

It is interesting but not surprising to note that one of the groups most negatively affected by heavy television viewing is economically advantaged children. Children from lower socioeconomic families benefit from the "window on the world" that television can sometimes provide. But children who watch a lot of television in spite of being economically advantaged tend to fall behind others in their peer group who spend time enjoying a range of cultural activities.

Television is one medium. Theater, opera, ballet, reading, and museums all provide other opportunities for kids to appreciate that the world offers many different forms of entertainment and enlightenment. Support the National Endowment for the Arts. If we sincerely want a better cultural environment, we will have to give our financial support to organizations that strive to expand our cultural opportunities. We pay for our children's toys, their clothes, and often their academic and spiritual educations; it is well worth a few dollars a year to pay for an improved cultural education as well.

All of my children were particularly fond of *Peter and the Wolf* when they were young. We went to *Peter and the Wolf* concerts, read *Peter and the Wolf* books, and even put on our own *Peter and the Wolf* dramas. It is this move from passive enjoyment to active imaginative play that is optimal for children. Each of my children, in his turn, constructed different wolves—sly ones, evil ones, greedy ones. Each relied on his particular personality and breadth of imagination to construct individual images. Play, which is the work of childhood, helps build the foundation for a lifetime of rich, flexible, and imaginative thinking.

Many youth organizations supply healthy and active alternatives to the television habit. Church or synagogue youth groups have traditionally provided a place for preteens and teens to spend time involved with each other as well as with community service projects. Similarly, organizations such as the YMCA offer a broad range of programs focusing on both individual development and social development. Outward Bound has provided over two hundred thousand teenagers with the opportunity to experience the outdoors in ways that are exciting and promote self-confidence and self-esteem. Participation in organizations such as these decreases your children's television viewing time and boredom; it also helps connect them to others with similar interests and to the community at large.

Hobbies and sports are important and healthy activities for children. My teenage son's television viewing was cut in half when he discovered the guitar. Life is not a spectator sport, and children should be encouraged to be active in things that interest them. Being involved with a child's particular hobby encourages family cohesion and shows that parents value participation rather than passivity.

Insist on Reading

Reading offers the mind unparalleled opportunities for expansion, diversion, and reflection. Study after study has shown that children who watch a great deal of television read less than their light-viewing counterparts.[14] Television does not displace all activities, but it tends to replace activities that have a similar purpose, such as entertainment, relief from boredom, and increasing knowledge. For example, we don't go to the movies instead of going to the bathroom, or instead of eating or sleeping, for that matter. But kids do watch television instead of playing or reading or drawing.

In *Amusing Ourselves to Death*, Neil Postman traces the rise of literacy in America and its decline due to mass electronic media in the twentieth century. From the title of his book, it is safe to assume that he does not see this as a change for the better. Postman notes that the founders of this country thought the idea of citizenship inconceivable without sophisticated literacy. He cites historians who have pointed out that although certain voting restrictions were "flexible," the ability to read was nonnegotiable. Literacy rates, which were quite high in colonial America, were one of the reasons the United States was able to rise to greatness. Being able to read means being able to use the mind in a manner that stresses objective, rational, and critical thinking.

Greater and greater technological advances do not *necessarily* mean greater understanding and advancement of the human condition. Children in particular need to slowly construct an understanding of the world based on experience and reflection. A father recently complained to me that when he took his fourteen-year-old son to San Francisco's Exploratorium, a hands-on multimedia learning environment, his son seemed interested only in things that "dazzled" him. Exhibits with flashing lights and loud music held his attention, while quieter and more complex exhibits were completely ignored. "If it's not as exciting as television, it just doesn't interest him," complained the father. I believe that this father had good reason to be concerned. Learning about life, whether through classroom academics, social interaction, or personal development, is a slow and demanding process. Children who sit back and say "entertain me" are bound to run into difficulty when they face the more rigorous tasks of learning that are always part of academic achievement. Reading, because it moves at a slower pace than almost all television programs, from *Sesame Street* to *Cops*, allows children to develop a more thoughtful, integrated, and personal style of learning.

Use Economic Power

In the media industry, one letter is generally acknowledged to represent the opinion of many thousands of people. Network executives say that short, reasoned letters are most likely to be taken seriously, and hastily written postcards or long ranting letters are typically ignored. Parents who want their voices heard by media executives must take the time to state their position forcefully and clearly. Huge corporations such as Johnson & Johnson, General Motors, and Ralston Purina have all canceled commercials when public pressure made these decisions financially inevitable. PepsiCo canceled a $5 million commercial featuring Madonna after her music video "Like a Prayer" (featuring burning crosses, sexual scenes with saints, and stigmata) offended large segments of the population.[15] A one-woman campaign by an angry Michigan mother who objected to the "blatant exploitation of women, sex and antifamily attitudes" on *Married . . . with Children* prompted Procter & Gamble, Kimberly-Clark, and McDonald's to cancel advertising on the top-rated Fox series.[16]

With a few exceptions, most notably PBS, the media are quite simply businesses. Television has only one product, and contrary to popular opinion, that product is not the shows that are produced; it is not even the products that are advertised. *Television's one product is you—the audience that is delivered to advertisers.* And it is at exactly this intersection, where the audience meets the advertiser, that parents are most likely to influence what is on television.

I have spent many hours interviewing network executives and can assure you that changes in programming will not come about because parents don't like violence; they will not come about because those in power feel a responsibility to use their power wisely. If the past thirty years of effort are at all predictive, changes will not come about through government regulation. Rather, any changes that come about in the entertainment industry will come about because someone's wallet was either fattened or flattened.

Be an Activist

Studies show that children grow up to be more like their parents than different from them. We teach our children how to live by the way we live our own lives. When I began researching this book, my children were less than thrilled with my "sticking my nose into other people's business." My teenage son perfected keeping just the right amount of distance between us, so that no one would suspect that we were related. I spoke with managers of fast-food restaurants, bookstores, toy stores, video stores, and record stores, asking questions, expressing concern, and frequently making known that I would not support an establishment that exploited the vulnerabilities of children. We walked out of places from McDonald's to Waldenbooks (both peddlers of Power Rangers), with my children alternately confused, amused, and embarrassed.

However, as my research proceeded, my two older children became increasingly interested in what I was so worked up about. My older son decided to do his yearlong social issues project on media violence and even tolerated my speaking to his high school assembly (no mean feat for a fifteen-year-old!). By the time he was seventeen, he decided that the controversy surrounding gangsta rap music would make an interesting and effective college essay. It is hard for our children not to be curious about those things that we are passionate about.

A week before I completed writing the first hardcover version of this book, my ten-year-old came home from a river rafting trip in Oregon. Jumping out of the car, he thrust a wrinkled McDonald's place mat in front of me. It was a picture of the six Power Rangers, each reciting a few disingenuous words of wisdom: "So find something you care about and make it happen!" "It takes time to be good at anything. Use the power of determination to see you through."

"I knew you'd hate this," said my son. Pointing to "With the power of education, you can think your way out of the toughest problems," he laughed and said, " 'and if that doesn't work, you can always kick some butt' is what they really mean." Crumpling the place mat, he threw it in the garbage can. "Not even little kids are that stupid," he added over his sunburned shoulder.

Involve your children as you become involved. Set a good example for them.

Petition Schools for Media Literacy Programs

Education serves many purposes, but first and foremost it provides children with the skills they will eventually need to deal with a large and complex world. We want our children to learn math, not only because it promotes a type of conceptual thinking but also because in the future they will have to add up grocery bills and balance checkbooks. We want our children to learn how to read not only because it will provide them with a lifetime of rich enjoyment but also because one day they will need to read a map, a medical report, or a mortgage contract.

It is incredible that, given the amount of time our children spend with electronic media, most schools do not have media literacy programs. Schools may bring their pupils to see powerful and historically important movies such as *Gandhi, Schindler's List,* or *Amistad,* but they tend to ignore the day-to-day influence of the media. This is a serious mistake. Parents who work at providing every educational advantage fail to realize that their children are being denied an essential part of their education when media literacy is not part of a school's curriculum.

Children who scream and cry for cheap plastic toys or demand the most nutritionally bankrupt cereal because it carries the name of their favorite superheroes are being conned by the most sophisticated propaganda machine the world has ever known—Madison Avenue. Girls who want to grow up to be as thin and pathetically dependent as the models they see on television and boys who think that physical prowess and intimidation are attractive and acceptable uses of power have all been exposed to repeated images that suggest that these are normal and desirable ways to live one's life.

Media literacy, by clarifying the ways in which the media exploit and manipulate their audience, helps children understand the nature of what they are seeing. This understanding makes them less susceptible to these manipulations. Critical viewing skills—the ability to understand and "read" the media—have become as necessary as knowing how to read a textbook. Former U.S. Commissioner of Education Ernest Boyer says, "It is no longer enough simply to read and write. Students must also become literate in the understanding of visual images. Our children must learn how to spot a stereotype, isolate a social cliché, and distinguish facts from propaganda, analysis from banter, and important news from coverage."[17]

Parents need to actively encourage schools to add media literacy courses and to make certain that the importance of the media is acknowledged by weaving it throughout the school's curriculum. Children love the opportunity to produce their own magazines, advertisements, and videos. This hands-on approach to media literacy helps guarantee that children will understand the behind-the-scenes reality of the media. It also encourages children to become active participants in the creation of media, so that perhaps in the future they will become producers of better media products.

Reestablish a Parent-Child Gradient

A parent-child gradient means that there is an inherent difference in authority and stature between children and adults. We may think of this gradient as a diagonal line with parents on the high end and children on the low end. This does not suggest that children are inferior to adults. However, by virtue of their age and experience, adults occupy a very different position in the hierarchy of the family than children do. Common sense tells us that a critical part of the job of parenting is for parents to maintain their position of authority and credibility. When a parent's legitimate authority is compromised or abandoned, families falter.

Most noticeable in my practice over the past eighteen years is the degree to which parental authority has been eroded. Many of us who were coming of age in the 1960s are now parents with children and often adolescents. Unfortunately, the 1960s zeitgeist of "do your own thing" has permeated our parenting. Families are not simply collections of people, each "doing their own thing." Family members are by necessity interdependent, and the family functions most effectively when there is a division of labor. Out of the 1960s came the recognition that this division of labor did not necessarily mean that Mom always washed the dishes and Dad always mowed the lawn. Although there has been some positive change and an increased flexibility in our thinking about the roles of mothers and fathers, there has also been some confusion about how to best apply these newly formulated definitions. While I strongly support the lessening of sex-role stereotypes, I also think that parents need to remember that their fundamental role as parent does not change, whether they are drying dishes or mowing the lawn.

In my office, I have witnessed countless discussions between a parent and a child that were conducted as if they were two adults. Negotiations worthy of our largest corporations have been carried out about everything from bedtime to allowance to household responsibilities. At times it has been hard to know who is the parent and who is the child.

We do our children a great disservice when we refuse to accept the authority of parenthood. If you don't like a program and think it is harmful or inappropriate for your child, then it is necessary for you to enforce your decisions, particularly if your child is young. All of us are often tired, stressed, and easily induced to take the path of least resistance. But when parents are uninvolved, children are frequently exposed to things they are ill-equipped to handle. *Ultimately, parental disengagement leads to a lessening of parental authority that invites our children into increasingly dangerous situations.*

The effects of the media on children are not small, and they are not incidental. We must approach decisions about our children's media viewing with the same deliberateness and seriousness we use when making decisions about other aspects of our child's well-being. We need to be as much a parent when we are deciding whether or not our four-year-old should be watching *Mortal Kombat* or our twelve-year-old should be watching *Scream* as when we are deciding whether jelly doughnuts are acceptable breakfast food or whether alcohol is a permissible beverage at our teenager's party.

Although this last suggestion about reestablishing a parent-child gradient is not particular to children and media, it is a crucial element in making all of the preceding suggestions viable. Parents need to maintain and in many cases reestablish their authority within the family. We are fooling ourselves if we think that muttering about the violence on *Power Rangers*, while allowing our children to parade around in Power Rangers T-shirts or eat Power Rangers–"endorsed" cereals, has a dampening effect on our child's enthusiasm for the program. There is no point in suggesting that the television be shut off if your teenager's response is "to hell with you." Parents need to regain their stature by providing clear, appropriate, and forceful guidelines for their children.

PARENTS' TO-DO LIST

- Watch TV with your kids. It increases comprehension, decreases stereotypical thinking, and increases prosocial behavior.

- Agree on a set number of hours or programs. After that, shut it off!

- Teach children to watch with a purpose. No channel-surfing!

- Not everything has to be "educational." Make sure your kids get to laugh. Make sure also that they are not laughing at the wrong things.

- Expose your children to other cultural opportunities, such as museums, the theater, and libraries.

- Insist that your children read, read, read.

- Remember, until your children leave home, you pay the bills and therefore you are the boss. You also get to decide on television rules. Use your authority wisely.

- Encourage your schools to offer media literacy. You wouldn't allow your child to be cheated out of learning about a revolution in math or science. You shouldn't allow them to be cheated out of learning about the communications revolution.

- Let your wallet speak. Support shows and advertisers who do good things. Boycott those who don't.

- Be an activist. Let your kids see you stand up for your beliefs. Walk out of a movie or store that offends you. Demand your money back.

10

Suggestions for Schools, Media, and Government

Contrary to popular opinion, television is not a window on the world. No form of mass media—commercials, newspapers, or movies—can present us with objective reality. Television shows, whether they are *National Geographic* documentaries or *Star Trek* reruns, are not reality. All media presentations have an agenda, and they construct a particular kind of reality, which is too often seen and accepted as real because it is so seamlessly authentic-looking. It is the job of media educators to teach our children that when it comes to the media, *what you see is not necessarily what you get.*

Children are immersed in television, movies, computers, and video games. They spend the single most significant block of time of their lives involved with media. Astounding as the statistics in this book are—that the average American child watches television three to four hours a day, that the average American household has the television on some seven hours a day—these numbers are still a gross underestimation of how involved children are with the media. My teenage son can read the sports section of our local paper with the TV on in the background and his latest musical obsession blasting from his room. He is logging time with three different types of media, with his attention drifting between them. This is not an unusual use of media. How often do we read a book or magazine, looking up for the opening stories of the evening news and maybe again for the weather? It is hard to believe that television is such a large part of our lives, and yet we remain so totally ignorant of its agenda.

Unfortunately, media studies have remained on the periphery of education in this country. This is a bizarre anomaly, considering that the media are the primary source of information for many people. For example, young adults say that the media are their main source of information about political matters. Our children are growing up in a world that is dominated by images, and yet they have absolutely no skills for understanding the meaning of those images in their lives. The power of the media rests on the fact that it can make things seem real, inevitable, and necessary. The media select their material, deliver a specific set of values, and are beholden to particular interests. Often what they don't show us is just as important as what they do show.

Without understanding these basic facts about the media, children and adolescents (adults too) are susceptible to a subtle process of indoctrination. Aside from the most obvious issues of promoting aggression, incivility, consumerism, and stereotypes, an uncritical reading of the media can have disastrous effects on our democratic processes. Already, political candidates are being merchandised much like breakfast cereals and laundry detergents. Ideologies are no longer the basis on which political candidates are elected; rather, the sound bite, the negative campaign, and the political spot drive an election. Neil Postman points out that Abraham Lincoln could have walked down the street virtually unnoticed.[1] He was known and judged by his ideas. But political images are far stronger and last longer than what little we know about our politicians' thinking: Gerald Ford tripping, Michael Dukakis looking ridiculous in a tank and hard hat, George Bush fainting at a state dinner in Japan. Repeated images such as these speak to our children with an immediacy and impact that print often lacks. More and more of our children's knowledge about the world will be derived from images rather than from print.

SCHOOLS AND MEDIA LITERACY

Why have schools been so reluctant to incorporate media literacy training into their curriculum? As a former teacher, I think that one of the things teachers like to believe is that they are the guardians of a higher culture than *Roseanne* or *Married . . . with Children*. There is an attitude that only "important" programs are worthy of class time, such as a Bill Moyers special or a BBC play. Many teachers would consider spending time on *Cops* or Arnold Schwarzenegger's latest movie a trivial use of class time. However, whether educators like it or not, children spend hours on end watching television and movies that are only partly understood. Schools are charged with educating our children and have the responsibility of preparing children to understand the world around them. A significant part of that world now includes various forms of electronic media.

Media literacy is not so much about content as it is about developing skills for decoding the messages that the media deliver. One could ask the same questions of *Married . . . with Children*, *Sesame Street*, *Face/Off*, or *Titanic:* "Why is this pleasurable?" "What are the implicit values?" "How is it marketed?" "Whose interests are being served?" "What information is being left out?" Media literacy is not simply about saying *Married . . . with Children* is bad and *Sesame Street* is good. It is about providing children with the tools they will need, in all subject areas and throughout their lives, to be able to understand the implicit as well as explicit agendas of the media.

I do not mean to suggest that the media, by definition, are evil and manipulative. Any medium must have a point of view. There is no way that we can reproduce reality because no two people see the world exactly alike. Even a photograph, the closest thing we can imagine to capturing reality, is influenced by an untold number of decisions that the photographer makes—the lighting, camera angle, and distance all convey a particular vision of what is being seen. The erotic lilies of Robert Mapplethorpe and the desolate tulips of Andre Kertesz hardly seem to exist in the same world. To say that each man photographed flowers is of course true but says nothing about the meanings they each saw and presented to their audience. Adults typically understand that they are being shown a particular version of reality; children, however, accept media at face value. Their experience with the world is limited, and as a result they have very little to compare to television or movie portrayals.

My father was a policeman, one of the most commonly depicted professions on television. He and I would watch police dramas, always looking out for mistakes and obvious distortions. My father would point out that much of police work was monotonous and routine, and he couldn't imagine anyone having the stamina to keep up with so many criminals. He was very proud of the fact that in twenty years on the police force, he had never once drawn his gun. So I suppose I learned early on that television policemen and real policemen had very little in common other than a predilection for coffee and doughnuts. With kids spending more and more time with the media and less time with competing sources of information, it becomes increasingly important that they understand to what extent the media are constructing rather than reflecting social reality.

We are at a point of tremendous social unease in our country. Increasingly, we find third world conditions existing within the United States. Poverty continues to increase and to affect a disproportionate number of African Americans, Hispanic Americans, and Native Americans. Even those who enjoy relative affluence find that their family structures have been disrupted. Economic necessity has forced many people to move from their homes in order to find jobs in other parts of the country, and many families are far removed geographically from where they were born. Our society has become fragmented. The institutions that have traditionally held families together—marriage, religion, patriotism—are weak at best. This leads to diffusion of responsibility for the society, fragmentation for the family, and isolation for the individual.

Television has enormous power to shape our views about other groups of people. For a long time, African Americans on television

were either athletic superstars or thugs. A series of situation comedies expanded that repertoire, but it wasn't until 1995 that *Under
One Roof*, the first dramatic series about African American families,
was briefly aired. Many white children in the United States have
very limited contact with black children. Although most of their
understanding derives from their families and from the mores of
their community, a great deal is also learned through the media.
The short-lived *All-American Girl*, about a Korean family, was the
first glimpse, for many children, of the similarities and differences
to be found in Asian culture. The potential of the media to explore
rather than exploit the experience of other cultures is deplorably
underutilized. Programs such as *Sesame Street*, with their emphasis
on multiculturalism, have taught several generations more than just
their ABCs. More important, they have taught that children everywhere are pretty much the same.

Media literacy teaches children that television constructs a version of social reality. Watching American television, an uninformed
observer would have to conclude that the majority of people in this
country are white men who rarely work but are always busy, that
women rarely live past the age of sixty-five, that almost everyone in
this country enjoys a high level of affluence, and that children
struggle with only the most trivial of problems. All of this is obviously false, but false with a purpose.

Television is not about raising social consciousness or even representing a more or less accurate view of reality. It is about selling
people to advertisers. What we see on television reflects successful
marketing techniques, not reality. We see lots of men, since men
hold more power and are seen as more authoritative; we see young,
beautiful women, since erotic feelings make us euphoric; and we see
people who are struggling with either outlandishly difficult or trivial
problems lest we be reminded of our own real life problems. Television encourages us not to think but to want. Everything about
television is constructed to optimize our willingness to spend money.

It is imperative that children and adolescents understand these
concepts. Media literacy teaches children that nothing the enter-

tainment industry produces is an unproblematic reflection of external reality. Media need to be "read" and analyzed in order to be understood. Children who acquire the skills to do this are at a great advantage. It means, for example, that adolescent girls can begin to understand that thinness or youth as an ideal is an arbitrary construction brought to them by a system that would like to see women spending lots of money on "improving" their appearance. Fully understanding this might help the young women of this country be more interested in improving their skills and their character as opposed to eradicating their cellulite. At every level of development, children can be taught skills for interpreting and understanding the media.

The schools have a wonderful opportunity to encourage children to become active participants in understanding how the media are constructed. Classes that allow children the opportunity to create their own media teach the importance, responsibility, and excitement of becoming producers as well as consumers.

WHAT THE MEDIA CAN DO

There are many things that the media can do to provide our children with a healthier and saner cultural environment. But I suspect that there will be few changes until the people in positions of power in the media are able to confront the dilemma that they face. On the one hand, the networks are charged to "serve the public interest, convenience, and necessity"; on the other hand, they are in business only as long as they deliver a demographically desirable audience to their advertisers and profits to their stockholders. This dual mandate, serving the interests of the public and the interests of corporate America, sometimes works smoothly but often engenders a conflict of interest. When there is a conflict, the American public tends to lose. We are talking show *business*.

I think that the media have the potential to do many wonderful things. In the meantime, however, I think that they do a lot of bad things. They perpetuate stereotypes and racism. They present limited options for girls while glorifying unacceptably violent options for boys. They make children fearful, pessimistic, and aggressive. Do I think that the people who produce these programs are bad people? It's a difficult question because, at heart, I believe that we cannot separate our values from the ways in which we lead our lives. So every writer, director, and producer has made choices about what to create and what not to create. I would say that they have made some very poor choices. As a result of making poor choices, they find themselves in the position of having to justify what they do.

People in the entertainment industry know full well that what they produce is not "just entertainment" in the dismissive sense of having no enduring value. Children do not watch television once a week or even one hour a day. Aside from sleep, children spend more time watching television than participating in any other activity, including school. Although I believe I have made it clear in this book that a parent's responsibility is to be his child's first line of defense, this does not suggest that the entertainment industry is without responsibility.

Recently, Secretary of Education Richard Riley appealed to Hollywood to "stop glamorizing assassins and killers. I urge you to see this issue through the eyes of parents instead of script writers, . . . through the eyes of teachers instead of advertisers."[2] Given the system of financing the media in this country, it is not likely that the entertainment industry can afford to stop looking through the eyes of advertisers. Media are businesses, and the sooner that fact is fully accepted, the sooner we can get to work on how to make entertainment that is both good for children and good for business. The two are not incompatible. Forrest Gump grossed $300 million, whereas the latest Nightmare on Elm Street brought in $18 million. From 1984 to 1993, R-rated movies grossed, on average, $10 million less than PG-rated films.[3] The Nielsen ratings illustrate that violence is not what the people want; of the top ten programs on a recent Nielsen rating report, not one is violent. Situation comedies such as *Home Improvement* and *Seinfeld* consistently score higher than violence-laden fare.

The realization that responsible programming could also be commercially successful is vividly illustrated by Sheryl Leach, the creator of *Barney & Friends*. A mother and teacher, she was disappointed by what television offered her young son. "I thought I could build a better mousetrap." And so Ms. Leach went about creating one of the most successful television programs for young children in broadcast history. "I knew about kids, about teaching, and about marketing. The only thing I didn't know anything about was video and television, but I figured I could learn." Recognized with the Socially Responsible Entrepreneur of the Year award in 1995, Ms. Leach considers one of her greatest accomplishments to be proving that television "doesn't have to be violent to be successful in the marketplace."[4]

By bringing issues such as spousal abuse, rape, incest, AIDS, and cancer to the public's notice, the media have been able to provide much-needed information. They have also provided models of healthy and appropriate responses to these problems. Calls to battered women's shelters rise substantially after shows depicting spousal abuse. Doctors report increased interest in mammography following breast cancer specials. The media is playing a significant role in helping reduce the number of Americans who smoke. Similarly, there has been a decrease in the rate of automobile deaths. While many factors contribute to this, such as improved auto safety and stricter drunk driving sanctions, the media's "designated driver" program is acknowledged to have played a role.

Though the media have willingly taken on the responsibility of tackling some of this country's most disturbing problems, they have steadfastly refused to acknowledge their own role in the creation of social problems. The media expect to be congratulated for occasional public service announcements, which are assumed to influence people's behavior, while at the same time denying the impact of incessant violent messages. In a moment of unbridled honesty,

Ted Turner of the Turner Broadcasting System said before a congressional subcommittee hearing on media violence, technology, and parental empowerment: "They [network executives] are guilty of murder as far as I can see. We all are. Me too."[5]

So how is it that bright, creative people insist that "violence is what sells," "we're just giving them what they want," or "my only job is to entertain"? In psychology there is the concept of *cognitive dissonance*. This powerful phenomenon, which has been well studied, shows that when a gap exists between what people believe and how they act, they fill in this gap by rationalizing their behavior. We all experience cognitive dissonance in everyday life. We're on a diet and have just eaten half a box of cookies—it doesn't matter because they were "low-fat." We get home and find that the department store sales clerk has given us an extra ten dollars in change, but we don't go back to the store because "it's a huge company and it doesn't make any difference." People work hard at coming up with rationalizations to legitimize their questionable behavior.

I believe that many people who work in the entertainment industry are exhibiting cognitive dissonance. Making movies that are sensational and gratuitously violent is hard to justify. An "artist" can hardly feel that he has contributed something worthwhile to the world after spending thousands of dollars to make a woman's decapitation appear real. Most of the people I spoke with in the entertainment industry have children of their own. When the kids ask, "Daddy, what did you do today?" do they respond, "Oh, I filmed a young girl being mutilated—my job was to make it look as realistic as possible"? This is the dilemma faced by people who often find themselves working on projects that have little redeeming value.

I believe that many people in the media live with themselves by simply denying the negative impact of their work. On a PBS *Frontline* special on the effects of media violence on children, George Vradenberg, executive vice president of Fox said, "Well, I tend to think that the studies have received really too much attention."[6] Can you imagine this point of view coming from an equally powerful figure in another field affecting our children? "We know that children are safer when they use car seats, but let's not pay so much attention to the studies." Or perhaps the Surgeon General saying, "We know teenage girls' rising cigarette consumption increases their risk of cancer, but let's just forget about all that scientific stuff." Mr. Vradenberg, like everyone else in influential positions in the entertainment industry, is well aware that there is a large, consistent, and damning body of evidence that says that watching a lot of violence makes children aggressive and fearful. My intention is not to single out Mr. Vradenberg for condemnation but simply to suggest that one must go through astounding psychological contortions to justify things that are unjustifiable.

I would like to suggest that the media demand a higher level of honesty from themselves. To all media executives who disingenuously insist that the media do not create attitudes and behaviors, please consider that the magnitude of advertising budgets speaks volumes about the power of the media to influence viewers' choices. The United States' largest corporations would not likely spend millions of dollars on advertising if they did not have overwhelming evidence that media messages can in fact alter attitudes and behaviors. To continue this debate only distracts from the real issue of what exactly is being sold and whose interests are being served.

At a recent conference I attended, a question was asked about why the immensely popular *Power Rangers* chose to highlight racial and gender stereotypes by casting an African American youth as the Black Power Ranger, an Asian youth as the Yellow Power Ranger, and a girl as the Pink Power Ranger.[7] Incredibly, the answer from Saban Entertainment executives was that the original drawings from Japan had a pink skirted costume, so the Pink Ranger had to be a girl. Although original footage from Japan was used early in the series, Saban could undoubtedly have afforded to change the costumes. It is infuriating when media executives treat parents who are genuinely concerned for their children's welfare with contempt. A real dialogue is possible only when the participants—be they parents, politicians, academics, advertisers, studio heads, or writers—are honest and forthcoming about their motivations and the demands placed on them.

Similarly, advertisers need to be forthright about the products they are peddling. Parents depend on the rating system and on well-known reviewers to provide some small measure of information about the movies and programs that their children see. Not even the most conscientious parent can preview all media offerings for their children. Deluding the public with false and misleading advertising is irresponsible and unethical. My adolescent son brought me enough positive advertising copy to convince me that he and I would enjoy seeing *Scream 2* despite its R rating. "One hell of a fun movie!" raved *Newsweek*. "It's a scream! A really fun movie done with great humor!" enthused *Good Morning America*. Even Siskel and Ebert gave it two thumbs up. "Fun, fun, fun!" insisted review after review. I thought we were going to see a cross between Bela Lugosi and Jim Carrey. Instead what we were treated to was over two hours of carnage and mutilation with just enough hip (and irrelevant) witticisms to occasionally obscure the fact that people were being stabbed through the head, crucified and shot, and slashed beyond recognition.

It is important to acknowledge that groups of people involved in the dialogue about children and the media have very different agendas. Parents have the greatest interest in the welfare of their children, but they may have other pressures as well, such as fitting in with community standards. Politicians need to be reelected, and academics need tenure. Studio heads need to keep advertisers happy, and advertisers need to sell their products. This doesn't mean that politicians or professors or those in the entertainment industry are unconcerned with children. Most of the people I met in the course of writing this book had a genuine interest and concern for the welfare of children. But it is naïve to assume that people aren't interested in keeping their jobs and paying their mortgages. The question for people in the media, and for our society as a whole, is how to encourage decisions that are moral as well as profitable.

We can learn a lesson from the ways other countries have expanded the pool of educational television available to children. France has a 3 percent tax on theater admission and a 2 percent tax on videotapes. These taxes go into a special fund that is made available to independent producers and helps provide breadth to the ideas and visions translated onto the screen. Such a system ensures that important, although not necessarily commercial, ventures can become part of a nation's cultural offerings. This modest redistribution of capital helps lessen the tremendous amount of centralized power that a handful of top media executives hold.

Finally, we must support the Public Broadcasting Service. Although politicians have chosen to make PBS a political football, it is one of our most valuable institutions. It assures us that some small corner of the media is safe from the demands of capitalism and is free to focus on the needs of the children it so richly serves. Ridiculous statements such as Newt Gingrich's "PBS is a playground for the rich" deserve comment only because his pronouncements carry weight. In fact, PBS is used by all children; its benefits to children of lower socioeconomic status are particularly notable, since these children have far fewer cultural opportunities than children from more financially comfortable homes.

I don't know how much of PBS's children's programming Mr. Gingrich has actually watched; I can only speculate. But after watching LeVar Burton's multicultural push for literacy on *Reading Rainbow* or Bill Nye's frenetic love affair with science on *Bill Nye the Science Guy*, I am hard pressed to figure out how Mr. Gingrich arrived at his conclusions. PBS is a national treasure, and it is nothing but classism that says that opera or theater or ballet is only the province of the rich. America's spending on public broadcasting is laughable compared to spending in other countries. In 1991 federal spending for public broadcasting in the United States was about $1 per person. By comparison, Japan spends $17, Canada spends $32, and Great Britain spends $38 per person. If we don't consider it worthwhile to foster a cultural environment that elevates our children, we may find ourselves with a cultural environment very much at odds with our values.

My invitation to the media is to work in collaboration with parents and experts on child development in order to ensure a healthier and more balanced presentation to our children. Several studies conclude that children are even more affected by prosocial messages than by antisocial messages. With all of the interest in media and violence, this compelling finding is often overlooked. A particularly useful suggestion for using the media's power to communicate positive messages comes from Professor Bernard Friedlander. He proposes "a major, long-term, highly sophisticated professional media campaign to promote many themes and actions that have the single purpose of protecting and being decent to children."[8] Just as Smokey the Bear raised consciousness about forest fires, Dr. Friedlander urges the media to help raise our national consciousness about the value and vulnerability of our children.

It is unrealistic and unnecessary to suggest that all violence be dispensed with, although I cannot see any particular reason for gratuitous violence. Movies like *Seven Years in Tibet* and television programs like *Law and Order* show that action and conflict, and even violence, can be portrayed without being irrelevant or gratuitous. The astronomical earnings of movies like *The Lion King* and *Forrest Gump* demonstrate that Americans are hungry for movies with a minimum of deaths, shootings, spectacular fires, explosions, and electrocutions. We want to know more about the human condition and how to deal with adversity. We are tired of being shell-shocked.

WHAT THE GOVERNMENT CAN DO

When I first began writing this book, I went to visit Ephraim Margolin, a constitutional and criminal attorney in San Francisco. He is well known as a man of principle and intellect and over the years has handled many First Amendment cases. At that time I was feeling so disgusted with what my children were watching that I asked what kinds of government restrictions a parent might hope for. Mr. Margolin shook his head and knitted his eyebrows in that kind of bemused gesture parents often use when their children ask questions that are off the mark. "Why in the world would you want the government involved in this? Are you looking to attack the problem in the most ineffective way possible?" he asked. At the time I was disappointed because I was not given a blueprint for government regulation. Years later, I understand the wisdom of Mr. Margolin's advice.

Since the earliest days of television, the government has threatened censorship, regulation, and interference. Reams of memos, hundreds of committee meetings, and thousands of political pronouncements have produced minimal results. Every ten years or so the government decides that "something must be done" about television and puts the networks on notice that if they don't clean up their act, they will have it cleaned up for them. This briefly changes the amount of violence in programming, which within months returns to its former level or surpasses it.

We have recently witnessed a particularly vigorous round of politicians' objections to the media. In 1990 former Senator Paul Simon authored the Television Violence Act, which allowed the major networks three years in which to show efforts at self-regulating the amount of violence on television. As the deadline approached with little apparent progress, Attorney General Janet Reno threatened that without further steps, "government action would be imperative." In January 1994, some two months after the expiration of the Television Violence Act, Senator Simon announced that he had reached an agreement with cable and broadcast networks on an "independent monitoring plan." "Independent" is an interesting choice of words, as the monitoring agencies were chosen and paid for by the cable industry.

However much politicians and parents demand changes in programming, networks have found ways to sabotage intentions and even legislation. The Children's Television Act of 1990, authored by Representative Edward J. Markey, mandated the networks to "serve the educational and informational needs of children." Unfortunately, the legislation did not specify how much programming was necessary to carry out this mandate, and "educational and informational" was only vaguely defined. The major networks initially increased the amount of educational programming, but the amount remained less than three hours a week, and claims for "educational content" soon became absurd. To understand the shameless lack of honesty of some network executives, one has only to look at the list of programs that were proffered as educational: *The Flintstones, The Jetsons*, and *G.I. Joe*, among others. Lynn McReynolds, a spokesperson for the National Association of Broadcasters, unabashedly said, "We don't like quotas period, which would make the government a judge of what shows are educational."[9] If McReynolds doesn't want government interference (a reasonable objection), then I suggest that broadcasters not offer *G.I. Joe* as an example of educational programming.

In response to parents' outrage over the corruption of the Children's Television Act, the Federal Communications Commission (FCC) moved to tighten regulations. The FCC mandated the major networks to show a minimum of three hours of children's educational and informational television programming per week. The three-hour minimum assures the networks of automatic reissuance of their licenses. Strangely, network licenses, which previously had been granted for three to five years, are now granted for eight, as if less, rather than more, scrutiny is in order. Although three hours per week is an anemic requirement, it does force the networks to acknowledge that children are a "special audience" in need of protection. The networks have attempted to comply with these requirements, and so we are seeing an improvement in children's programming. After all, three hours of decent programming does mean that there is three hours' less junk. However, the networks still have a long way to go in their understanding of what constitutes education for children. As this book goes to press, both *Sports Illustrated for Kids* and *101 Dalmatians* have been offered as educational programming. Both are reasonably good programs. Recreational? Yes. Educational? Give me a break!

Representative Markey's "V-chip" remains one of the most interesting ideas about how to protect children without introducing government regulation into network decisions. His bill became law when it was added as an amendment to the Telecommunications Act of 1996. The bill requires that the V-chip be installed in all new televisions with screens measuring over thirteen inches. Entrepreneurs are also preparing to market the V-chip as an add-on to existing sets. This chip would allow parents to screen out programs that contain violent or sexual materials unsuitable for their youngsters. On the surface, it's hard to imagine much objection to this plan. It's voluntary and, with an appropriate rating system, would simply give parents more control over what their children are viewing. Not surprisingly, the networks opposed the V-chip.

We should be suspect of the motives of individuals who oppose parents' obtaining more information and exerting legitimate control over their children's viewing. Fox executive Lucy Slahany is unaccountably frightened by the prospect of parental control. "Quite frankly, the very idea of a V-chip scares me."[10] Jack Valenti, president of the Motion Picture Association of America, also opposes the V-chip and has put forth the excuse that parents should be making decisions on violence on a case-by-case basis. "I'm opposed to indictment without appraisal. Parental discretion means it ought to be done individually."[11] In fact, networks who oppose the V-chip do so because they fear that parents may "indiscriminately" program out all violent shows for their children. Since violence represents a significant portion of programming, the potential of lost revenues to sponsors is great. Newton Minow, former FCC commissioner, recognizes that "the real fear is that the V-chip will chip into revenues."[12]

The V-chip became law in February 1996. The networks, which had threatened to challenge the constitutionality of the V-chip, instead did a 180-degree turnaround (with some encouragement from the White House) and volunteered to create the rating system that would accompany the V-chip. After all, the V-chip is only as effective as its rating system, because it is the rating system that supplies information about what exactly parents might find inappropriate for their children. From this information, parents then decide whether to program the V-chip to block out certain programs. Having the entertainment industry produce the rating system is, in the apt phrasing of George Gerbner, like having the fox guard the chicken coop.

The entertainment industry, led by Jack Valenti, insisted on using the same sort of rating system as the movie rating system, a system based solely on the age of the viewer, with no information on content. Television ratings were designated as PG, PG-13, and M. Parents were justifiably angered by this indifference to their concerns. In poll after poll, parents insisted on a rating system that indicated the content of the program, not simply some television executive's view of how old the viewer should be. I, like most parents, feel very differently about movies and programs that are blood-baths, those that have love scenes, and those with bad language. Within each of these categories, I need even more information to make my decision. Is the love scene grounded in emotional connection and shown sensitively, or is nudity used for shock value and exploitation? Is the violence shown in a context and with appropriate consequences, or is it gratuitous and consequence-free?

The entertainment industry was immovable, insisting that neither governmental nor parental pressure would influence its rating system. Mr. Valenti introduced his discredited system in late 1996. Parental opposition was intense, and in the end, the industry was forced to concede to the demands of parents—sort of. Though the industry was willing to provide reasonably inclusive content ratings for adult programming—V (for violence), S (for sex), L (for adult language), and D (for suggestive dialogue)—it was willing to provide only limited ratings for children's programming. Children's programs could carry one of only three possible ratings: TV-Y (programs suitable for all youngsters), TV-Y7 (programs suitable for youngsters aged seven and older), and TV-Y7-FV (programs for children seven and older that portray fantasy violence). As always, the industry's concessions to common sense carried a stiff price. In exchange for the content-based ratings, key members of Congress agreed, for the time being, not to press for any new legislation regulating the networks.

Despite this rather long description of the progress made in getting parents the most basic information about what their children are watching, in the end a network cannot be denied a license because of noncompliance with the rating system. Both NBC and Black Entertainment Television on cable have refused to participate in the rating system at all. Although the V-chip is law, the rating system is voluntary. Such shenanigans should try the patience of us all. Bob Wright, head of NBC, has said that no one cares about the rating system. Have a spare minute? Look in the back of this book for NBC's address or contact your local affiliate and let NBC know that we do care. Networks that refuse to be parent-friendly will not have the support of friendly parents.

In the end, I don't believe that government or technology will solve this problem for us. Although this book has at times drawn a rather dark picture in broad strokes, the fact is that there are many bright spots on television. Television can teach tolerance and cooperation. It can reduce prejudice and increase helpful behavior. It can introduce children to different people, cultures, and ideas. The media can be used to develop community, to reinforce the values of honesty and integrity, and to educate children to be citizens of the world. As I have pointed out several times, the media do not "just tell stories." They are tied into a larger agenda that includes cultivating opinions and attitudes that facilitate aggression, consumerism, and a nonreflective reading of our environment. Nevertheless, it is not the responsibility of the media to raise morally healthy children. Certainly the media should contribute to this goal, but in the final analysis, the development of a child's conscience is the responsibility of parents.

Each one of us—parents, educators, child professionals, and media executives—makes decisions every day that affect the well-being of America's children. It is tempting for parents to point fingers at network executives, network executives to point fingers at advertisers, and advertisers to point fingers back at parents. Bathing our children in violence and stereotypes in order to sell products degrades us all. Levels of aggression and incivility rise as our children become increasingly insensitive and intolerant. A country that is willing to sacrifice its children's welfare for the pursuit of money is bound to unravel. Ultimately, it is the responsibility of each and every one of us to insist that the welfare of our children come before profits.

Resource Directory

NATIONAL TELEVISION NETWORKS

ABC, Inc.
2040 Avenue of the Stars
Los Angeles, CA 90067
Telephone: (310) 557-6655
Web site: www.abc.com

CBS Entertainment
7800 Beverly Boulevard
Los Angeles, CA 90036
Telephone: (213) 460-3000
Fax: (213) 653-8266
Web site: www.channel2000.com

Fox Broadcasting Company
P. O. Box 900
Beverly Hills, CA 90213
Telephone: (310) 369-1000
Web site: www.fox.com

NBC Entertainment
3000 West Alameda
Burbank, CA 91523

Telephone: (818) 840-4404
Web site: www.nbc.com

Public Broadcasting Service
1320 Braddock Place
Alexandria, VA 22314
Telephone: (703) 739-5040
Fax: (703) 739-5295
Web site: www.pbs.org

Turner Broadcasting System
1 CNN Center
Atlanta, GA 30303
Telephone: (404) 885-4291
Web site: www.turner.com

GOVERNMENT AGENCIES

The best way to make your views known is to contact your senators
and congressional representatives directly. If you don't know who
they are or how to contact them, the main Capitol switchboard, at
(202) 224-3121, will be able to provide you with names and phone
numbers. You can obtain the same information on the Internet:
House of Representatives Web site: www.house.gov
Senate Web site: www.senate.gov

Consumer Product Safety Commission
Washington, DC 20207
24-hour hotline: (800) 638-2772
This agency handles complaints about a wide range of products,
including toys (for example, toy guns that look like real guns).

Federal Communications Commission
Mass Media Bureau, Enforcement Division
2025 M Street

Washington, DC 20554
Telephone: (202) 418-1430
Web site: www.fcc.gov
Division of the FCC charged with handling complaints. Be aware that most callers are simply told to call the networks. Charged with implementing the Children's Television Act of 1990, which requires the FCC to review the educational programming efforts of the networks.

Federal Trade Commission
Attention: Marketing Practices, Room 238
6th Street and Pennsylvania Avenue, NW
Washington, DC 20580
This agency handles complaints related to advertising and marketing. Complaints have to be in writing or can be faxed to (202) 326-2050.

United States House of Representatives
Subcommittee on Telecommunications and Finance
2125 Rayburn Building
Washington, DC 20515
Telephone: (202) 225-2927
Web site: www.house.gov/com

United States Senate
Subcommittee on Communications
227 Hart Senate Office Building
Washington, DC 20510
Telephone: (202) 224-5184
www.senate.gov/~commerce/

MEDIA LITERACY

Center for Media Literacy
4727 Wilshire Boulevard, Suite 403
Los Angeles, CA 90010

Telephone: (800) 226-9494
Fax: (213) 931-4474
Web site: www.medialit.org
The Center for Media Literacy is a nonprofit membership organization providing leadership, training, and a direct mail clearinghouse of books, videos, and teaching materials for the growing
media literacy field. Issues covered include children and television,
tobacco and alcohol advertising, and the acclaimed *Beyond Blame:
Challenging Violence in the Media*, a video-based community education curriculum for all ages.

Citizens for Media Literacy
Wally Bowen
34 Wall Street, Suite 407
Asheville, NC 28801
Telephone: (704) 252-0600
A nonprofit, educational organization dedicated to linking critical
thinking about media and advertising to citizenship and civic participation. Through workshops, comic books, and other teaching
materials, this organization shines a light on the structure of media.
It emphasizes the fact that although we have many consumer choices,
we have few citizen choices.

National Association for Family and Community Education
Children's Television Project
P. O. Box 835
Burlington, KY 41005
Telephone: (606) 586-8333
Fax: (606) 586-8348
Web site: www.nafce.org
The goal of this grassroots organization is to strengthen individuals,
families, and communities through education, leadership, and ac-
tion. Provides media literacy materials.

Media Watch
P.O. Box 618
Santa Cruz, CA 95061
Telephone: (408) 423-6355
E-mail: mwatch@cruzio.com
Web site: www.mediawatch.com
This nonprofit organization focuses on challenging sexism and violence in the media through education and action. Produces educational videos and an international newsletter aimed at helping consumers be more critical of the media.

National Telemedia Council
120 East Wilson Street
Madison, WI 53703
Telephone: (608) 257-7712
Web site: danenet.wicip.org/ntc
A professional organization promoting media literacy education through partnership with educators, media producers, and consumers across the country. This nonprofit membership organization publishes *Telemedium: The Journal of Media Literacy* and is the home of the Media Literacy Clearinghouse and Center.

ADVOCACY AND REFORM GROUPS

Adbusters
1243 West Seventh Avenue
Vancouver, British Columbia
V6H 1B7 Canada
Telephone: (604) 736-9401
E-mail: adbusters@adbusters.org
Publishes *Adbusters*, an irreverent and thought-provoking networking tool for teachers and activists interested in media reform. Particularly useful for teachers.

Center for Media Education
1511 K Street, NW, Suite 518
Washington, DC 20005
Telephone: (202) 628-2620
Fax: (202) 628-2554
Web site: www.cme.org/cme
A nonprofit organization dedicated to safeguarding the needs of
children. Organizes and educates consumer groups and nonprofit
organizations on issues of public policy and the media. The Center's
Campaign for Kids' TV is aimed at improving the quality of chil-
dren's television.

Children's Advertising Review Unit
Council of Better Business Bureaus
845 Third Avenue
New York, NY 10022
Telephone: (212) 705-0124
This agency deals only with advertising. Its mission is to promote
responsible, truthful, and accurate advertising to children under
twelve and to ensure that advertisers are sensitive to the particular
nature of their audience. However, compliance with agency guidelines is voluntary. Prefers to receive complaints in writing.

Children Now
1212 Broadway, Suite 530
Oakland, CA 94612
Telephone: (510)763-2444
Web site: www.childrennow.org
A nonpartisan policy and advocacy organization for children. Children Now is spearheading a national commitment to improve the
quality of media for children. The goal of the Children and Media
Program is to help raise awareness among leaders in the news and
entertainment industries about the needs of children and to encourage more effective portrayals of and services to young people.

Cultural Environment Movement
P. O. Box 31847
Philadelphia, PA 19104
Telephone: (610) 642-3061
CEM is an educational nonprofit corporation made up of a broad coalition of media, professional, labor, religious, environmental, health-related, women's, and minority groups working for a "freer and saner cultural environment." Focus is on reducing concentration of control by small number of media conglomerates and expanding input of less affluent and more vulnerable groups.

FAIR (Fairness and Accuracy in Reporting)
130 West 25th Street
New York, NY 10001
Telephone: (212) 633-6700
E-mail: fair@igc.apc.org
The national media watch group that offers well-documented criticism of media bias and censorship. Advocates for greater diversity in the press and scrutinizes media practices that marginalize public interest, minority, and dissenting viewpoints. FAIR believes that structural reform is needed to break up the dominant media conglomerates and establish independent, nonprofit sources of information.

Foundation to Improve Television ✗
60 State Street, Suite 3400
Boston, MA 02109
Telephone: (617) 523-5520
Fax: (617) 523-4619
This is a nonprofit, public interest organization working to reduce the amount of violence shown on television. The foundation works to raise public awareness, contacts business leaders to enlist their support in reducing the attractiveness of advertising on shows that feature unnecessary violence, and initiates legal proceedings to

ensure that regulators fulfill their mandate that television broadcasting is to serve the public interest.

Parents' Choice
119 Chestnut Street
Newton, MA 02164
Telephone: (617) 965-5913
Publishes a quarterly review of children's books, toys, videos, TV programming, computer programs, movies, and music. Parents' Choice Awards help parents identify the year's best in all fields of children's media.

MEDIA RESEARCH AND POLICY

Mediascope
12711 Ventura Boulevard, Suite 280
Studio City, CA 91604
Telephone: (818) 508-2080
Web site: www.mediascope.org
Nonprofit public policy organization founded to promote constructive depictions of health and social issues in media. Provides tools and information to help the entertainment community to be more socially responsible without relinquishing creative freedom.

Notes

Introduction

1. Communications Act of 1934, sec. 310(d); Code of Federal Regulations, Title 47; FCC Children's Television Report and Policy Statement, 1974.

Chapter 1: What We Know

1. L. D. Eron, testimony before the Senate Committee on Government Affairs, *Congressional Record*, June 18, 1992.

2. House Energy and Commerce Committee, Subcommittee on Health and the Environment, July 11, 1994.

3. B. Weinraub (*New York Times*), "Hollywood Scoffs at Dole's Rebuke of Show Business," *San Francisco Chronicle*, June 2, 1995.

4. "Senator Dole Calls Oliver Stone a 'Modern-Day McCarthy,'" *San Francisco Chronicle*, June 2, 1995.

5. S. Garbarino, "Do Movies, Music Trigger Violent Acts?" *Newsday*, Aug. 10, 1992, p. 38.

6. Sgt. David Thompson, Manteca, California, Police Department, personal communication, Feb. 1996.

7. Garbarino, "Do Movies, Music Trigger Violent Acts?"

8. G. Comstock with H. Paik, *Television and the American Child* (Orlando, Fla.: Academic Press, 1991).

9. N. Postman, *The Disappearance of Childhood*, 2nd ed. (New York: Vintage Books, 1994), p. 97.

10. H. F. Waters, "Life According to TV," *Newsweek*, Dec. 6, 1982.

11. "Would You Give Up Your TV for a Million Bucks?" *TV Guide*, Oct. 10–16, 1992.

12. "Parents' Guide to Kids' TV," *TV Guide*, Mar. 4–10, 1995.

13. L. Bogart, *Commercial Culture* (New York: Oxford University Press, 1995), p. 232.

14. "Cobain Suicide Copycats," *Scottish Daily Record & Sunday Mail Ltd. Daily Record*, Oct. 20, 1994.

15. "Violence on TV," *TV Guide*, Aug. 22–28, 1992.

Chapter 2: Television in the USA

1. M. Chen, *The Smart Parent's Guide to Kids' TV* (San Francisco: KQED Books, 1994), p. 58.

2. E. B. White, cited in E. L. Boyer, *Ready to Learn: A Mandate for the Nation* (Princeton, N.J.: Carnegie Foundation for the Advancement of Teaching, 1991).

3. Mike Mills, "Congressional Insight," *Harper's*, Mar. 5, 1990.

4. Michael Miller, "Music Rocks into Political Arena," Reuters Information Services, June 18, 1992.

5. R. J. Harris, *A Cognitive Psychology of Mass Communication* (Hillsdale, N.J.: Erlbaum, 1994).

6. G. Gerbner, M. Morgan, and N. Signorielli, "Living with Television: The Dynamics of the Cultivation Process," in J. Bryant and D. Zillmann (eds.), *Perspectives on Media Effects* (Hillsdale, N.J.: Erlbaum, 1986).

7. B. Bagdikian, *The Media Monopoly* (Boston: Beacon Press, 1992).

8. N. N. Minow, address to the National Association of Broadcasters, Washington, D.C., May 1961.

9. N. N. Minow, *How Vast the Wasteland Now?* (New York: Gannett Foundation Media Center, Columbia University, 1991).

10. Plato, *The Republic*, 2nd ed., trans. D. Lee (London: Penguin Classic, 1987).

11. S. Burns, "Tax Policy Works Against Family Values," *Dallas Morning News*, July 11, 1993.

12. T. Williams, *The Impact of Television* (Orlando, Fla.: Academic Press, 1986).

Chapter 3: Research and Theory

1. "Mom Blames Fatal Fire on 'Beavis,'" *Cincinnati Post*, Oct. 9, 1993.

2. *San Jose Mercury News*, Oct. 2, 1993.

3. R. Harris, *A Cognitive Psychology of Mass Communication* (Hillsdale, N.J.: Erlbaum, 1994).

4. A. Bandura, "Influence of Model's Reinforcement Contingencies on the Acquisition of Imitative Responses," *Journal of Personality and Social Psychology*, 1965, *1*, 589–595.

5. D. G. Singer, "Does Violent Television Produce Aggressive Children?" *Pediatric Annals*, 1985, *14*, 804–810; A. Bandura, D. Ross, and S. Ross, "Imitation of Film-Mediated Aggressive Models," *Journal of Abnormal Social Psychology*, 1963, *66*, 3–11.

6. "26 People Shot Themselves Through Head Imitating Scene from *Deer Hunter*," *Los Angeles Times*, Aug. 22, 1987.

7. L. R. Huesmann, K. Lagerspetz, and L. D. Eron, "Intervening Variables in the TV Violence-Aggression Relation: Evidence from Two Countries," *Developmental Psychology*, 1984, *20*, 746–775; A. Dorr, "Television and Affective Development and Functioning: Maybe This Decade," *Journal of Broadcasting*, 1981, *25*, 335–345.

8. B. S. Greenberg and C. Atkin, "Learning About Minorities from Television: A Research Agenda," in G. Berry and C. Mitchell-Kernan (eds.), *Television and the Socialization of the Minority Child* (Orlando, Fla.: Academic Press, 1982).

9. P. G. Christenson and D. F. Roberts, "The Role of Television in the Formation of Children's Social Attitudes," in M.J.A. Howe (ed.),

Learning from Television: Psychological and Educational Research (London: Academic Press, 1983).

10. T. D. Cook, H. Appleton, R. F. Conner, A. Shaffer, G. Tabkin, and J. S. Weber, *Sesame Street Revisited* (New York: Russell Sage Foundation, 1975).

11. Bandura, "Influence of Model's Reinforcement Contingencies."

12. L. Berkowitz, R. Corwin, and M. Heironimus, "Film Violence and Subsequent Aggressive Tendencies," *Public Opinion Quarterly*, 1963, 27, 217–229; L. Berkowitz and R. Geen, "Stimulus Qualities of the Target of Aggression: A Further Study," *Journal of Personality and Social Psychology*, 1967, 5, 364–368.

13. S. Milgram, *Obedience to Authority* (New York: HarperCollins, 1974).

14. E. Donnerstein, D. Linz, and S. Penrod, *The Question of Pornography: Research Findings and Policy Implications* (New York: Free Press, 1987).

15. S. Hearold, "A Synthesis of 1043 Effects of Television on Social Behavior," in G. Comstock (ed.), *Public Communication and Behavior*, Vol. 1 (Orlando, Fla.: Academic Press, 1986).

16. S. Feshbach, "Reality and Fantasy in Filmed Violence," in J. Murray, E. Rubinstein, and G. Comstock (eds.), *Television and Social Behavior*, Vol.2 (Washington, D.C.: U.S. Department of Health, Education, and Welfare, 1972).

17. J. Cantor, "Fright Responses to Mass Media Productions," in J. Bryant and D. Zillmann (eds.), *Responding to the Screen* (Hillsdale, N.J.: Erlbaum, 1991).

18. J. Cantor and S. Reilly, "Adolescents' Fright Reactions to Television and Films," *Journal of Communication*, 1982, 32(1), 87–99.

19. J. L. Singer, D. G. Singer, and W. S. Rapaczynski, "Family Patterns and Television Viewing as Predictors of Children's Beliefs and Aggression," *Journal of Communication*, 1984, 34(2), 73–89.

20. Federal Bureau of Investigation, *Crime in the United* States. Washington, D.C.: U.S. Government Printing Office, 1993.

21. G. Gerbner, L. Gross, M. Morgan, and N. Signorielli, "The 'Mainstreaming' of America: Violence Profile No. 11," *Journal of Commu-*

nication, 1980, *30*(3), 10–29; G. Gerbner, M. Morgan, and N. Signorielli, *Television Violence Profile No. 16: The Turning Point* (Philadelphia: Cultural Environment Movement, 1994).

22. Gerbner, Morgan, and Signorielli, *Television Violence Profile No. 16*.

23. Ibid.

24. G. Gerbner, "Television Violence: The Art of Asking the Wrong Question," *The World and I*, July 1994, p. 396.

25. A. L. Kellerman and D. T. Reay, "Protection or Peril? An Analysis of Firearm-Related Deaths in the Home," *New England Journal of Medicine*, 1986, *314*, 1557–1560.

26. D. K. Osborn and R. C. Endsley, "Emotional Reactions of Young Children to TV Violence," *Child Development*, 1971, *42*, 321–331.

27. R. E. Goranson, "Media Violence and Aggressive Behavior: A Review of Experimental Research," in L. Berkowitz (ed.), *Advances in Experimental Social Psychology*, Vol. 5 (Orlando, Fla.: Academic Press, 1970).

28. R. Lazarus, J. Speisman, A. Mordkoff, and L. Davison, "A Laboratory Study of Psychological Stress Produced by a Motion Picture Film," *Psychological Monographs*, 1962, *76*.

29. V. B. Cline, R. G. Croft, and S. Courrier, "Desensitization of Children to Television Violence," *Journal of Personality and Social Psychology*, 1973, *27*, 360–365.

30. A. Bandura, E. B. Blanchard, and B. Ritter, "The Relative Efficacy of Desensitization and Modeling Approaches for Inducing Behavioral, Affective, and Attitudinal Changes," *Journal of Personality and Social Psychology*, 1969, *13*, 173–199.

31. R. S. Drabman and M. H. Thomas, "Does Media Violence Increase Children's Toleration of Real-Life Aggression?" *Developmental Psychology*, 1974, *10*, 418–421.

32. S. L. Gaertner and J. F. Dovidio, "The Subtlety of White Racism, Arousal, and Helping Behavior," *Journal of Personality and Social Psychology*, 1977, *35*, 691–707.

33. M. H. Thomas, R. Horton, E. Lippincott, and R. S. Drabman, "Desensitization to Portrayals of Real-Life Aggression as a Function

of Exposure to Television Violence," *Journal of Personality and Social Psychology*, 1977, 35.

Chapter 4: The Cartoon Dilemma

1. D. Berlyne, "Curiosity and Exploration," *Science*, 1966, *153*, 25–33.
2. E. Erikson, *Childhood and Society* (New York: Norton, 1993), pp. 255–258.
3. G. Gerbner, M. Morgan, and N. Signorielli, *Television Violence Profile No. 16: The Turning Point* (Philadelphia: Cultural Environment Movement, 1994).
4. L. Elber, "TV Summit: All Talk, Some Grumbling, No Action," Associated Press, Aug. 3, 1993.
5. R. DeVries, "Constancy of Generic Identity in the Years Three to Six," *Monographs of the Society for Research in Child Development*, 1969, *34*.
6. J. L. Singer and D. G. Singer, "Family Experiences and Television Viewing as Predictors of Children's Imagination, Restlessness, and Aggression," *Journal of Social Issues*, 1986, *42*, 113.
7. Federal Communications Commission, "Broadcast Deregulation Order," *Federal Register*, 1984, *49*(165), 33599 et 67.
8. "EPM Communications," *Billboard*, July 6, 1996.
9. B. C. Nossiter, "The FCC's Big Giveaway Show," *The Nation*, Oct. 26, 1985, p. 402–404.
10. G. Robertson, "Law for the Press," in James Curran (ed.), *The British Press: A Manifesto* (New York: Macmillan, 1978), p. 205.
11. T. Engelhardt, quoted in T. Gitlin, *Watching Television* (New York: Pantheon Press, 1986), p. 90.
12. J. Elicker, M. Englund, and L. Sroufe, "Predicting Peer Competence and Peer Relationships in Childhood from Early Parent-Child Relationships," in R. Parke and G. Ladd (eds.), *Family Peer Relationships: Modes of Linkage* (Hillsdale, N.J.: Erlbaum, 1992).

13. A. N. Meltzoff and M. K. Moore, "Imitation of Facial and Manual Gestures by Human Neonates," *Science*, 1977, *198*, 75–78.

14. A. N. Meltzoff, "Imitation of Televised Models by Infants," *Child Development*, 1988, *59*, 1221–1229.

15. R. J. Desmond, J. L. Singer, and D. G Singer, "Family Mediation: Parental Communication Patterns and the Influences of Television on Children," in J. Bryant (ed.), *Television and the American Family* (Hillsdale, N.J.: Erlbaum, 1990), p. 301.

16. A. Bandura, D. Ross, and S. Ross, "Vicarious Reinforcement and Imitative Learning," *Journal of Abnormal Social Psychology*, 1963, *67*, 601–607.

17. L. Friedrich and A. Stein, "Aggressive and Prosocial Television Programs and the Natural Behavior of Preschool Children," *Monographs of the Society for Research in Child Development*, 1973, *38*, 1–64.

18. J. L. Singer, D. G. Singer, and W. S. Rapaczynski, "Family Patterns and Television Viewing as Predictors of Children's Beliefs and Aggression," *Journal of Communication*, 1984, *34*(2), 73–89.

19. Ibid.

20. Bandura, Ross, and Ross, "Vicarious Reinforcement and Imitative Learning."

21. Desmond, Singer, and Singer, "Family Mediation."

22. S. Chess and A. Thomas, *Temperament in Clinical Practice* (New York: Guilford Press, 1986).

23. J. Flavell, "The Development of Children's Knowledge About the Appearance-Reality Distinction," *American Psychologist*, 1986, *41*, 418–425.

24. J. L. Singer and D. G. Singer, "Imaginative Play in Early Childhood: Some Experimental Approaches," in A. Davids (ed.), *Child Personality and Psychopathology* (New York: Wiley, 1974).

25. D. G. Singer and J. L. Singer, *House of Make-Believe*. (Cambridge, Mass.: Harvard University Press, 1990).

26. G. Salomon, "Effects of Encouraging Israeli Mothers to Co-Observe 'Sesame Street' with Their Five-Year-Olds," *Child Development*, 1977, *48*, 1146–1151.

27. J. Johnston and J. Ettema, "Using Television to Best Advantage: Research for Prosocial Television," in. J. Bryant and D. Zillmann (eds.), *Perspectives on Media Effects* (Hillsdale, N.J.: Erlbaum, 1986).

28. J. H. Bryan, "Model Affect and Children's Imitative Behavior," *Child Development*, 1971, *42*, 2061–2065.

29. J. L. Singer and D. G. Singer, *Executive Summary on Barney and Friends* (New Haven, Conn.: Family Television Research and Consultation Center, Yale University, 1995).

30. Ibid., pp. 107–124.

Chapter 5: Middle Childhood

1. J. Elicker, M. Englund, and L. Sroufe, "Predicting Peer Competence and Peer Relationships in Childhood from Early Parent-Child Relationships," in R. Parke and G. Ladd (eds.), *Family Peer Relationships: Modes of Linkage* (Hillsdale, N.J.: Erlbaum, 1992).

2. A. C. Huston, C. J. Carpenter, and J. B. Atwater, "Gender, Adult Structuring of Activities, and Social Behavior in Middle Childhood," *Child Development*, 1986, *57*, 1200–1209; L. Hoffman, "Changes in Family Roles, Socialization, and Sex Differences," *American Psychologist*, 1977, *84*, 712–722.

3. J. H. Block, "Personality Development in Males and Females: The Influence of Different Socialization," *Master Lecture Series of the American Psychological Association* (New York: American Psychological Association, 1979); M. Sadker and D. Sadker, *Failing at Fairness* (New York: Simon & Schuster, 1994).

4. J. Daven, J. F. O'Conner, and R. Briggs, "The Consequences of Imitative Behavior in Children: The 'Evel Knievel Syndrome,'" *Pediatrics*, 1976, *57*.

5. J. Cantor and B. L. Omdahl, "Effects of Fictional Media Depictions of Realistic Threats on Children's Emotional Responses, Expectations, Worries, and the Linking for Related Activities," *Communication Monographs*, 1991, *58*, 384–401.

6. J. Cantor, "Confronting Children's Fright Response to Mass Media," in D. Zillmann, J. Bryant, and A. Huston (eds.), *Media, Children, and the Family* (Hillsdale, N.J.: Erlbaum, 1994).

7. B. S. Greenberg and J. E. Brand, "Cultural Diversity on Saturday Morning Television," in G. Berry and J. Asamen (eds.), *Children and Television* (Newbury Park, Calif.: Sage, 1993).

8. E. Maccoby, *Social Development* (Orlando, Fla.: Harcourt Brace, 1980).

9. D. Baumrind, "Rearing Competent Children," in W. Damon (ed.), *Child Development Today and Tomorrow* (San Francisco: Jossey-Bass, 1988), pp. 349–378.

10. A. Baldwin, R. Cole, and C. Baldwin, "Parental Pathology, Family Interaction, and the Competence of the Child in School," *Monographs of the Society for Research in Child Development*, 1982, *47*(5).

11. W. Emmerich, "Structure and Development of Personal-Social Behaviors in Economically Disadvantaged Preschool Children," *Genetic Psychology Monographs*, 1977, *95*, 191–245.

12. W. Becker, "Consequences of Different Kinds of Parental Discipline," in M. Hoffman and L. Hoffman (eds.), *Review of Child Development Research*, Vol. 1 (New York: Russell Sage Foundation, 1964).

13. L. R. Huesmann, "Psychological Processes Promoting the Relation Between Exposure to Media Violence and Aggressive Behavior by the Viewer," *Journal of Social Issues*, 1986, *42*, 125–139.

14. L. R. Huesmann, L. D. Eron, M. M. Lefkowitz, and L. O. Walder, "The Stability of Aggression over Time and Generations," *Developmental Psychology*, 1984, *20*, 1120–1134.

15. L. R. Huesmann and L. D. Eron, *Television and the Aggressive Child* (Hillsdale, N.J.: Erlbaum, 1986), pp. 78–79.

16. Ibid., p. 9.

17. Ibid., p. 5.

18. L. D. Eron, L. R. Huesmann, E. Dubow, R. Romanoff, and P. Yarmel, "Aggression and Its Correlates over 22 Years," in D. Crowell, I. Evans, and C. O'Donnell (eds.), *Childhood Aggression and*

Violence: Sources of Influence, Prevention, and Control (New York: Plenum, 1987).

19. S. Stein, H. Kraemer, and D. Spiegel, *The Impact of Media Coverage of a Violent Crime on Children in Three States,* in press.

20. E. E. McGhee, "Children's Appreciation of Humor: A Test of the Cognitive Congruency Principle," *Child Development,* 1976, *47,* 420–426.

21. A. Dorr, "No Shortcuts to Judging Reality," in J. Bryant and D. Anderson (eds.), *Children's Understanding of Television* (Orlando, Fla.: Academic Press, 1983).

22. R. Hawkins, "The Dimensional Structure of Children's Perceptions of Television Reality," *Communication Research,* 1977, *4,* 299–320.

23. T. Lickona, *Raising Good Children* (New York: Bantam, 1983), p. 140.

Chapter 6: Older Childhood

1. L. B. Ames, F. L. Ilg, and S. M. Baker, *Your Ten to Fourteen Year Old,* Gesell Institute of Human Development (New York: Dell, 1988), p. 21.

2. D. Ruble, "The Development of Social Comparison Processes and Their Role in Achievement-Related Self-Socialization," in T. Higgins, D. Ruble, and W. Hartup (eds.), *Social Cognitive Development* (Cambridge, Mass.: Cambridge University Press, 1983).

3. M. Rosenberg, *Conceiving the Self* (New York: Basic Books, 1979).

4. E. Erikson, *Childhood and Society* (New York: Norton, 1993), pp. 258–261.

5. M. L. Hoffman, "Altruistic Behavior and the Parent-Child Relationship," *Journal of Personality and Social Psychology,* 1975, *31,* 937–943.

6. M. Radke-Yarrow, C. Zahn-Waxler, and M. Chapman, "Prosocial Dispositions and Behavior," in P. Mussen (ed.), *Handbook of Child Psychology* (New York: Wiley, 1983).

7. G. Spivack, J. Marcus, and M. Swift, "Early Classroom Behaviors and Later Misconduct," *Developmental Psychology,* 1986, *22,* 123–131.

8. C. S. Dweck, W. Davidson, S. Nelson, and B. Erra, "Sex Differences in Learned Helplessness: 2. The Contingencies of Evaluation Feedback in the Classroom, 3. An Experimental Analysis," *Developmental Psychology*, 1978, *14*, 268–276.

9. C. Gilligan, *In a Different Voice* (Cambridge, Mass.: Harvard University Press, 1982).

10. R. L. Huesmann, "Learning of Aggression from Television Violence," paper presented at the Third International Conference on Standards in Screen Entertainment, London, Mar. 1992.

11. P. A. Williams, E. H. Haertel, G. D. Haertel, and H. J. Walberg, "The Impact of Leisure-Time Television on School Learning: A Research Synthesis," *American Educational Research Journal*, 1982, *19*, 19–50.

12. M. Fetler, "Television Viewing and School Achievement," *Journal of Communication*, 1984, *34*(1).

13. S. Hearold, "A Synthesis of 1043 Effects of Television on Social Behavior," in G. Comstock (ed.), *Public Communication and Behavior*, Vol. 1 (Orlando, Fla.: Academic Press, 1986).

14. L. Berkowitz and E. Rawlings, "Effects of Film Violence on Inhibitions Against Subsequent Aggression," *Journal of Abnormal and Social Psychology*, 1963, *66*, 405–412.

15. A. Bandura, "Influence of Model's Reinforcement Contingencies on the Acquisition of Imitative Responses," *Journal of Personality and Social Psychology*, 1965, *1*, 589–595.

16. E. Donnerstein and L. Berkowitz, "Victim Reactions in Aggressive-Erotic Films as a Factor in Violence Against Women," *Journal of Personality and Social Psychology*, 1981, *41*, 710–724.

17. Berkowitz and Rawlings, "Effects of Film Violence."

18. S. Feshbach, "Reality and Fantasy in Filmed Violence," in J. Murray, E. Rubinstein, and G. Comstock (eds.), *Television and Social Behavior*, Vol. 2 (Washington, D.C.: Department of Health, Education, and Welfare, 1972).

19. G. Gerbner, L. Gross, M. Morgan, and N. Signorielli, "The 'Mainstreaming' of America: Violence Profile No. 11," *Journal of Communication*, 1980, *30*(3), 10–29.

20. J. L. Singer, D. G. Singer, and W. S. Rapaczynski, "Family Patterns and Television Viewing as Predictors of Children's Beliefs and Aggression," *Journal of Communication*, 1984, *34(2)*, 73–89.

21. R. Ebert, *Roger Ebert's Video Companion* (Kansas City, Mo.: Andrews McMeel, 1998).

22. G. Gerbner, "Television Violence: The Art of Asking the Wrong Question," *The World and I*, July 1994, pp. 385–397.

23. G. Gerbner, *The Amplifier* (Washington, D.C.: American Psychological Association, 1994).

24. L. D. Eron, "Prescription for Reduction of Aggression," *American Psychologist*, 1980, *35*, 244–252.

25. Ebert, *Roger Ebert's Video Companion*.

26. J. Mander, *Four Arguments for the Elimination of Television* (New York: Quill, 1978).

27. Gerbner, Gross, Morgan, and Signorielli, "The 'Mainstreaming' of America."

28. J. Clemente, "The Vulnerable Viewing Violent Visions: Victims Become Victimizers," paper presented at the International Conference of Child and Adolescent Psychiatry, San Francisco, Aug. 1994.

29. R. S. Drabman and M. H. Thomas, "Does Media Violence Increase Children's Toleration of Real-Life Aggression?" *Developmental Psychology*, 1974, *10*, 419.

Chapter 7: Early Adolescence

1. E. Erikson, *Childhood and Society* (New York: Norton, 1993), p. 261.

2. E. Douvan and J. Adelson, *The Adolescent Experience* (New York: Wiley, 1966); R. Montemayor, "Parents and Adolescents in Conflict," *Journal of Early Adolescence*, 1983, *3*, 83–103.

3. M. Rutter, P. Graham, O. Chadwick, and W. Yule, "Adolescent Turmoil: Fact or Fiction?" *Journal of Child Psychology and Psychiatry*, 1976, *17*, 35–56.

4. E. H. Uhlenhuth and others, "Symptom Checklist Syndromes in the General Population: Correlations with Psychotherapeutic Drug Use," *Archives of General Psychiatry*, 1983, 40, 1167–1173.

5. R. Helfer and C. H. Kempe, *Child Abuse and Neglect: The Family and the Community* (Cambridge, Mass.: Ballinger, 1976).

6. L. Zinn, "Teens: Here Comes the Biggest Wave Yet," *Business Week*, Apr. 11, 1994, pp. 76–86.

7. F. Hechinger, *Fateful Choices: Healthy Youth for the 21st Century* (New York: Hill and Wang, 1992), p. 177.

8. C. Moog, "The Selling of Addiction to Women," *Media and Values*, 1991, 54–55, 20–22.

9. K. Montgomery, "Alcohol and Television," *Media and Values*, 1991, 54–55, 18–19.

10. Hechinger, *Fateful Choices*, p. 110.

11. C. Cooper, H. Grotevant, and S. Condon, "Individuality and Connectedness in the Family as a Context for Adolescent Identity Formation and Role-Taking Skill," in G. D. Grotevant and C. Cooper (eds.), *Adolescent Development in the Family* (San Francisco: Jossey-Bass, 1983).

12. L. A. Fingerhut, *Firearm Mortality Among Children, Youth, and Young Adults 1–34 Years of Age: Trends and Current Status.* (Atlanta: Centers for Disease Control and Prevention, 1993), p. 231.

13. "Charges Expected in Boy's Killing, Union City Teenager Allegedly Shot 9-Year-Old in the Head," *San Francisco Chronicle*, Nov. 23, 1994.

14. Office of Juvenile Justice and Delinquency Prevention, *Juvenile Offenders and Victims: 1997 Update on Violence*, Aug. 1997, p. 1.

15. AIDS Information Clearing House, 1994.

16. S. Jhally, *Dreamworlds: Desire/Sex/Power in Rock Video* (Northampton, Mass.: Media Education Foundation, 1995). Videotape.

17. E. Donnerstein, "Aggressive Erotica and Violence Against Women," *Journal of Personality and Social Psychology*, 1980, 39; N. Malamuth, S. Haber, and S. Feshbach, "Testing Hypothesis Regarding Rape: Exposure to Sexual Violence, Sex Differences, and the

'Normality' of Rapists," *Journal of Research in Personality*, 1980, *14*, 121–137.

18. Josephson Institute of Ethics, *Ethics in Action* (Marina del Rey, Calif., 1994).

19. L. D. Eron, J. Gentry, and P. Schlegel, *Reason to Hope* (Washington, D.C.: American Psychological Association, 1994).

20. "Mr. MTV," *W*, May 1995.

Chapter 8: Adolescence

1. E. Erikson, "Autobiographic Notes on the Identity Crisis," *Daedalus*, Fall 1970.

2. J. McCord, "Problem Behaviors," in S. Feldman and G. Elliot (eds.), *At the Threshold: The Developing Adolescent* (Cambridge, Mass.: Harvard University Press, 1990).

3. B. C. Miller and P. Dyk, "Sexuality," in P. Tolan and B. Cohler (eds.), *Clinical Research and Practice with Adolescents* (New York: Wiley, 1993).

4. A. L. Kellerman and D. T. Reay, "Protection or Peril? An Analysis of Firearm-Related Deaths in the Home," *New England Journal of Medicine*, 1986, *314*, 1557–1560.

5. D. F. Roberts, "Adolescents and the Mass Media: From 'Leave It to Beaver' to 'Beverly Hills 90210,'" *Teachers College Record*, 1993, *94*(3).

6. C. Gilligan, *In a Different Voice* (Cambridge, Mass.: Harvard University Press, 1982).

7. E. Erikson, *Childhood and Society* (New York: Norton, 1993), p. 262.

8. Snoop Doggy Dogg, "Gin and Juice," *Doggy Style*, Death Row Records, 1993.

9. B. S. Greenberg and others, "Sex Content on Soaps and Prime Time Television Series Most Viewed by Adolescents," in B. S. Greenberg, J. D. Brown, and N. L. Buerkel-Rothfuss (eds.), *Media, Sex, and the Adolescent* (Cresskill, N.J.: Hampton Press, 1993).

10. M. Miedzian, *Boys Will Be Boys* (New York: Doubleday, 1991), p. xxiii.

11. E. Donnerstein, D. Linz, and S. Penrod, *The Question of Pornography: Research Findings and Policy Implications* (New York: Free Press, 1987), p. ix.

12. E. Donnerstein, L. Berkowitz, and D. Linz, "Role of Aggressive and Sexual Images in Violent Pornography," unpublished manuscript, University of Wisconsin, Madison, 1986.

13. Donnerstein, Linz, and Penrod, *The Question of Pornography*, p. 136.

14. L. D. Eron, J. Gentry, and P. Schlegel, *Reason to Hope* (Washington, D.C.: American Psychological Association, 1994), p. 171.

15. N. Postman, *The Disappearance of Childhood* (New York: Vintage Books, 1994).

16. Ibid., pp. 104–105.

Chapter 9: What Parents Can Do

1. D. Walsh, *Selling Out America's Children* (Minneapolis: Fairview Press, 1994).

2. K. Heintz-Knowles, "Television's Image of Children," study commissioned for Children Now, 1995.

3. R. H. Frank, "Shaping Our Children's Values: The Role of the Entertainment Media," presented at the national Children Now Conference, Stanford University/UCLA Center for Commercial Policy, Stanford, Calif., Mar. 2–4, 1995.

4. Family Research Council, Sept. 1993.

5. Josephson Institute of Ethics, "Aspen Declaration," 1992.

6. R. J. Desmond, J. L. Singer, and D. G. Singer, "Family Mediation: Parental Communication Patterns and the Influences of Television on Children," in J. Bryant (ed.), *Television and the American Family* (Hillsdale, N.J.: Erlbaum, 1990).

7. S. Hearold, "A Synthesis of 1043 Effects of Television on Social Behavior," in G. Comstock (ed.), *Public Communication and Behavior*, Vol. 1 (Orlando, Fla.: Academic Press, 1986).

8. L. K. Friedrich and A. H. Stein, "Aggressive and Prosocial Television Programs and the Natural Behavior of Preschool Children,"

Monographs of the Society for Research in Child Development, 1973, 38, 1–64.

9. J. L. Singer and D. G. Singer, *Executive Summary on Barney & Friends* (New Haven, Conn.: Family Television Research and Consultation Center, Yale University, 1995).

10. W. A. Collins and S. K. Getz, "Children's Social Responses Following Modeled Reactions to Provocation: Prosocial Effects of a Television Drama," *Journal of Personality*, 1976, 44, 488–500.

11. L. K. Friedrich and A. H. Stein, "Prosocial Television and Young Children: The Effects of Verbal Labeling and Role-Playing on Learning and Behavior," *Child Development*, 1975, 46, 27–38.

12. Hearold, "Synthesis of 1043 Effects."

13. W. H. Dietz, "You Are What You Eat—What You Eat Is What You Are," *Journal of Adolescent Health Care*, 1990, 11(1), 76–81.

14. G. Comstock with H. Paik, *Television and the American Child*. (Orlando, Fla.: Academic Press, 1991).

15. "Madonna's Commercial for Pepsi Off," *Oregonian*, Apr. 7, 1989.

16. "How One Woman Pushed Big Firms to Kill Ads," *San Jose Mercury News*, Mar. 3, 1989.

17. E. Boyer, "Working Toward Media Literacy," National Telemedia Council, Madison, Wisconsin.

Chapter 10: Suggestions for Schools, Media, and Government

1. N. Postman, *Amusing Ourselves to Death* (New York: Penguin Books, 1985), p. 63.

2. R. Riley, "Turning the Corner: From a Nation at Risk to a Nation With a Future" (Second Annual State of American Education Address), Arlington, Virginia, Feb. 1, 1995.

3. Paul Kagan and Associates, "From 1984 to 1993, R-Rated Movies Grossed Less Than PG," *Washington Post*, Feb. 27, 1994.

4. Sheryl Leach, personal communication, June 1995.

5. Ted Turner, speech before the Subcommittee on Telecommunications and Finance, May 12, 1993.

6. "Does TV Kill?" *Frontline*, Public Broadcasting System, Jan. 10, 1995.

7. Children Now Conference, Mar. 2–4, 1995, Stanford University, Palo Alto, California.

8. B. Friedlander, "Community Violence, Children's Development, and Mass Media," in D. Reiss, J. Richter, M. Radke-Yarrow, and D. Scharff (eds.), *Children and Violence* (New York: Guilford Press, 1993).

9. D. Abrahms, "FCC Seeks to Improve Quality of TV for Kids," *Washington Times*, Apr. 6, 1995.

10. F. Swertlow, "Fox Executive Fears High-Tech Devices May Lead to Censorship," *Daily News of Los Angeles*, July 12, 1993.

11. House Energy and Commerce Telecommunications Subcommittee Hearing, July 1, 1993.

12. N. N. Minow, "How to Zap TV Violence," *Wall Street Journal*, Aug. 3, 1993.

The Author

Madeline Levine is a clinical psychologist in private practice in Marin County, California. She earned a B.A. degree (1969) and a M.Ed. degree (1972), graduating cum laude and Phi Beta Kappa, from the State University of New York at Buffalo. She holds both an M.A. degree (1972) and a Ph.D. degree (1979) in psychology from the California School of Professional Psychology at Berkeley. Dr. Levine spent several years teaching at the elementary and secondary levels before becoming a psychologist. She has been a consultant to many preschools and elementary schools in the San Francisco Bay Area and has taught child development at the University of California, San Francisco Medical Center.

Dr. Levine is a frequent and popular lecturer on the topic of media effects on children and has written extensively on this issue. Her first book *Viewing Violence* was published in 1996 by Doubleday.

Dr. Levine lives in Kentfield, California, with her husband and three sons. She considers her house a living laboratory and admits that on occasion her kids watch junk, which they have taken to calling "research."

Index